Y0-BYF-717

# GLOBAL CORPORATE REAL ESTATE MANAGEMENT

# GLOBAL CORPORATE REAL ESTATE MANAGEMENT

## A HANDBOOK FOR MULTINATIONAL BUSINESSES AND ORGANIZATIONS

M. A. HINES

HD
1394
. H56
1990
West

QUORUM BOOKS

NEW YORK • WESTPORT, CONNECTICUT • LONDON

**Library of Congress Cataloging-in-Publication Data**

Hines, Mary Alice.
Global corporate real estate management : a handbook for
multinational businesses and organizations / M. A. Hines.
    p. cm.
Includes bibliographical references.
ISBN 0–89930–530–X (alk. paper)
1. Real estate management.  2. International business enterprises.
3. International agencies.  4. Office buildings—Management.
5. Commercial buildings—Management.  6. Industrial buildings—
Management.  I. Title.
HD1394.H56  1990
658.2—dc20        90–32722

British Library Cataloguing in Publication Data is available.

Copyright © 1990 by M. A. Hines

All rights reserved. No portion of this book may be
reproduced, by any process or technique, without the
express written consent of the publisher.

Library of Congress Catalog Card Number: 90–32722
ISBN: 0–89930–530–X

First published in 1990

Quorum Books, 88 Post Road West, Westport, CT 06881
An imprint of Greenwood Publishing Group, Inc.

Printed in the United States of America

The paper used in this book complies with the
Permanent Paper Standard issued by the National
Information Standards Organization (Z39.48–1984).

10  9  8  7  6  5  4  3  2  1

# CONTENTS

# EXHIBITS

# PREFACE

Global business has long been important to prosperous societies. Europeans traded with the Chinese for their silk fabrics and ceramic goods before the birth of Christ. The merchants of Florence developed their business empires by trading with the countries surrounding the Mediterranean Sea. The Japanese have traded with other Asian countries for centuries. The British Empire thrived on the trade between the Commonwealth and other countries around the world. In like manner, the Dutch, French, Portuguese, and Spanish built their empires around international trade. In each instance, businesses have required globally located manufacturing facilities, warehouses, office buildings, and retail premises from which to conduct commerce.

## THE IMPORTANCE OF GLOBAL CORPORATE BUSINESS

No one country can be self-sufficient. Important natural resources are unevenly distributed around the world so that no one country has all that it needs to carry on in today's sophisticated society. The most highly industrialized and developed nations today depend on foreign trade for natural resources, semifinished goods, and imported finished goods.

When countries develop surpluses of certain goods and services, they must market them abroad. Most advanced economies produce more goods and services than their domestic markets can consume. The rest is sold abroad.

Some countries deliberately produce goods for foreign markets. If the national market has not been developed adequately, some goods will not serve domestic market needs, but only overseas ones. For example, Chinese businesses, particularly joint ventures with foreign companies, produce goods primarily for foreign sale. Domestic productivity may serve foreign markets to the benefit of the companies and the national government.

Global businesses have attained high profitability by operating in many national markets. The trends point to an even higher level of global business by multinational firms based in the United States, Europe, or Asia. The integration of separate nations into the European Community is stimulating more new multinational businesses. A company that wishes to serve the twelve nations of the European Community (EC) will find it easier to do so once the trade barriers among the various EC nations are reduced. The buying power of the new Europe with its population of 345 million entices multinational business operation based throughout the world.

Most global businesses require administrative and sales-oriented premises in each country where they do business. They may manufacture, assemble, or process goods in various countries, and thus require manufacturing and warehousing buildings. As global business increases, the number of properties required also increases. As a multinational corporation extends its manufacturing and/or marketing to new countries, more locations are needed.

Technological changes require redefinition of the building space needed. As the numbers of global business properties increase, the architecture necessary for the properties changes. For example, the development of energy conservation and transnational communication has promoted the demand for "intelligent" commercial buildings with built-in sophisticated communications and energy conservation systems. A multitenant office building may have a central computer system for its business occupants rather than separate computer systems for each corporate office.

Global business at a high sales volume prompts the use of the corporate business structure rather than partnership or proprietorship structures. Major multinational businesses seek limited financial and legal liability, continuous legal life, numerous employees and managers in complex organizational structures, and a flexible and accommodating financial structure. The corporate form of business organization has been found to be the best. Partnerships and proprietorships generally do not have structures that can accommodate a business spread across multiple governmental entities, languages, cultures, legal systems, tax and accounting systems, and financial systems.

When a nation has positive trade balances with many other countries, its economy is healthy. When exports exceed imports, a positive trade balance results, and the nation tends to be a creditor, not a debtor. Therefore, a global corporate business that generates a positive trade balance for its home country benefits its government. Japan and West Germany are creditor nations today because of their positive trade balances around the world, while the United States is a debtor nation with a high, negative trade balance. The relatively high standard of living in the United States is supported by imported goods. United States exports have been increasing with the devalued U.S. dollar, but the trade deficit persists. As U.S.-based global enterprises increase their exports, they may deploy more properties in more countries to increase their overseas manufacturing, wholesaling, and retailing operations.

In summary, the importance of global corporate business lies in its accessibility to needed natural resources, in the marketing of surplus productivity overseas, in bolstering the national economy by production for foreign markets, in attainment of higher profitability by operations in many national markets, and in strengthening the domestic economy through export promotion for positive trade balances. Exploitation of global business opportunities involves the use of industrial and commercial properties that must reflect architectural designs appropriate to the current stage of business technology and locations that fit current demand and supply patterns. The corporate form of business organization fits the requirements of global business better than partnership or proprietorship forms.

## THE SIGNIFICANCE OF GLOBAL CORPORATE REAL ESTATE HOLDINGS AND THEIR VALUES

The financing of cross-border mergers and acquisitions has often been based on the real property values of the company being acquired. The money from the sale of property is added to the proceeds from "junk-bond" financing to reach the acquisition price of the target company.

As multinational companies seek to protect themselves from hostile takeovers, they have restructured their assets and liabilities as means of defense. Attractive real property holdings may attract the attention of the "corporate raider." If the property is refinanced, the corporate raider may be repelled. Some companies have recently restructured for takeover defense by selling prime corporate property and leasing it back. The company itself capitalizes on the value of the real estate. The cash must then be wisely used or the cash surplus will attract the corporate raider who could use the cash to acquire the company.

Many global corporations are worth more than their balance sheets may indicate. The stock value might not reflect the company's real asset values. Many multinational corporations carry their properties at depreciated historical costs. The market value of the properties may far exceed the book value of those assets as shown on the corporate balance sheet. Japanese corporations, particularly, undervalue their commercial properties in Japan, where property values have multiplied since the reconstruction following World War II.

In summary, the significance of global corporate real estate holdings may be associated with the expansion of the growing multinational firm, the financing of the corporation seeking to acquire another cross-border major firm, and the defense against hostile corporate takeovers. A multinational firm may be undervalued because its real property is valued at depreciated historical cost for financial statement presentation rather than at current market value.

## READER USES FOR THIS BOOK

The director of real estate for the wholly domestic corporation can view the corporate real estate management process as it is applied to global corporate real estate. By reading the examples of successful real estate operations of these multinational firms, a company could avert some errors.

Some corporations currently do business in only a few countries outside of their home country. Before venturing into additional countries, the corporate director of real estate would benefit from this book's presentation of a variety of overseas challenges and how problems can be averted or lessened with preparation and organization.

Corporate real estate trade associations may want to adopt the book for seminars for their members who are involved in global business operations and properties. U.S.-based corporate real estate trade associations are finding that their members are vitally interested in discovering what bearing global expansion of business has on their corporate real estate interests. Appropriate seminars and conferences can help solve global real estate problems common to most of their association members. The subject matter presented by seminar speakers can be enhanced by a book that substantiates and elaborates on the seminar themes.

Through reading this book, those who supply international real estate services will learn of the interests of the global corporate real estate community. Their consulting, marketing, accounting, tax, financial, and investment services may be more closely matched to the interests of their prospective clients. The client's global property interests tend to take on different dimensions than the domestic property interests. The suppliers of international real estate services include commercial and industrial brokers; chartered surveyors; valuers and appraisers; tax, marketing, and financial consultants; accountants; and commercial and investment bankers.

College students are often interested in corporate real estate management at home and abroad. Academic real estate programs include courses in international real estate and corporate real estate management. For example, the International Real Estate Institute and the International Real Estate Federation, including their U.S. chapters, offer courses and seminars for real estate professionals on topics such as global corporate real estate management.

On the university level, the major accrediting body of American Collegiate Schools and Colleges of Business promotes the expansion of international business courses and the expansion of international topics within regular U.S.-oriented business courses. *Global Corporate Real Estate Management* can be used as the text for a course with a similar name or as a supplementary international text for a U.S.-oriented undergraduate or graduate real estate course. It could also be used as a supplementary text for a global business management course. The book presents the use of basic management practices for the special problems of global real estate.

## ACKNOWLEDGMENTS

I would like to thank the following people for their valuable contributions to this book: Mike Cissell of Philip Morris Kraft General Foods Company; Edward W. Lewis of Motorola; Rick Rogers of Abbott Laboratories; John Havelock of Amoco; R. Price Lindsay of Morton Thiokol; Armand DuPont of IBM France; Mark Ahn of FMC Corporation; Bill Tropiano and Thomas A. Mulhern of AT&T; Michael Masters of Warner Lambert; John Novomesky of John Novomesky & Associates; Joe Rooney of Xerox; Reinhardt Kleff and Rebecca E. Bray of United Parcel Service; Ronald Bauman and John W. Fitzpatrick of Union Carbide; Wib Sutherland, Michael Fischer, and John Callard of McDonald's Corporation; Harry S. Thomes of E. I. DuPont de Nemours & Company; and Lee Lanselle of Walt Disney Productions (Eurodisneyland).

Other important contacts and contributors include Terry Rees, United Technologies; Victor Wood, Volume Shoe Corporation; H. Mark Norton and Gerard Taieb of Larry Smith Consulting; Robin E. Kaplan and Antonio Serrachio of Citicorp Real Estate, Paris and Milan, respectively; Jean de Launoy of Bourdais Consultants; Patrick Taylor of FGV, Frankfurt; Abraham de Koning of Rodamco France; Robert S. Orr and Wendy Thomas of Jones Lang Wootton, Frankfurt; Robert Waterland of Jones Lang Wootton, Paris; Peter Evans of Debenham Tewson & Chinnocks, London; Russell Schiller of Hillier Parker May & Rowden, London; Tim Keese of Citibank, Frankfurt; Michael von Zietzewitz of Deutsche Bank, Frankfurt; Nicholas Knowland of Healey & Baker, Paris; Michel Haskel of Commercial Credit of France, Paris; Jean Meynial of Arc Union, Paris; Mr. Chenand, Parly Duo Shopping Center, Versailles, France; Vincent Bouee of Societe Generale, Paris; and Andrew Irvine of FIABCI (International Real Estate Federation), Paris. This represents only a partial listing of the many corporate and real estate leaders across the world who over the years have contributed to my writings on international real estate.

Several members of the Industrial Development Research Council also have contributed significantly to the research for this book. Members of the Building Owners and Managers Association (BOMA) International of Washington, D.C., and NACORE International (International Association of Corporate Real Estate Executives) contributed data both by questionnaire and in person. On more than one occasion, the executive staff of BOMA Japan in Tokyo has provided data for my international real estate and corporate research. Washburn University research grants and advances from Quorum Books and the International Real Estate Institute have financed by research.

My parents have constantly offered encouragement and moral support during the writing of this and the other books. They assisted with the driving around the United States during the summer of 1989 to visit the corporate headquarters of many major U.S.-based multinational companies. They also helped with the driving for the comprehensive Western European real estate research in 1983. My mother went around the world with me in 1985, including a three-week trip through the People's Republic of China. Without their encouragement and assistance, the research for this global corporate real estate book could not have been done as efficiently and thoroughly.

# GLOBAL CORPORATE REAL ESTATE MANAGEMENT

# 1

## INTRODUCTION

As their corporations expand worldwide, managers seek to gain the highest productivity from their assets, including land and buildings. Most corporations have historically considered the productivity of their real property holdings secondary to the productivity of their principal lines of business. The real estate is thought to serve the primary functions of the multinational company. Therefore, the corporate goals are associated with the profitability of manufacturing, wholesaling, and/or retailing certain lines of goods and services. The profitability of the real estate is usually not considered. Investment returns are not expected from the real estate that the company uses. But management expects the real estate to promote the corporate profit interests. Profits are generated from company use of the real estate.

### THE IMPORTANCE OF CORPORATE REAL ESTATE

For many of the multinational corporations, their assets are dominated by inventories of raw materials, semifinished goods, machinery, and equipment. Their real estate may be a high percentage of their assets if they own numerous manufacturing plants, warehouses, office buildings, and retail buildings. Some multinational companies are very capital intensive with large holdings of real estate. Even though all global businesses use large amounts of real estate to keep their companies going, some use less land and buildings than others. Some multinational companies lease their land and buildings to a large extent so real property does not assume such a place of importance on the asset side of the corporate balance sheet.

### COMPANY OBJECTIVES AND REAL ESTATE MANAGEMENT

The global business usually focuses its attention on the profitability from its lines of business such as steel or auto manufacturing, chemical processing, or oil exploration, refining, and distribution. Its objectives relate to such factors as current return on assets and sales, trends in their profitability, and market share per product line.

### The Effect of the Merger and Acquisition Movement

Hostile overtures toward multinational companies by prospective acquirers have turned the thoughts of the target companies toward their net worths, their cash balances, the market value of their real estate holdings, the value of their proprietary technologies, the effectiveness of their management systems and personnel, as well as other management considerations. The question that arises for management is: What does the prospective acquirer see in this company that promotes its multimillion- or multibillion-dollar offer? Some of these large corporate offers of purchase are welcomed by the target companies; others are not. Recently hostile takeovers have dominated the multinational corporate scene. Therefore, the target company has sought to defend itself from the actualization of the prospective purchase. It tries to analyze its company's operations and financing as the acquiring company would.

There has been a flurry of corporate mergers and acquisitions since the mid–1980s in the United States and abroad. The 1970s were also marked by a corporate merger and acquisition movement, but the mergers and acquisitions of the 1980s tend to be different from those of the 1970s. Leveraged buyouts and management buyouts have characterized many of the multimillion- and multibillion-dollar buyouts of the 1980s in the United States. U.S. investment bankers have been taking their talents in these financial areas to Western Europe where international corporate mergers and acquisitions are prompted by the integration of the European Community into a single trading market. At this point the international business combines of Europe are somewhat comparable to the interstate businesses of the United States. But many of the newly formed multinational companies of Europe plan to become major global corporate players.

The acquiring company must plan for the payment of the acquired company. Numerous alternative financing plans are considered as they are presented to corporate management by numerous investment bankers from the United States and abroad. Oftentimes junk bonds become an important financial component of the acquisition financing package. These junk bonds are debentures that have relatively low financial ratings by Standard & Poor's and Moody's. The breadth and depth of the possible investor community for prospective junk bond issues must be assessed before this financial avenue becomes a firm component of the acquirer's financial package.

The prospective acquirer usually looks to the cash reserves and real estate values of the target company for financing the acquisition. What could be used to pay off the assumed corporate indebtedness which is necessary to finance the major corporation acquisition? The target company's cash reserves might be available for immediate use as a part of the acquirer's equity. Is the target company real estate available for sale or collateralized financing? Is its real estate undervalued or full-valued at market prices and uses? The equity interest in prime properties of the target company might be sold easily to finance the corporate purchase. If the target company property is carried on the books at depreciated historical cost, there may be "hidden value" in the real estate of the company being acquired. The acquirer could capitalize on the real estate's "hidden value" by selling these assets for market prices. Or the properties appraised at market value may support collateralized financing for the company acquisition. Either by selling the real estate or using it as collateral for loans, the acquiring company can gain cash to finance the acquisition.

### The Effect of Company Restructuring on Global Property Management

For a number of reasons a multinational company may restructure itself for future operations and purposes. Financial weakness resulting from a period of high interest rates and strong competition might promote financial restructuring. Financial strength could also be protected by restructuring that might involve real estate. Management restructuring may result from the addition or deletion of product lines, company expansion into new domestic and overseas markets, or the development of new business policies for the company's future. Antitakeover strategy could also promote organizational changes.

Restructuring a company can take many forms depending upon the reasons for the restructuring and reorganizing. Since corporate real estate serves the basic functions of the company, the needs and productivity of the company's real estate depend on the changes in the company's financial and management structure. Leasing real estate rather than owning it may free up capital to increase the financial strength of the company. As an antitakeover defense, the real estate strength of a company may be dissipated by engaging in sale leasebacks and by spinning off company property or leasehold estates into real estate funds open to outside investors. Union Carbide, for example, recently sold its headquarters building in Danbury, Connecticut to a West German investor and leased it back as an antitakeover defense and for other reasons. Amoco Corporation is establishing a real estate fund involving some of its prime real estate for some of the same reasons. After selling several product lines, Union Carbide has restructured its management into three distinct and important product lines. AT&T is adding to its management structure as it expands its operations overseas, including Europe and the Far East. Xerox decided to leave land development and investment so it has revised its organizational structure to eliminate this functional area.

### Decentralization of the Corporate Real Estate Function

The corporate real estate function is often highly centralized into a corporate service area. A director of corporate real estate with his or her staff may serve the entire global company. But the global company may be restructured to wholly or partially decentralize the real estate functions and management of its real estate holdings. At Union Carbide the three newly created business units—chemicals and plastics, industrial gases, and carbon products—will have management control over their real estate. The centralized global real estate function will act in two capacities: (1) to consult to the three business units and (2) to approve all corporate real estate-related expenditures. The partial decentralization at Union Carbide changes the need for centralized office locations and permits the manager of its major units to deploy its real assets in ways that prove most profitable and beneficial to each unit's operations.

### Split-up of a Global Corporation

The real estate function may be split into two or more parts if a company is split up. As of July 1, 1989, Morton Thiokol became two independent companies: Morton and Thiokol. Instead of one centralized corporate real estate function for the entire global company, each of the two companies will decide the type of worldwide real estate management that it needs for its independent company.

## TRENDS IN GLOBAL BUSINESS

Global businesses thrive on their sources of global comparative advantage. They seek to retain comparative advantages that result in substantial profits. The shifts in business comparative advantages associated with country economies determine the national trends in global competition. Global business trends affect global property use, its management, and its value.

### Sources of Global Comparative Advantage

Comparative advantages held by global companies may be derived from economies of scale in production, transportation, marketing, and purchasing. They could be derived from labor and natural resource availability at relatively low cost and from proprietary technology that is protected from competitors. The labor supply may be unusually productive and labor relations congenial.

Companies that realize favorable economies of scale in production tend to be capital intensive. Plants automated for shorter product runs and flexible production systems prove advantageous in today's market which requires wide varieties within a product line and customized products. Robotic production equipment may provide the needed mass production under controlled production budgets with flexible adaptation to numerous product variations. If a company is not particularly capital intensive, it may gain economies of scale in production from skilled and trainable labor that is cost effective over relatively long individual working hours per week.

Production economies of scale connected with automated factories are generally associated with the advanced economies where the labor force is costly and unionized and where appropriate skilled personnel are relatively scarce in the industrialized sector. Less capital intensive industries that desire the services of direct labor usually find economies of scale by plant location in the underdeveloped countries of East, South, and Southeast Asia. For this reason, major industries from all over the world have relocated in the Republic of Korea (South Korea), the Republic of China (Taiwan), Hong Kong, the People's Republic of China, India, Malaysia, and Philippines, and also in the Caribbean Islands.

If a global company seeks transportation or logistical economies of scale, that company will tend to locate worldwide in areas of good transportation facilities. Transportation facilities tend to be the most advanced in Japan, Western Europe, the United Kingdom, Canada, Australia, and the United States.

Global companies with marketing economies of scale to support their profitability also tend to be associated with the advanced economies. Here the corporate and personal buying power per company or per capita is the greatest. If a product is a basic necessity of relatively low cost per unit, the marketing economies of scale may be found instead in the most populous countries that are less economically developed. The same product may sell to consumers in all countries due to the population relationship associated with basic necessities. Marketing economies of scale of industrial goods tend to be associated with the advanced economies because manufacturing and wholesaling establishments tend to be more distant from each other in less developed economies of the world.

Purchasing economies of scale for global companies are usually associated with the locations of raw materials or natural resources, the locations of manufactured semifinished goods, and the locations of plants producing marketable finished products. Since Latin America and Africa contain many valuable natural resources, purchasing requirements of global companies may be met through volume purchases in these regions of the world.

Other less developed countries such as South Korea, China, Taiwan, and Hong Kong also represent countries whose companies may provide high volumes of semifinished and finished goods for marketing worldwide by multinational businesses based elsewhere.

Advances in technology and its proprietary use are usually associated with the research and development facilities of the United States and Japan. Substantial research and development is conducted in Western Europe, the United Kingdom, and the USSR and its satellite countries. But private business has access to the advanced technology derived from labs and high-tech facilities in the United States, Western Europe, and Japan. Generally the Communist countries—including Cuba, Ghana, Zambia, East Germany, Poland, Hungary, Yugoslavia, and the USSR—tend to exchange information about developed technology within their own system of nations. These lesser developed nations continually try to obtain advanced technology from the capitalistic countries which are well advanced economies.

Comparative advantage among global real estate companies tends to be associated with the deployment of educated and trained staff in offices spread across the world. They tend to use advanced office technology for the pursuit of their research duties and marketing responsibilities. Since the international real estate firms tend to specialize in commercial and industrial property marketing, they gain economies of scale from locating near concentrations of commercial and industrial business. Some economies of scale are gained from the global real estate firms dealing with global industrial, transportation, and service firms. Therefore, Jones Lang Wootton based in London, is located in the United States, Australia, Hong Kong, Japan, Singapore, and in most countries of Western Europe. These are advanced economies where most of the global corporations are headquartered.

### Trends Affecting Global Competition

The comparative advantages that global corporations have in economies of scale related to production, transportation, marketing, and purchasing change over time. South Korea's labor costs are rising as are the labor costs of Japan. There are fewer economies of production to be gained by relocating plants to South Korea and Japan. Neither of these highly productive economies tends to protect copyrights and patents as do the laws and regulations of other developed countries, such as the United States. Production technology may not be protected as well by foreign-based companies in these countries who actively seek ideas for advanced technology.

Hong Kong's productive labor force which is employed for six-day work weeks at relatively low wages may not be as accessible after the takeover of Hong Kong in 1997 by the People's Republic of China. Hong Kong becomes a separate administrative district of China, but China will maintain a military presence in Hong Kong after 1997. China already exerts economic direction over Hong Kong business and industry which has not proven disastrous to its global trade at this time. The dampening of capitalistic economic tendencies promoted by Deng Xiaoping in the early 1980s is affecting labor force morale in the colony. Middle management and other Hong Kong workers with foreign passports have been streaming out of Hong Kong for Australia, Canada, the United States, and the United Kingdom since the 1997 agreement was signed in the mid–1980s.

Because Japan has encouraged development of its domestic economy and government infrastructure since the mid–1980s, its domestic market has proven to be a good marketplace for global corporate marketing. At the same time, Japan continues to export far more than it imports each year. This creditor nation of entrenched industrial and corporate wealth does business with most countries of the world from its vantage point of trade surpluses with most countries.

The integration of the 12 European countries into a united Europe with minimal internal trade barriers may prove a new competitive force. The united Europe will represent the buying power of approximately 345 million residents who maintain high standards of living on relatively high personal incomes. Japan represents approximately 115 million residents and the United States, approximately 250 million residents with high per capita incomes and buying power. Global companies may easily find it advantageous to be well represented in Western Europe as well as in Japan and the United States, the leading economic regions of the world.

The adoption of the glasnost and perestroika economic policies by the USSR has given impetus to greater global trade among the Communist and non-Communist countries of the world. Within the Communist bloc, elements of capitalism are showing up in the promotion of global trade between the Eastern bloc and the West and Asia. Capitalist corporations are signing more joint venture agreements with Russia, Poland, and Hungary for the establishment of manufacturing, distribution, and hospitality and resort facilities within their national boundaries. If the Communist parties of these Eastern bloc nations reverse their policies, global business would take a step backward. But right now, global corporations are anxious to carry out the new agreements which involve new locations within the Communist countries.

*The Impact of Advances in Telecommunications.* As telecommunications develop, the world marketplace becomes smaller. Better communication prompts plant, office, warehouse, and retail facility changes. It is not as necessary to be located in the expensive central business district of the major business center. Location in the suburbs near appropriate transportation hubs may be preferable to central business district locations where sale prices and rents tend to continue to increase with overall space demand. With better communication, a manager's geographical span of control may widen. More management control over a wider area is possible with less travel and direct person-to-person relationships. Advances in international facsimile are permitting the transmission of documents for review and negotiation. Overnight document and package delivery to all corners of the world permits rapid delivery of valuable documents. Better telephone communication reduces the need for direct person-to-person communication. Like facsimile, telex messages can be delivered around the clock as long as the receiving equipment is operational and free of other message transmission.

*Impediments to Global Competition*. Those who have reason to transfer technology to companies elsewhere in the world want copyright and patent protection that is satisfactory for the original owner's protection. Even though there are international treaties supporting copyright and patent protection, the regulation and enforcement do not satisfy most owners of valuable proprietary technology.

Legal systems of Communist countries do not protect private property rights. Property is generally owned by the state and allocated to the various government sectors including the residential and agricultural communes. Foreign corporations find that land and buildings are only available by lease. Private land ownership is not available. Most building space is only available under lease, also.

Some countries outside the Communist bloc do not allow foreign entities to buy property, but permit only the leasing of land and building space. Singapore's property purchase restrictions are probably related to its scarce land area. Countries of the Middle East such as Bahrain do not permit foreign ownership of land. These land ownership restrictions are impediments to global company location and competition.

Regional economic development associations tend to create trade among the member countries and to restrict trade with outside entities and countries. There are long-established regional trading blocs in Latin America, the Caribbean, the Middle East, the Communist bloc, Western Europe, Southeast Asia, and North America. Even though the European Economic Community has been an established trading bloc for some years, the current European economic integration by 1992 is considered more of a threat to free global trade than the previous organization. In fact, some wonder if "Fortress Europe" is not being created to the detriment of global trade involving the United States and Japan. Therefore, many U.S. and Japanese corporations, including major financial institutions, are trying to establish a presence in Western Europe before "the closing of the Fortress door" in 1992.

### The Importance of Global Business

If an economy is to thrive, it must achieve a net export balance. This applies to the economy of a community, a state, or a nation. If an economy serves only the domestic or internal needs of the community, that economy will soon decline and eventually disappear. That productive community must provide for its own needs plus produce surplus goods and services to supply the needs of other communities, states, or countries. The United States once represented such a vibrant, creditor nation. Now that the United States has become a debtor nation although still highly productive, Japan and West Germany have taken its place as net exporters of goods and services. While Japan restrained the economic development of its own people and domestic businesses and industries while creating huge trade surpluses, West Germany has provided well for its citizenry, businesses, and industries since the Second World War while maintaining a trade surplus. (A trade surplus represents a surplus of exports over imports for a country.)

The Latin American and African countries have arrived at critical economic impasses due to their negative trade balances with their major trading partners. Most of the countries must import far more than they export since they lack the needed production systems to satisfy their own needs. To pay for the imported goods and services, they have accumulated huge debts that they cannot pay within the foreseeable future. The World Bank continues to help these countries develop their individual economies, reschedule debt payments with creditors, and restructure their financial systems to restore reasonable levels of inflation, higher economic productivity, and higher standards of living.

*The Need for Net Export Balances of Trade.* Global business development stimulates exports. At the same time, goods and services are imported to meet the needs of the country. To manage the trade balance toward a positive balance, the government must strive to keep economic conditions conducive to high levels of exporting. In the United States, the government's financial authority, the Federal Reserve System, has permitted the devaluation of the U.S. dollar to make the prices of U.S. goods for export cheaper in world markets. Many government steps taken to stimulate exports have resulted in more U.S. industrial production and a lower trade deficit. Foreign investment in the United States has been stimulated by higher levels of U.S. economic activity and higher overall yield on investments in many areas of business.

*Exportation of Goods Generated by Excess or Normal Capacity.* When an economy reaches a point of excess capacity, it can lower its unit costs by marketing the goods and services to other nations. Higher output from a given industrial input can result in lower unit costs. Profits may be gained from sales abroad and added to the profits realized at home for higher profitability and productivity. Most advanced economies, such as the United States, produce goods and services that companies and consumers in other countries wish to purchase. For example, pharmaceutical companies may successfully market proprietary drugs, nonprescription health care products, and gums, mints, and candy to many other countries. Warner

Lambert is one such pharmaceutical company engaged in a high level of exporting. The company markets cereals, processed coffee, spaghetti, candies, processed cheeses, frozen foods, salad dressings, and processed meats to foreign countries. One food conglomerate company might sell tobacco products, food, and beer to various overseas customers. Philip Morris Companies, which includes the newly acquired Kraft General Foods Division, represents the latter situation.

*Exportation of Goods Partially Produced Abroad.* Global businesses may also export goods derived in part from overseas sources. Many products are assembled in one or more countries and then exported by the company that has managed the profitable assembly and marketing process. Generally such corporate management operations involving several foreign subassembly processes are associated with the advanced economies of the United States and Japan.

Many countries have developed free trade zones for the importation of raw materials or partially assembled goods for further assembly or completion and ultimately for exporting to other countries. As the government providing the free trade zones realizes higher employment of its citizens and greater profitability for its companies operating in the free trade zones, it approves reduced import and export tariffs and lower space and occupancy costs for the companies operating in the designated zones.

## THE EVOLUTION OF GLOBAL BUSINESS AND GLOBAL CORPORATE REAL ESTATE MANAGEMENT

Most multinational corporations started as one-country based companies. When overseas marketing opportunities appeared, they marketed their goods and services to the prospective foreign clients from their home bases. Then overseas distributors such as manufacturers' representatives and agents may be employed to market their products along with others as a full product line. Company marketing representatives have supplemented this channel of distribution. Joint ventures with established wholesalers or acquisition of established distributors might be considered. Retail channels of distribution might have been considered on the same basis— marketing agreements with established foreign retailers, acquisition of established retailers in order to introduce the new products, or joint ventures with retailers. Many channels of distribution may eventually be employed as the company's products become established in individual foreign markets. Increasing market share and profits over time may require several channels of distribution, so overseas production is eventually considered. This is prompted by production, transportation, and marketing factors. The foreign market may resist foreign-produced goods. Production and transportation costs might be lower for locally produced products.

Fast food companies based in the United States have participated in part of the described evolution toward global business. McDonald's Corporation was well entrenched in the United States with their systematized management before they ventured abroad. They first gave operating licenses to a prospective owner-operator in France. After trying this channel of distribution for several years in France, the United Kingdom, and West Germany, they turned to store ownership and a corporate management director. Due to logistical problems, the company wanted local food supplies. When locally produced food products were found to lack the quantity and quality specifications of the corporation, local suppliers were encouraged to produce products to higher quality and quantity specifications. Once each of the company- or licensed-owned outlets hired employees and managers and acquired locally produced food products, some of the production, logistical, and marketing problems were alleviated. Now McDonald's seeks half of their sales from overseas business. The overseas market for their fast food business is growing more rapidly than the U.S. market for the same products in general.

### The Evolution of Global Corporate Real Estate Management

The evolution of global corporate real estate management is similar to that of global business in general. If the corporation does business only in its home country, the real estate managers face opportunities and challenges only from the management of home-base distribution outlets and production plants. When the corporation moves abroad into one or more countries, the real estate manager receives expanded responsibility and authority for the few overseas properties. These properties are actively managed by the domestic manager who uses the available telecommunications systems and transportation media between the home office and the foreign locations. The company might use an alternate management system immediately, though, upon full expansion. Instead of local management of even the first overseas properties, the company might employ overseas property managers. The home-office real estate manager would retain only supervisory management responsibilities under this alternative management arrangement.

The home-office director of real estate may retain complete responsibility and authority over all the overseas properties as the corporation expands its production and distribution into countries around the world. This management plan is not ordinarily used by major corporations. The usual arrangements are the preservation of supervisory management by the home-office real estate director or the preservation of overseas project managers as consultants who oversee the properties.

In many multinational companies all the project proposals and budgets are supervised by the home-office real estate directors and associated production, marketing, and financial departments. As a corporation strives to make each unit a profit center and to change even support service divisions such as real estate management into profit centers, the corporation may leave financial authorization with the real estate division but change the remaining supervisory authority to a consultative function for a fee. Union Carbide, for example, has changed its real estate department into a consultative department, primarily as a result of the multinational corporation's antitakeover defense and overall restructuring. In contrast, AT&T supports a hands-on, active management function for each of its worldwide properties from its corporate real estate headquarters in Basking Ridge, New Jersey. Unlike Union Carbide, AT&T is merely entering its global development phase. Where AT&T derives relatively little revenue from overseas operations, over 30 percent of Union Carbide's revenues come from outside of the United States.[1]

### The Role of International Trade Associations

The challenge of the global side of corporate real estate management are being explored by trade association memberships in new series of professional seminars and conferences involving corporate real estate and facilities managers from around the world. These newly created international seminars and conferences are staged in the United States and abroad. For example, the International Facility Management Association just held its First International Symposium on Facility Management in Washington, D.C., from May 10 through May 12, 1989. Delegates from Australia, Canada, England, Japan, the Netherlands, Switzerland, West Germany, and the United States attended. An observer from Mexico also attended this international facility management meeting. The speakers discussed trends, concerns, and opportunities that the various national delegates share in their corporate and government facility management.

After changing the trade association name from the National Association of Corporate Real Estate Executives to the International Association of Corporate Real Estate Executives, the association scheduled an important international corporate real estate conference in Brussels in October 1989. The founder of the association, Joseph Bagby, believes in the future of the global corporate real estate thrust for the programming and publications of the association.

A number of years ago the Building Owners and Managers Association (BOMA) International sponsored the formation of overseas affiliate organizations and conferences for participating delegates from each of the affiliate groups. Japan BOMA is particularly active. Its membership is drawn principally from office building managers and owners whose properties are located in Japan.

The membership of the International Real Estate Institute of Scottsdale, Arizona also represent global corporate real estate interests. Their numerous conferences and annual World Congresses scheduled for locations in the United States and abroad delve into multinational corporate real estate matters. The International Academy of Real Estate Studies, in recent years held in Stockholm, Geneva, and Copenhagen, normally involves global corporate real estate leaders from such industries as fast food chains and hotels.

These multinational corporate real estate organizations help train and educate corporate real estate managers who are on the job. The memberships benefit from airing their problems and from opportunities to meet with other professional real estate people. Organizations based in the United States—as mentioned above—serve particularly well the domestic and international corporate real estate industry. Some managers overseas do not have such organizational opportunities to meet and discuss common problems with their colleagues. A West European corporate real estate manager commented that he could not find local meetings of trade association members specializing in corporate real estate or property management. This manager, who represented a rapidly growing multinational company in the document and parcel delivery business, expressed an interest in having such organizational meetings available.

## APPLICATION OF GENERAL MANAGEMENT FUNCTIONS TO GLOBAL CORPORATE REAL ESTATE MANAGEMENT

In most organizations, management consists of planning, organizing, and controlling the personal, real property, and other resources of the organization. The performance of these management functions should be directed toward the objectives and goals of the organization. Policies must be set so that the organization will move quickly toward the objectives and goals in a logical and consistent manner. The available resources need to be used efficiently, economically, and advantageously. These management methods apply to both private and public organizations and to departments and divisions within the organizations. So the corporate real estate department should apply good management principles just as the entire multinational organization should.

### The Planning Function and the Global Corporate Real Estate Department

The planning function is related to the department management in several different ways in the multinational firm. First, top management must plan what functions will be delegated to the corporate real estate department. Top management must also decide whether the department will be a profit or service center. How should the real estate department be expected to grow as the assets of the growing multinational company increase?

How should the company's properties and the real estate department be financed in order for top management to pursue the overall goals of the entire firm? How should real estate work be approved for implementation by the real estate department? How should the project expenditures be approved before action is taken by the department and outside consultants?

The planning function for the multinational corporation is normally accomplished by top management with the guidance and approval of the board of directors. Some of this planning work may be assigned to the corporate planning department or the economic planning and research department. Strategic long-term planning may be accomplished on a preliminary basis by the corporate planning department, but the decisions about corporate goals and objectives will normally be made by top management and the board of directors. Since the acquisition, leasing, and divestiture of corporate real estate is a part of the planning function, the director of real estate or facility planning should be a part of the corporate planning process. The director of real estate may be a part of the top management team. If a lesser role is taken in the corporate planning process, the director of real estate should be informed of the general directions of the multinational company's latest plans. The director of real estate needs lead time to change the real estate inventory worldwide in order to support the new plans and directions for the growth of the company. Most real estate changes consume large amounts of time if reasonable purchase prices, sale prices, and leases are negotiated. If appropriate real estate must be purchased quickly, exorbitant or above-market prices might be paid. The same thing is true for leased space. Finding the best space in the best possible location at a good price or rent on good contract terms usually requires time. In like manner, if property has to be sold quickly— perhaps to release invested corporate capital—the price may be relatively low. "Fire sales" normally bring lower-than-market prices. Therefore, it is in the best interests of the director of real estate or the real estate department head to know the overall corporate plans as far in advance as possible.

Quicker response to general corporate plans may be possible for the real estate department if the properties involved in corporate changes are located in the headquarters' country. Overseas real estate changes can involve the headquarters department, plant and project managers and their associates at the overseas site, and outside professional people. Many company resources may be necessary for overseas real estate activity.

Today within many companies there tends to be a gap in the information flow regarding global plans for expansion, restructuring, and divestiture. The corporate real estate director often must merely react on short notice to requests for overseas property changes. Often top management's plans for their global business are not relayed quickly to this supporting service or consultative department. If the planning time of the corporate real estate director is shortened, the costs of doing real estate business overseas may increase significantly. Purchase and sale of property at good prices takes time. The company and the corporate real estate director are both more flexible if property is leased. High costs, though, may be encountered in breaking the longer leases that may be found in Western Europe. When a new appropriate plant site must be located in a rather short period, the problem of site scarcity complicates the situation and adds cost.

A number of corporate real estate departments are run by a single administrator. All real estate functions related to a large multinational corporation may be performed by this person with secretarial assistance. The planning function tends to be short-circuited in such situations. This person must primarily react quickly to numerous problems. Solutions must be found quickly since the passage of time will bring more problems needing immediate solutions.

In contrast, some multinational corporate real estate departments are staffed with people assigned to company real estate affairs in various regions of the world. For example, McDonald's Corporation has a Latin American real estate representative in its Chicago headquarters. This Latin American real estate representative does work in the United States and elsewhere when time permits. The real estate planning function may be properly carried out if adequate global real estate staff is available and there is good communication between the real estate department and top management about changes in global plans and policies.

The top management perception of the importance of the corporate real estate function varies among multinational corporations. If well-located real estate is particularly important to the success of the overall business, the real estate function may be assigned a major role. The real estate director will probably be directly involved in top management's plans for the company. If well-located real estate is important to the global company but is considered much less significant than product development, patent and copyright protection, production economies, global marketing management, corporate advertising and public relations, and financing for takeover protection, the real estate function may be assigned a secondary or less important role in the organization. Advance or long-term planning for the real estate function becomes difficult. The personality and tenure of the real estate director may give a real estate department more importance than it would normally attain. When the real estate director is a long-term respected employee and well acquainted with top management, he or she may be privy to immediate changes in global corporate plans which could permit the real estate department to plan for more efficient and economical operation. This is the case at Motorola where the director of real estate assumes the view of Motorola's top management in his business relationships.

*Planning for the Growth Cycle of the Company and Its Real Estate.* The responsibilities and duties of the corporate real estate department tend to increase as the overall company increases in size and business. When the real estate department is first established, few properties may be needed for the company that has just initiated a growth policy. Those properties may be located within the headquarters' country. In order for the company to stay flexible, the right approach for the real estate director might be to lease property as often as possible. Once the domestic business is stabilized at reasonably good total revenue and profits, domestic properties might be purchased with a plan for some normal expansion. Fast corporate growth tends to preclude acquisition of land and buildings unless flexibility and expansion ideas are built into the corporate real estate plans. Most fast growth industrial and financial corporations want to commit capital to product development and marketing and production rather than to ownership of real estate in the initial stages of expansion.

Whenever top management is unsure about the prospects for a particular production or distribution location, the corporate real estate manager may wish to lease space in that particular location. When the company has long-term plans for a production plant, the company will probably benefit from an ownership position or a long-term sale-leaseback. IBM France has generally assumed this planning pattern for the multiple production plants and distribution facilities in France. The uncertainty about the long-term need for a building stems partially from the current growth patterns within the same multinational corporation. As growth in sales and profits in various product sectors occurs and as production and distribution conditions change worldwide, the company may seek flexibility in real estate so that new locations can be explored.

In like manner, when the company goes overseas for the first time, the real estate department needs to plan for expansion from a small global real estate position to a substantial global real estate position. Leasing property may give the company more flexibility during the global growth phase. Departmental plans may focus on short-term leases of three to five years where the terms for vacating the property will not be onerous if better properties at better locations appear in the near future.

As the global business expands, the plans for the product lines of the company will generally determine where the new properties need to be located. Leasing plans may be explored if locational flexibility is needed as new markets are entered. Once the product line is established and the demand for the products is determined to be long term, the distribution center could be purchased from an initial lease-purchase plan or the distribution center might be relocated to an owned facility. If top management decides on long-term production for a major production plant, a leased space of small dimensions may be exchanged for a company-owned major plant with specially designed built-in features for anticipated expansion.

Perhaps the anticipated profit from the production and marketing of the associated products will pay for the company facilities over a long period.

*The Real Estate Department's Role in Creating or Developing New Space.* When new production and/or distribution facilities are needed by the manufacturing and marketing managers of the company, the expertise of the real estate staff may be employed to advantage in the planning phase. Some companies employ the team approach in all space planning, development, and construction. In such companies, the corporate real estate function may be a part of the engineering, architectural, and cost estimation work that falls under a corporate facilities management department. There are several labels given the department established for the team approach to corporate real estate planning, leasing, designing, developing, and constructing. Leading multinational telecommunications, pharmaceutical, and diversified chemical companies plan for global real estate facilities with such a team approach within a single, multifunction department.

*The Real Estate Functions That Require Planning.* Corporate real estate at home or abroad requires certain real estate services. The real estate department, division, or area may provide all or part of these services:

Maintenance and repair of buildings

Leasing buildings and space within buildings

Lawn, shrub, and tree care and maintenance

Landscaping

Administration of building equipment maintenance contracts

Budgeting of operating and other building expenses

Tax administration

Personnel recruitment, management, retention, and training

Land and building acquisition

Building design, development, and construction

Environmental pollution analysis and preparation of impact reports

Negotiation of project planning approvals

Maintenance of building records

Timely payment of property management expenses

Highest and best use analysis

Real estate appraisal

Interior design of offices, work stations, warehouses and plant space, and retail stores

Site selection

Real estate financial analysis

Acquisition and maintenance of energy conservation systems for buildings

Foreign exchange management

Purchase and leasing of building equipment and furnishings

Parking lot preparation, striping, lighting, and maintenance

Administration of building renovation and reconstruction programs

Marketing the real estate department's services to other business units

Administration of employee relocation services

Management of overseas expatriate housing programs

Selling and leasing excess space and properties

Management of building demolition

Other functional responsibilities

Top management must decide who will perform and be held accountable for the administration of these services. This planning involves outside consultants, the real estate department, the treasury department, plant management, the engineering departments, and other operating and service support units. The brokerage, property management, appraisal, maintenance, and other real estate work must be done. As the company expands worldwide, the real estate work may have to be reassigned to equalize the work loads and to contain employment increases.

*The Roles Assigned Outside Consultants.* Consultants may be seldom used by a major global firm. Or they could be used extensively, particularly for overseas property acquisition and leasing. A global company might use outside consultants only to supplement the talents and capabilities of the corporate real estate and engineering staffs. If a special study needs to be commissioned for which the regular staff has little time, a special consultant may be employed.

If the global company has ample in-house real estate and engineering staff, it may avoid the use of outside consultants. AT&T represents such a global telecommunications firm. Large multinational fast food chains have little need for outside consultants due to their specialized real estate staffing. The international oil companies often have sufficient specialized staff to handle the majority of their real estate work in-house. If a multinational company has grown chiefly through the acquisition of on-going, successful local companies, the current personnel of the acquired local companies may be able to handle real estate problems as they occur without the aid of outside consultants.

Major multinational companies that severely restrict the number of in-house real estate staff they employ count heavily on the assistance of outside consultants. In these instances, the brokerage contacts and information systems of the international real estate companies are used to accomplish some overseas work that would otherwise be required of the headquarters staff. In a similar manner, personnel of outside firms are employed locally to do property management work that headquarters staff would otherwise have to do on an on-going basis. Even one person placed permanently overseas to represent the home-office real estate department may be extremely costly, according to a leading U.S.-based telecommunications company real estate manager.

## GENERAL CORPORATE REAL ESTATE POLICIES

As part of the planning function, top management and the corporate real estate director must consider several areas for real estate policy making. It is usually the position of top management to make the policies that are approved by the board of directors, but the real estate director of the global firm should contribute to the discussion of policy determination. No one else is as knowledgeable about the real estate functions that are necessary to smoothly running and profitable firms. After corporate policy is set, policy decisions will tend to change with the course of the global business. Financial circumstances change, as do the goals and objectives of the firm. Since policies are subject to change, the real estate director should again be consulted when matters concerning the management of the corporate real estate are considered. The real estate director should be prepared to discuss the need for policy changes that affect his or her specialty area.

Here are a few of the corporate real estate areas that need policy determination by top management:

Acquire property or lease property

Property management by the company or by outside contractors

Profit center or staff service facility

Property held only for corporate use or property for investment return as well as property for corporate use

Need for property market value monitoring

Use of joint ventures

Importance of environmental protection and analysis

Importance of personnel health and safety within company buildings

Need for general company property standards

Need for architectural policies

Urban locational policies for building ownership and lease

Control and management of overseas properties

Litigation policies

Real estate accounting policy

Company policy toward political risk and its property locations

Approach to foreign land use approval

### Property Ownership or Lease Policy in General

Some global companies want to own all their properties. Most multinational companies want to own their manufacturing facilities so that they can fully control their premises and their total manufacturing operations including security. A few global companies wish to lease property as much as possible to keep assets off the balance sheet. They do not want to use significant amounts of their credit for acquisition of real property; they want to preserve the bulk of their credit for financing the manufacturing and the distribution of their important products. (The term "products" is intended to represent both goods and services.)

The company that prefers to own its own properties globally may, on occasion, lease premises (1) until a preferable permanent location becomes available, (2) until a new product's profit meets the test of time and the market and the associated properties become permanently necessary to the company, and (3) because appropriate locations are unavailable in a tight real estate market. Then such a company may choose between locations with short-term leases available and locations with longer-term leases available. Short-term leases lend the greatest corporate flexibility, but the particular local real estate market may not be accustomed to short-term leases. For example, multinational corporations find that the Frankfurt, West Germany real estate market is not accustomed to short-term commercial leases. Only recently have U.S. developers introduced short-term leases to the Frankfurt Class A office building market. Most major multinational companies prefer new Class A office premises when they select administrative space in a financial capital or a foreign city such as Frankfurt.

### Property Management by the Company or by Outside Contractors

Most multinational corporations tend to do their own property management with internal staff on site. Manufacturing plants are best managed by their corporate owner-users. Since warehouses are often computerized and stocks are picked and stored by robots, the company may readily manage its own warehouse space. If a company prefers to own its office buildings, it is probably financially able to employ managers for the office buildings. Many major global firms maintain high credit ratings and ample financial capacity no matter what their country of origin. In fact, the property manager may have had a large portion of the responsibility for the development, construction, floor layout, and equipment and furnishing of the premises before the long-term property management duties began. The property managers of major global computer companies are examples of this management situation.

There may be multiple reasons why a major corporation tends to manage its own buildings from production plants to office buildings and retail stores. The property management industry has not developed a high level of sophistication in many countries of the world. But multinational companies have had to develop, construct, furnish, and maintain and repair for decades. The British Commonwealth companies were located worldwide centuries ago, not just decades ago. They used all types of properties to serve their manufacturing, national resource exploration, mining, exporting and importing, and distribution functions. Yet today the property management industry is not well developed in Western Europe. It is not highly organized with many specialized companies and professional managers. The same can be said for many other parts of the world. Property management is developed to a professional level only in the United States, the United Kingdom, Japan, and a few other countries. In these countries, the large multinational firms could contract with outside property management firms for services that could equal or exceed those provided within the companies.

The British chartered surveyors and estate agents have taken property management talents and managerial skills to many countries of the world. International real estate firms, such as Jones Lang Wootton, Richard Ellis, Knight Frank & Rutley, and Debenham Tewson & Chinnocks, can offer property management services to major industrial and financial corporations on a worldwide basis.

## Profit Center or Staff Service Facility

Most corporate real estate departments continue to be part of the supportive service area for the corporate holding company. When a business or operating unit has a real estate problem, it may call upon the services of the corporate real estate department just as it might call upon the corporate treasury department to receive a forecast of currency values for a particular country whose future business is undergoing analysis. The small real estate staff usually handles the assigned jobs as quickly as they can. A number of domestic and international properties can be managed effectively only by a small holding company staff who have specialized in real estate matters and the general status of the markets where the company's properties are located.

Corporate takeover threats and close company profit analysis have contributed to the change in the real estate function from a staff service function to a profit center or consulting role. A few companies have changed their real estate departments into totally or partially independent consulting offices. Union Carbide's International Real Estate Department operates as an independent consulting office within the corporation. Union Carbide has reorganized its corporate real estate staff into a partially independent consulting office. Some corporate service is still required of the Carbide real estate office in addition to the consulting.

### Property Held Only for Corporate Use or for Both Corporate Use and Investment Returns

The multinational corporation usually manufactures and/or distributes goods and services worldwide. Its management is focused on gaining profitability from the sale of goods and services; it is not focused primarily on real estate investment profitability. Therefore, most global corporations acquire, build, and lease property only for their own use. As mature global corporations have continually reassessed their profit centers' performance and future sources of profits, they have noted, in some cases, that the real estate department could gain profitability from leasing excess space to outside entities and from managing investment properties acquired or developed by the corporate real estate department. The department's expertise in real estate might encompass investment real estate. Xerox Corporation entered into investment real estate with a joint venture with VMS Realty in the early 1980s and then spun off the development and investment joint venture subsidiary in the latter part of the 1980s. The venture into investment realty by the major office equipment manufacturer and distributor did not turn out as successfully and profitably as forecasted. A major package delivery firm is now contemplating entrance of its real estate department into investment and corporate real estate. This growing international firm may capitalize on property value and rental growth rates in various dynamic locations in the world. Their package delivery business gives them access to profitable investment real estate markets. They already have the management and brokerage expertise in the same markets.

### Need for Property Market Value Monitoring

Industrial corporations generally are not interested in the current market values of their worldwide properties. They use the properties to produce products from which they derive corporate profitability. The managers of the business units are not compensated for the "paper profits" derived from the increase in value of their manufacturing plants, research and development facilities, warehouse buildings, office buildings, or retail or wholesale buildings. And accounting practices do not require the companies to place the current market value of their real properties on their publicly distributed balance sheets. Neither do privately held corporations have to report market values for their corporate properties in most countries. Therefore, few corporations have monitored the current value of their real assets.

In an era of multinational corporate acquisitions through management buyouts and leveraged buyouts by outside concerns, top management has become more interested in the current value of its properties. The understatement of corporate properties may attract hostile corporate acquirers who could replace the current management of the existing corporation after buyout. Therefore, more major corporations are examining the value of their properties as they prepare takeover defenses and restructure their firms for better profitability. Hostile corporate raiders often see the chance to turn around a company for greater profitability and to sell off valuable real estate in order to finance the acquisition.

## Use of Joint Ventures for the Holding of Real Estate

If a company wishes to dispose of valuable real estate interests, it may select property for disposal in total or in part. Many corporate property sales involve the total freehold interest. Other sales involve sale-leasebacks through joint venture agreements, which assure the real estate partner that the current property owner will continue to manage the property for a time with, perhaps, a corporate lease on the premises. The original owner may be given the right to sell the corporate interest after a certain period so that the new partner will hold the total ownership.

Since land cannot be depreciated by the tax law of most countries, the corporate property owner usually prefers to sell off valuable land instead of valuable building space which can be depreciated. The building may or may not have been fully depreciated by the current corporate owner. If it has been, there may be little reluctance to sell off the building and the land. Depreciation expense may reduce the otherwise taxable income of the company.

Entering into a joint venture involving currently owned corporate property will give the current owner a source of cash, will remove part of the property value from the balance sheet, and will complicate the ownership of the valuable real estate from the viewpoint of a potential hostile corporate raider. The acquired cash can be put back into the company's main line of the business for more efficient and profitable management.

## Importance of Environmental Protection and Analysis

Some companies decide to take an aggressive stance in assuring environmental protection as related to their company operations around the world. Other companies take a defensive stance and respond with environmental pollution analysis only when called upon to do so by outside entities. Some companies engage in manufacturing processes that tend to pollute the air or water. The operations may generate industrial waste that must be disposed of; toxic industrial waste may pose disposal problems in environmentally sensitive areas. Some businesses generate noise and light at night which may disturb nearby residential areas. If the company realizes that it is prone to create environmental hazards, that company may choose either an aggressive or a defensive environmental policy position. The company's selection may depend upon the stringency of the environmental protection regulations and enforcement system of the community, state, commune, province, and country. The company's policy may depend on the corporate conscience of the firm's management and board of directors. Some managements are very jealous of their worldwide images and seek to preserve good government, stockholder, consumer, union, and personal relationships.

The corporate environmental protection policy may vary from country to country. Generally, in developing countries environmental protection legislation has been lax. The government leadership has wished to maintain the best possible business relationships with large employers in the world industrial community. Only recently have governments voiced preference for nonpolluting high technology industry for their newly created industrial areas and newly built industrial buildings. Heavy industry with its polluting processes and with its large employment levels has heard this type of government opposition. So they have gravitated to the developing countries that will tolerate some environmental pollution in order to gain high export quotas and employment of its citizens. This is one reason the shipbuilding, steel making, and auto production industries have been drawn to South Korea and Taiwan. In the past India has not had stringent environmental protection regulations so multinational chemical companies located within its borders for this and other reasons. A corporation can develop flexible environmental protection policies depending on the country locations involved. Some countries require expensive waste water treatment plants or capping of smokestacks to reduce air pollution. In those countries the corporation may follow more rigid environmental protection policies.

### Importance of Employee Health and Safety within Company Buildings

Some companies have high level standards for health and safety of their employees who work within their buildings. Management may subscribe to a high standard of outside and inside lighting for each office building even before the local government or union imposes such a standard. Some companies want at least two exits from each office floor. If one exit cannot be used in case of fire or other emergency, another exit will be available. Good ventilation and year-round air conditioning and heating may be requirements for the buildings of some multinational companies. Some multinational companies may subscribe to the local building standards for heating, air conditioning, and ventilation. The local building standards might be much lower than those of the headquarters country. Office building standards tend to be lower in developing countries than in economically advanced countries.

### Need for General Company Property Standards

It may be important to a multinational company to establish and maintain general property standards that are applied worldwide to all its properties. International Business Machines has tended to fit this pattern. Other companies do not find the need for such worldwide property standards. The top management of these companies leave decisions about building standards to the real estate department. Generally the director of real estate would prefer more concrete guidance from top management in this policy area.

Here are some of the areas in which company property standards may be useful:

Fire protection

Air conditioning, heating, and ventilation

Natural light for each office worker

Office sizes by company rank

Ceiling heights

Work space per employee type

Building standards differ along these lines around the world. For instance, the property standards of Latin America tend to be lower than those of Western Europe. Japanese office building standards tend to be different from those of North America, and Italian standards tend to be different from those of France. The multinational company's top management may seek to establish general building standards so that their employee productivity, health, and safety are assured in all company locations.

### The Need for Architectural Policies

Major global firms may wish to establish building architectural policies. Among the major firms, top management tends to differ on the place of architecture within the company. Some companies wish to "make a statement" with spectacular or avant garde architecture such as Bouygues' Grand Arch office building in La Defense of Paris. Hongkong & Shanghai Bank has attracted attention with their new Hong Kong Central headquarters building. Deutsche Bank and Tishman & Speyer, developers, also plan to "make a statement" with the Messeturm Tower of Frankfurt which will be the highest office building in Europe when it is completed.

The architecture of the office buildings of a global corporation may

establish, in part, the image of the company. High-technology office build-
ings are usually associated with high-technology companies such as Digital
Equipment Corporation, Hewlett-Packard, IBM, and Intel. The GAN
Building, the highest in La Defense of Paris, projects the outstanding image
of European pension and investment funds including RODAMCO and
ROBECO, large Dutch institutions.

Should the building's architecture primarily enhance the functions performed by the company whose shelter it provides? Most companies would
agree to this architectural requirement. At the same time, most company
top management would agree that the architecture should adapt to the
environment. In rural or suburban areas the buildings may be lower and
blend in with the topography and foliage.

### Urban Locational Policies for Building Ownership and Leasing

For the guidance of the real estate department, top management needs
to make policy about the urban locations of its properties. Of course, the
properties must lie within areas that are properly zoned for the land use,
or the owner must receive a variance from established zoning for a non-
conforming property. Policy should also be set about the general urban
location, particularly for office and retail buildings. Most industrial buildings must be located in industrially zoned areas of the center city, of certain
suburbs, and of outlying rural areas. New industrial buildings are not permitted in any central business district. But office and retail buildings can
be located in prime central business districts, in secondary locations of the
central business district, in center city office and retail corporations, and
in suburban areas of office and retail concentrations.

Urban locational policies are related to the company's architectural policies. If the company wishes to make statements with their office buildings,
they might want conspicuous office buildings so the company name and
logo atop a magnificent building can be seen far and wide. The urban
location will be part of "corporate image maintenance." The company's
top management may consider this type of spectacular location an important part of its advertising. Many multinational financial institutions, such
as Hongkong & Shanghai Bank, Citicorp, and Deutsche Bank, have this
policy. Other major multinational companies have historically shied away
from spectacular building architecture in prime central business districts.
Some multinationals that deal only with other manufacturers and wholesale
distributors and not directly with consumers fit this corporate locational
preference. In past years E. I. du Pont de Nemours Inc., a diversified
chemical company, has followed this corporate policy. It has deliberately
selected good office locations in the more obscure suburban areas of major
foreign cities with little architectural exposure to the general public. Recently this company had deliberately changed its policy. The du Pont real

estate area, which is located within the materials and logistics department, will be seeking and constructing new office buildings in more publicly noticeable central business districts in foreign cities.

## Control and Management of Overseas Properties

Top management may decide to totally manage and control its overseas properties from the home office. Or it may decide to retain supervisory or consultative authority for its home office and relegate management and control of overseas properties to company people at the particular location or to outside brokers and property managers who are supervised by the on-site company personnel. Sometimes a combination of these two approaches will be employed. Most major multinational companies with immense inventories of industrial, office, warehouse, and retail properties simply cannot manage their properties from the home office. These large companies may maintain supervisory control over expenditures and other matters, but they must depend on regional or local real estate managers overseas for the day-to-day management activity. Multinational companies with small inventories of property overseas may attempt to manage the properties, with the help of local plant managers, from the home office. Or the home office could manage certain foreign properties and then delegate the rest of the worldwide properties to regional real estate representatives or plant or divisional managers. No one pattern fits all multinational companies.

The home-office real estate director may supervise all expenditure requests from all domestic and foreign properties. Or the director may approve only the requests over a certain base amount, say $200,000.

## Litigation Policies

Top management may decide that contestable real estate matters should be settled amicably by the disputing parties if possible before any long, drawn out litigation. Legal disputes are associated with real estate activities in any country. The Japanese businesses are particularly averse to litigation, since their culture is based on discussion, negotiation, and compromise. In comparison to the large legal community in the United States, Japan has very few attorneys—only 14,000—to deal with all domestic and foreign business matters for a population of 125 million.

## Real Estate Accounting Policy

Top management may wish to monitor the current value of its real estate. Most multinational firms do not revalue their properties for yearly financial statements. Generally they focus on their manufacturing and distribution interests and pay little attention to the high values of their real estate. Corporate policy may be turning to annual appraisals of all corporate property as the company tracks each property closely by computer analysis. Generally the major multinational corporations have insufficient in-house appraisal staff to do annual appraisals of all properties.

### Company Policy toward Political Risk and Its Property Locations

The company's top management may aggressively take on political risk as it seeks new manufacturing plant, office, warehouse, and retail locations. The perception of market demand may override perceptions of political risk. A company might seek to serve new overseas markets and assume that it can handle any political risks that may be encountered. For example, most multinational corporations have entered or are entering the market of the People's Republic of China if they perceive Chinese market demand for their products. After the Chinese student uprising in May and June of 1989 and the government punishment of offenders and reassignment of students to rural areas, most multinational corporations proceeded with their plans and operations in that country. Admittedly, most companies pulled their threatened personnel out of Chinese locations temporarily while the government sanctions were imposed, but most of the companies had no intention of withdrawing from that communist market. In like manner, most companies with an opportunity to enter the Eastern European bloc and Russia do not hesitate even though political risk is apparent.

Most of the properties used by global firms in politically risky communist environments are leased from government entities. Seldom do communist government agencies permit private land and building ownership especially for foreign investors, manufacturers, and distributors of products.

Political risks in Central and South America and Africa are assumed by global firms as they seek profits from product sales and from manufacturing, natural resource exploration, processing, and product assembly. As a policy, the firms generally plan to deal with the risk as it appears. Major multinational companies build, buy, and lease properties on these continents with little hesitation.

Some global company real estate personnel take the possibility of company and asset nationalization by a foreign country rather lightly. If one government nationalized the properties of a global company with a worldwide presence and a large inventory of properties, that government would probably take only a very small portion of the company's overall property investment. Of course, a multinational company with few properties in a few countries would perhaps have a different perception of government nationalization of their assets.

## Approach to Foreign Land Use Approval

All global real estate directors are confronted with the local land use approval system as they attempt to develop property. Even land and building purchase transactions may be complicated by the local land use approval process. Some global firms plan to work within the local system and eventually get the land rezoned for their intended land use. The major company plans to wait it out and get what they want with time. Other companies who do not wish to wait for the desired government approvals are frustrated and seek other alternatives. It is difficult to speed up the regular government approval process without encountering extra payments for services. Firms based in the United States understand that their government forbids by law such extraordinary payments that may be defined as bribes of government and other officials.

The foreign company may have a policy of employing local people who are knowledgeable in the local land use approval system and who know the people involved. With the assistance of a person employed perhaps only for this duty, the corporation can proceed as if it believes the necessary approval will be forthcoming. Temporary consultants may be employed for this purpose.

The company may, as a policy, enter into joint ventures in new country locations so that the domestic company can facilitate such negotiations. The joint venture partner who in the past has successfully gained similar land use approvals may expedite the often time- and money-consuming process.

## Organization for Global Real Estate Administration

In an era of global and national corporate takeovers and asset-based financing through global capital markets, there is a need for the integration of global real estate into multinational corporate strategy. The U.S. trade associations are suggesting in various reports the integration of real estate into corporate strategy. Joel R. Parker has recently discussed the need for this strategy established by the 1988 report, *The Corporate Real Estate Profession: Tasks and Resources*, published by the Industrial Development Research Council.[2] The integration of real estate into overall corporate strategy is suggested for three reasons: (1) fast-changing product lines, (2) shorter product cycles, and (3) corporate acquisitions. The obstacles in the formulation of a long-term facilities plan that could be integrated into corporate strategy include: (1) limited corporate level long-term planning, (2) resistance from operating divisions, (3) top management indifference, (4) imminent corporate restructuring, (5) real estate department's placement in the corporate structure, and (6) other considerations. One half of the companies surveyed by the Industrial Development Research Council did not have a company-wide facilities management plan and planning goals. So the integration of real estate into corporate strategy has just begun.

### Centralized versus Decentralized Real Estate Management

My research points to decentralization of global corporate real estate management of the majority of U.S.-based multinational companies. The majority of Fortune 500 multinational corporations let their overseas plant managers manage the real properties within their market jurisdictions. Perhaps a third of these major global companies actively manage their overseas properties from the corporate headquarters. Some of the companies manage the finances for the overseas properties actively from the home office. But the property management, acquisition, leasing, and other such duties involving the overseas real estate may be left to the project and plant managers of the area in which the properties are located. The overseas division or group may or may not do the actual management; they may contract with local real estate firms for the property management, acquisition, and leasing functions. The foreign partners of the multinational corporation may take care of the foreign real estate. The home office may assign the property management duties to a real estate firm that operates in the area of the foreign real estate.

The decentralization of the global corporate real estate may be managed on a regional or country basis. A major telecommunications company is restructuring its real estate organization to form a worldwide regional structure. A major diversified chemical company is organized on the basis of three worldwide offices. Each office is given responsibility for several regions for real estate administration. A major multinational computer company is organized by country. The general manager for the country's computer operations also assigns his or her staff the management of the company's real properties within the country.

Global real estate management may be totally centralized. The total centralization may reflect initial forays into multinational operations, long-term global business, or an in-between stage of multinational corporate development. As Anheuser Busch, a major alcoholic beverage firm, moves into the European market, it has centralized its real estate management at the St. Louis, Missouri home office. It is developing a large tract on the northern portion of the eastern coast of Spain, a site southeast of Barcelona. The major mixed-use project is being managed actively from the U.S. corporate headquarters. In contrast, Warner Lambert, a diversified pharmaceutical company, has a fully centralized real estate department that manages U.S. and overseas properties. Multinational operations are nothing new to this well-entrenched global firm. The fully centralized real estate management of Warner Lambert is also represented in Abbott Laboratories, another multinational pharmaceutical company. The major oil companies tend to have fully centralized real estate management, also.

Companies that are rapidly establishing global operations may be fully centralized for real estate management. The multinational courier companies tend to represent this "in-between" position. These companies are not new to multinational business, but they are not historically entrenched in global business like Royal Dutch Shell or Exxon.

### The Position of Corporate Real Estate within the Multinational Company

The recent report, *The Corporate Real Estate Profession: Tasks and Resources*, which appeared to focus on major corporations operating primarily in the United States, revealed that the manager of corporate real estate reports directly to the chief executive officer (CEO) in only one percent of the responding companies. At 44 percent of the responding companies, there was one reporting level between the manager of corporate real estate and the CEO. In 39 percent of the cases, there were two reporting levels between the manager of corporate real estate and the CEO. Three reporting levels were between the manager of real estate and the CEO in 14 percent of the cases.[3] At a major multinational chemical company there are far more than three reporting levels between the CEO and the corporate real estate department.

### The Organizational Structure of Corporate Real Estate Itself

At least part of the corporate real estate function may be incorporated while the rest falls directly under the corporate organizational "umbrella." Sometimes the special real estate board or corporation is designed to permit the company to develop property for sale to other entities in national and global markets. A number of corporate real estate departments function as profit-making land developers. Their joint venture and other financing programs induce risks and other financial features that may be best accommodated by the special real estate board or corporation. For example, AT&T has a special real estate board that reports to the chairman of AT&T, the second-ranking officer of the total AT&T organization.

More often than not, corporate real estate falls under an administrative or support services function. In one multinational company, real estate, purchasing, education and training, and support services report to the manager of contract services. Within this structure, real estate represents 500 people while support services represents 7,500 of the total 8,000 people working within the contract services organization. Or a vice president may manage both the real estate and the general services division, as occurs at the Xerox Corporation. Occasionally corporate real estate falls within a materials and logistics department that reports to the purchasing department. Even though industrial and plant engineering, which works closely with corporate real estate, may report to an operations department manager, corporate real estate may answer to the finance department. Or corporate real estate, construction engineering, and facilities planning may all report to engineering administration.

Corporate real estate may encompass tax, currency, and political risk management and insurance, but it usually does not. Rarely is there an association with the foreign exchange or treasury department. Normally both property and project management fall within the jurisdiction of corporate real estate. Finance, including real estate finance, seldom is integrated into the real estate department. Land development may be, but few multinational corporations have for-profit land development functions. Most of their land development serves their corporate needs, not the needs of outside firms and clients. National and global employee relocation might rest within the corporate real estate department.

One might say that the principal functions of global corporate real estate are (1) facility planning, (2) leasing, (3) property acquisition and disposition, (4) property and record management, (5) project development and management, and (6) real estate services, such as employee relocation. These corporate functions may be performed as a staff function or on a consulting or advisory basis. The multinational corporation usually needs these services, but they may be managed in a variety of ways, often changing the department from a staff function to a profit-making consultant function.

## SELECTED MANAGEMENT CHARACTERISTICS OF THE CORPORATE REAL ESTATE FUNCTION

Let us look over the approval of corporate real estate financial requests, use of the services of other departments of the company, employee relocation programs, and other employee financial assistance. Several of the corporate real estate functions are broken down into more detailed functional areas.

### Approval of Real Estate Expenditure Requests

Most corporations require that all the people associated with a corporate real estate budget request sign off on the individual financial request. A plant manager or other corporate person initiates a request for funds for real estate. The real estate department may review the request initially to see what other corporate managers are involved. For example, if the plant manager needs more space due to increased sales, several people are financially involved in the request. Perhaps seven or eight people must give approval to a single financial request before the director of real estate takes the necessary actions to implement the planned expansion and/or divestiture program. Steps must be taken to get the building constructed or the space leased. An older, obsolete building may have to be sold and then new premises procured. This is a typical "sign-off" approval system for real estate expenditures at major multinational corporations.

### Utilization of Other Company Personnel

The headquarters office may or may not be involved in the approval of all real estate expenditure requests. One of the major U.S.-based aircraft manufacturers for worldwide markets and one of the major chemical companies must approve or deny every request for real estate expenditure no matter what the amount in U.S. dollars. The real estate headquarters of a major food processor and distributor approves only expenditures of $5 million or more. The headquarters real estate office of a major office equipment manufacturer and distributor approves only expenditure requests of $500,000 or more. Decisions about the smaller budget requests are made by local overseas company officials such as the corporate manager of the company's operations.

Some real estate departments may utilize the services, on a temporary basis, of other corporate departments. This "matrix system" requires interdepartmental cooperation to further the corporate objectives.

Corporate real estate staff may be temporarily assigned to countries for which they are not primarily responsible. For example, in Brazil, in order to develop an appropriate building for a corporate headquarters plant or office building, a staff real estate member may be borrowed temporarily from a Chilean office. This experienced real estate person could set up the construction or leasing program that will give the company the needed production or administrative premises. Some fast food companies borrow two or three real estate staff from established company operations for the setting up of the first few retail outlets in a new country. After local managers and employees are hired, the "borrowed" personnel are moved back to their original office locations. Thus the multinational real estate expansion continues to take place.

### Employee Relocation and Other Financial Services

As employee relocation costs have risen so extremely in the 1970s and 1980s, corporations have developed programs to financially assist their personnel in moving to worldwide locations where the companies need their services. If the employee is asked to move from a lower cost area to the higher cost one, the company will meet resistance from the employee unless the new compensation program for the employee makes up for the cost differences. If the person's salary cannot be increased enough to cover the cost differentials, the company may need to help with the increased living costs in another way. Therefore, the employee relocation programs were devised and implemented. The real estate department often administers the program.

What costs are involved in moving an employee to another country or to another area of the same country? The new house for the employee's family might cost substantially more. A move from anywhere to Tokyo definitely means a very significant house or apartment price increase for generally less space. The moving costs include temporary housing for the family members during the search for a home and after the new job starts but before the new home is available for occupancy. Often the existing home must be sold before the household can afford to buy the new home. Most workers find it difficult to pay for two home mortgages at the same time plus all other personal living costs. The costs of a moving van, packing at the existing home, and unpacking at the new home are substantial, particularly if the move involves relocation to another country perhaps overseas. Then the personal belongings, including furniture and cars, must be shipped by ocean, which requires money and time.

First, the employee relocation office usually gives the employee an incentive to sell his or her existing home. If the home is not sold by the time the employee must start work at the new location, the company's relocation office will generally have the home appraised by three independent appraisers and will pay the employee a reasonable amount for the home. The company then sells the home to recoup the price paid to the employee plus cover the other corporate expense. The company assumes the risk of selling the property at a reasonable price.

Other overseas employee programs provide expatriate housing facilities, transportation subsidies when the employee faces extraordinary commuting costs, housing and housing upkeep subsidies, and school tuition payments for private overseas schools that cater to multinational employee children. In Hong Kong, the tight housing situation prompts corporate provision of expatriate housing that can be rented for relatively short periods of overseas duty. In Singapore, local property laws prohibiting foreign purchase of Singapore land and housing force corporations to provide rental housing for their expatriate employees. Transportation, housing, housing maintenance, and school payments are common expenses for the maintenance of expatriate households in costly areas where the public schools are administered in a language other than the employee's normal language.

*More Detailed Structuring of the Corporate Real Estate Function.* There are a variety of ways of structuring the corporate real estate function of the multinational corporation. A major multinational food company breaks the real estate function into employee relocation, tax management, insurance, and industrial and commercial real estate. A major telecommunications company breaks the real estate function into (1) planning and finance, (2) international real estate, (3) real estate development, and (4) project management. Under the planning and finance function, the managers deal with international and domestic planning and finance. For this same company, there is a director of international real estate who has several real estate district managers. Real estate development is divided into the following regions: Canada, Europe, the Middle East, Africa, the Far East, Japan, and Latin America. Under project management, several construction project managers work. A major office equipment firm is reducing the principal functional areas of corporate real estate from three to two. After development and investment have been eliminated, the two functions remaining will be (1) acquisition and divestiture and (2) leasing.

Project management may entail the following functional areas:

Lease acquisitions

Land and facility purchases

Surplus property disposal

Long-range facility studies and recommendations

Space design and construction (field locations)

Building design and construction

Property management and operations may entail the following functional areas:

Utilities operations

Contract services such as

   cafeteria
   janitorial
   window washing
   scavenger
   snow removal
   indoor plants
   exterminating
   elevators
   non-lab office furniture

Building maintenance

Security

Architectural services

Building administration such as

   capital and expense budget administration and coordination
   financial and control budgets
   annual audit and expense escalation
   planning, scheduling, and control of construction and maintenance work

furniture inventory
purchasing, invoice processing, tenant buildings
food service coordination

### Controlling the Administration of Corporate Real Estate

Various methods are used for controlling the administration of corporate real estate. If the company retains good profitability over the long term, top management will assume, to some extent, that the company's real estate holdings and rented premises are accommodating the principal company operations. Actually the stockholders, the owners of the business, look to the trends in sales and profits as well as to dividend distributions.

If the corporation seeks to monitor the profit performance of the real estate function directly, it may turn the real estate department into a consulting group. Each project taken on by the real estate group must generate a market-competitive fee for services. The costs of the real estate group operation must be paid out of the service fees paid by corporate divisions and groups and non-corporate, outside clients. Personnel must be hired, trained, promoted, and retrained with the monies available from the consulting fees. From the income, the company must be compensated for the space used by the consulting group. The cost and operating expense of the business equipment and computer software must also be covered. In essence, all costs of the group must be covered by the revenues. The group as a profit center must generate profits for dividend and bonus payments.

If the real estate department is a staff function and not a profit center, periodic analyses of performance may reveal to the top management the efficiency and competence of the individuals employed by the real estate department. Each of the employees may be evaluated once or more often per year against the individual objectives that each have set for themselves. Top management may also subject itself to individual evaluation on a periodic basis. If each of the associates of the individual being evaluated comments about the recent service given by the individual, a rather complete picture of the individual's productivity will be gained. Generally the management and employee evaluations are forerunners to annual salary and bonus compensation schemes. The corporate real estate department may have an established annual salary with an additional increment for group real estate performance and an additional increment for individual performance within the real estate group. Promotions may also be based on these corporate evaluations.

## INTERNATIONAL COMMUNICATIONS

Global real estate planning, organizing, and controlling revolve around a well functioning international corporate communications system. For example, the Mitsui international trading company established a multi-media communications center in its corporate office in Tokyo. This costly communications center is essential to its worldwide operations. Companies such as Mitsui & Co. use telex, international facsimile, international telephone, and other such services. If the real estate department is well equipped with personal and main frame computer systems, overseas electronic mail may be used for interoffice communications.

## SUMMARY

Since global business is important to the world's economy, the real estate that supports global business is important to the world's economic success. The real estate of global business must accommodate the objectives of the multinational company. Changes in corporate real estate are taking place due to changes in corporate structures and due to multinational corporate expansion. There is a worldwide merger and acquisition movement in progress that affects the major and smaller corporations in most industries in most countries. The companies that are not yet experiencing corporate takeover overtures by potential corporate acquirers are trying to defend themselves from hostile takeovers by restructuring their companies and real properties. The companies with decentralized management of their properties are tending to reanalyze their real estate management on a more centralized basis. Many of the corporate takeovers are being financed through the sale of the real estate of the acquired corporation. Most corporate real estate is valued on the corporate books at historical cost so there is widespread understatement of market value. Some global corporations have deliberately been split up as a corporate defense against possible takeover. Therefore, valuable real estate may be split into two or more independently listed companies or autonomous corporate groups.

Global business is expanding for a number of reasons. Global competition is fostered by the advances in telecommunications. Many impediments exist for global competition and the expansion of multinational businesses. To bolster national economies, each country usually strives for a positive overall balance of trade where export volume exceeds import volume. The exportation of goods is generated by excess or normal capacity of home industries and by exchange rates that foster exports. For example, the steep devaluation of the U.S. dollar was a major stimulant to the recent growth in the U.S. exports of goods and services. The prices of U.S. goods and services become cheaper to foreign buyers. Some goods are partially produced in several countries and then sold in many countries as demand dictates.

As global business expanded, the methods of global corporate real estate management became more important. The challenges of global corporate real estate have been noticed by the international trade associations that appeal to multinational corporate real estate members. They have recently established international conferences to help the global directors of real estate to meet the challenges of their expanding jobs. International conferences on the development of an integrated Europe by 1992 are particularly popular with trade association members. The mergers, acquisitions, and corporate restructurings are giving a lot of work to real estate directors who increasingly acquire, divest, and lease space in Western Europe.

The general management functions of planning, organizing, and controlling may be applied to global corporate real estate management. There should be real estate and facility planning for the anticipated growth cycle of the multinational company. The real estate department has the major role in the creation and development of new space for the company. All of the functions performed by the real estate department require planning. Some of the functions may be performed by outside consultants and real estate companies. Some global businesses employ international real estate companies for various selected services.

Company policies can be established to guide the corporate real estate department in its worldwide work. The policies may pertain to (1) property ownership or leasing, (2) property management by company or outside contractors, (3) profit center or staff corporate real estate facility, (4) property held only for corporate use or for rental or sale to outside entities for an additional profit, (5) property market value monitoring, (6) use of joint ventures for property holding, (7) environmental protection inspections and management, (8) importance of employee health and safety within company structures, (9) general company property standards, (10) architectural policies, (11) urban locational policies, (12) control and management of overseas properties, (13) real estate accounting, (14) attitude toward political risk assumption, and (15) approach to foreign land use.

Global real estate may be administered on a centralized or a decentralized basis. Real estate strategy should be integrated into overall corporate strategy, but more often than not today, it is not. The corporate real estate function may be organized in a number of ways. Real estate expenditure requests need established policies for efficient management. Employee relocation, employee subsidies for higher-than-normal overseas living expenses, and other employee financial services may be a part of the functions of the real estate department.

The ability of top management to control the administrative real estate function revolves around the profitability and profit trends of the company. Periodic personnel evaluations can aid the administration of compensation programs. Establishing the real estate area as a profit center can help in management control. Most real estate departments are staff functions of the overall holding or operating company. International communications require full-service communications equipment and corporate centers for this special purpose. The real estate department may particularly benefit from such corporate services and equipment in the control of its operations.

## SUMMARY OF BOOK CONTENTS

Recently the management of global corporate real estate has been spotlighted by the use of corporate real estate to finance major corporate takeovers. The majority of the hostile and friendly takeovers have involved Fortune 500 multinational corporations with large inventories of real estate. After the merger or acquisition, the acquiring company has sold the prime real estate for prices much higher than the book values carried in the company's financial statements.

Expanding multinational companies usually acquire or build new industrial plants to gain more production space. When the company restructures for changing markets and changing competitive relationships, they may dispose of some properties and buy others that are better located or designed or offer more space. Therefore, Chapter 2 covers the acquisition and disposition of foreign corporate property.

If the company does not acquire space for its expansion into a new market, it leases space. Many multinational companies lease office space for their administrative headquarters. They may also engage in sale-lease-backs of industrial plants and warehouses. This is covered in Chapter 3, entitled "Leasing Space."

Chapter 4 deals with the taxes of multinational corporations which can be managed for the reduction of corporate tax incidence. Property sales revenue, net cash flows from the rental of excess space in owned buildings, and property acquisitions and sales are affected by income taxes, capital gains taxes, value added taxes, wealth taxes, rent taxes, transfer taxes, and other such taxes which are levied by federal, state, commune, region, province, and local governments. As funds are repatriated to the home country from property rental and sale, these funds are subject to withholding taxes on dividends, royalties, interest, management fees, and other such payments to the headquarters office.

Many risks are encountered by corporate real estate managers. The various risks are enumerated and possible solutions are mentioned in Chapter 5, entitled "Risk Management."

Chapter 6, "Performance Measurement and Portfolio Management," reports on current methods of performance measurement and the application of global portfolio management. Since corporate real estate facilities are not the main business of the multinational corporation, little attention has been given these topics until recently. The performance of the real estate portfolios of multinational companies has attracted the attention of potential acquirers of "understated" or "undervalued" companies. Then, some companies, in moves to ward off hostile takeovers, have changed their real estate thrusts to centers for real estate consulting and development for other land users as well as for their own additional profit.

## NOTES

1. 1988 corporate annual reports of Union Carbide and AT&T.
2. Robert H. Pittman, "Integration of Real Estate into Corporate Strategy: A Progress Report," *Site Selection*, February 1989, pp. 2–3.
3. Ibid.

## BIBLIOGRAPHY

Bingham, Bruce B. "Managing Corporate Real Estate in a Takeover." *Site Selection*, February 1988, pp. 6–9.

Brown, Bob. "International Network Helps UPS Set Sights on Global Market." *Network World*, October 10, 1988, p. 55.

Cox, James. "A Crack in the Golden Arches?" *USA Today*, July 27, 1989, p. 3B.

Donahue, John J. "A Site-Selection Case in Sydney, Australia." *Site Selection*, June 1989, pp. 20–22.

"End Seen in Olivetti AT&T Tie." *International Herald Tribune*, July 15–16, 1989, p. 9.

Gabetti Agency. *The Italian Real Estate Market in 1988*. Milan, Italy: Research Department, Gabetti Agency, 1988.

King, Resa W. "UPS Isn't About to Be Left Holding the Parcel." *Business Week*, February 13, 1989.

Labich, Kenneth. "Big Change at Big Brown." *Fortune*, January 18, 1988.

Love, John F. *McDonald's: Behind the Arches*. New York: Bantam Books, 1986.

Lublin, Joann S., and Craig Forman. "Battle of Britain: Europe's Merger Boom Triggers an Invasion by U.S. Deal Makers." *Wall Street Journal*, August 23, 1989, pp. A2, A8.

Messenger, Bob. "Campbell Gears Up for Global Battleground." *Food Business*, October 14, 1988.

Peltz, Curtis. "Integrated Building Data Base." *Building Operating Management*, July 1989, pp. 51–53.

Pittman, Robert H. "Integration of Real Estate Into Corporate Strategy: A Progress Report." *Site Selection*, February 1988, pp. 2–3.

Porter, Michael E., ed. *Competition in Global Industries*. Cambridge, Mass.: Harvard Business School Press.

Rees, Terry L. "Site Selection in Europe—A Case Study." *Site Selection*, October 1988, pp. 13–15.

Richardson, Michael. "Japanese Industry Boosts Southeast Asian Base." *International Herald Tribune*, July 15–16, 1989, p. 9.

Silverman, Robert A., ed. *Corporate Real Estate Handbook*. New York: McGraw-Hill, 1987.

"Site Net Dramatically Expands Geo-Economic Coverage." *Site Selection Handbook*, February 1988, p. 267+.

Welle, David, and Thomas Hauschild. "Integrating Real Estate into Corporate Strategic Planning." *Coopers & Lybrand Real Estate Newsletter*, Spring 1988, pp. 1–4.
Wood, Allen F. "Site Selection Trends—1989–2000." *Site Selection*, June 1988, pp. 12–13.

# 2

# ACQUIRING AND DISPOSING OF FOREIGN CORPORATE PROPERTY

Multinational corporations acquire properties to gain profits from the production and distribution of various products. When an industrial plant is established, the investment is usually long term. An industrial plant will serve the production and distribution systems of the company. A warehouse can be built quickly or purchased readily if appropriately designed storage and distribution space is available at the right location. Until the company changes its production and distribution systems significantly, the warehouse space is satisfactory. Office space may be acquired with the warehouse construction or purchase. Otherwise, an office building may be built or purchased at a location appropriate for company and personnel purposes. Like the warehouse, the office space or building is useful in its current location until production and distribution systems change significantly. In other words, warehouse and office space tends to have shorter useful life than industrial plants that are built for a unique manufacturing process. Warehouses and office buildings are usually not built according to unique specifications. While it may be difficult to dispose of an industrial plant built for a specific purpose, it usually is not hard to dispose of warehouse and office buildings because they can serve various occupants.

## TRENDS IN MAJOR OIL COMPANY PROPERTIES

When a multinational company expands worldwide, it may buy or build more properties to serve the primary company objectives. When the primary company objectives change, the company may have to dispose of their properties. For example, when retail marketing of gasoline products became relatively unprofitable, many multinational companies disposed of a large number of their service stations. In the 1970s, these major oil companies closed and sold off many neighborhood stations; they developed large real estate staffs just for the disposition of properties in various regions of the United States. Many of the service stations became fast food or fast photo-processing locations. Other service stations were demolished for new land uses on the valuable corner sites. Some of the service stations were bought by smaller oil distributors who closed down the unprofitable car service bays. Today, in all parts of the world, there are far fewer "filling stations" to serve neighborhoods than there were in the 1950s, 1960s, and 1970s.

## TRENDS IN WORLDWIDE IRON AND STEEL INDUSTRY PROPERTIES

The iron and steel community of Western Europe was an important force that required extensive amounts of real property before the Second World War. After the bombing of Europe during that war, there was need for iron and steel products to rebuild Europe. Ample property was again devoted to the iron and steel industry, particularly in the Düsseldorf-Cologne general area. Then competition from South Korea and Japan began to affect the profitability of the iron and steel industries of Western Europe and the United States. Many industrial plants became obsolete due to the advancement in technological processes in South Korea and Japan and due to the incline in profitable business. The European companies started to dispose of unnecessary industrial plants, warehouses, and office buildings associated with the declining European industry. They saturated the market with obsolete and unneeded space. As this occurred, the various European governments developed programs for the "rationalization" of the vacant industrial and commercial space. New land uses were sought for these properties.

## TRENDS IN AUTO COMPANY PROPERTIES

When the mass production assembly-line process was developed in the auto industry worldwide, one-story production plants which spread endlessly across land were built to expand auto production. When the robotic systems using computerized machine tools were developed, the older mass production assembly line plants became obsolete. The property acquisition process was reversed. The auto companies tried to sell the uniquely constructed assembly plants. When that idea generally failed because the market was saturated with obsolete auto plants, they started redeveloping the old buildings for partially robotic and computerized processes. With advanced technology, the global auto companies designed and built new premises in new locations to cut costs per unit of production. The Japanese encouraged the latter trend by building computerized auto plants in new areas of the United States and Europe. They avoided plant locations in unionized metropolitan areas and sought inexpensive rural land where local labor was trainable and anxious to work. The advancement of technology

**Exhibit 2.1**
**Total Assets, Net Property, Plant, and Equipment, and Percentage of Total Assets Represented by Net Property, Plant, and Equipment of 14 Selected U.S.-Based Multinational Corporations, 1988**

| U.S.-Based Multinational Corporation | Total Assets (Millions of Dollars) | Net Property, Plant and Equipment at Cost (Millions of Dollars) | Percent Represented by Net Property, Plant and Equipment of Total Assets |
|---|---|---|---|
| Philip Morris including Kraft General Foods Group | $36,960 | $ 8,648 | 23.4% |
| Motorola | 6,710 | 2,854 | 42.5 |
| Abbott Laboratories | 4,825 | 1,952 | 40.5 |
| McDonald's | 8,159 | 6,800 | 83.3 |
| Morton Thiokol | 1,920 | 760 | 39.6 |
| Amoco | 29,919 | 23,095 | 77.2 |
| Campbell Soup | 3,610 | 1,509 | 41.8 |
| Warner Lambert | 2,703 | 1,053 | 38.9 |
| United Parcel Service | 6,936 | 5,025 | 72.4 |
| duPont | 30,719 | 17,221 | 56.1 |
| Xerox | 26,441 | 2,008 | 7.6 |
| Union Carbide | 8,441 | 4,416 | 52.3 |
| FMC Corporation | 2,749 | 1,268 | 46.1 |
| AT&T | 35,152 | 15,280 | 43.5 |

Source: 1988 corporate annual reports.

and the changes in production costs led to changes in industrial plants, warehouses, and office buildings associated with the worldwide auto industry.

## THE HOLDINGS OF NET PROPERTY, PLANT, AND EQUIPMENT OF MULTINATIONAL CORPORATIONS

The significance of net property, plant, and equipment to a company depends on many factors including the nature of the industry and management policies. Exhibit 2.1 shows a range from 83 percent of the total assets of McDonald's Corporation to seven percent of Xerox Corporation. The fourteen sample global companies had generally 35 to 45 percent of their assets devoted to net property, plant, and equipment in 1988. In this sample the average percentage of total assets represented by net property, plant, and equipment is 47.5 percent. The significance of global corporate real estate is partially shown by this percentage.

Actually, in market terms, the percentage devoted to net plant, property, and equipment is higher than the average of 47.5 percent. While the other assets of the firm are carried at market value, real properties are normally carried at historical cost. At their historical costs, the fourteen multinational companies had committed over U.S. $30 billion to investment properties, land and improvements, buildings, and construction in progress. At the same time, the total assets of the fourteen companies, according to 1988 annual financial statements, was over U.S. $205 billion. Since net property, plant, and equipment at cost represented over U.S. $91 billion, the value of the equipment carried on the books was approximately U.S. $60 billion. Very little of the global corporate property was represented by investment properties—less than one percent among the fourteen global companies (Exhibit 2.2).

## TRENDS IN CORPORATE REAL ESTATE NEEDS

Expansion of multinational companies is focused in certain areas, but the expansion affects all areas of the world. For example, various kinds of companies, including diversified chemical companies, continue to establish plants and distribution outlets in South Asia including India. The huge market for products and the existence of trainable labor are particularly appealing to many companies. In the People's Republic of China, we find the same corporate appeal. While India is forecasted to have one billion people within ten years, China surpassed the one billion population mark recently.

With the approach of 1997, companies currently producing and distributing products in Hong Kong are considering relocation north to Taiwan and Japan or west to Singapore, Malaysia, and Thailand. They may also be considering various locations in Australia to serve both the South Pacific and Asian markets. But the market is small and labor is expensive in Australia and New Zealand.

The unified Europe represents a formidable market and production site to many multinational companies, including those already established in Europe. The growth countries of Europe that appeal to manufacturers and distributors are Spain and Portugal. More corporate expansion will take place in these countries due to relatively low labor costs, the availability of skilled and trainable labor, the increasing incomes and standards of living, the political encouragement of foreign investment, and their en-

**Exhibit 2.2**
**Types of Property and Total Property Value Net of Depreciation of 12 Selected U.S.-Based Multinational Corporations, 1988 (Millions of Dollars)**

| U.S.-Based Multinational Corporation | Investment Properties | Land and Improvements | Buildings | Construction in Progress | Total Net Properties |
|---|---|---|---|---|---|
| FMC Corporation | | $113.2 | $ 214.6 | $ 68.5 | $ 396 |
| AT&T | | | | | 7,468 |
| Union Carbide | | 415 | 762 | 471 | 1,648 |
| Xerox | | 480 | 773 | 179 | 1,432 |
| United Parcel Service | $290.2[a] | 441.5[a] | 1,456.8[a] | 254.1 | 2,442.8[a] |
| Warner Lambert | | 30.2[a] | 640.5[a] | -0- | 670.7[a] |
| Campbell Soup | | 53.2[a] | 735.5[a] | 126.6[ab] | 915.3[a] |
| Morton Thiokol | | - - 483.4[ac] - - | | 96.8[a] | 580.2[a] |
| McDonald's | | - - 7,244.4[ac] - - | | | 7,244.4[a] |
| Abbott Laboratories | | 52.9[a] | 770.8[a] | 171.0[a] | 994.7[a] |
| Motorola | | 107[a] | 1,420[a] | | 1,527[a] |
| Philip Morris | | 612[a] | 3,422[a] | 761[a] | 4,795[a] |
| Total . . . . . . . . . . . . . . . . . . . . . . . . . . . . | | | | | 30,114.1 |

[a]Historical (not depreciated) cost of property. The company carries accumulated depreciation for "property, plant, and equipment" altogether as one amount.
[b]Projects in progress.
[c]Represents land, improvements, and buildings.

*Source*: 1988 corporate annual reports. Data were not available for Amoco or DuPont during the same time period.

trance into the "tariff-free" European market of the mid–1990s. Italy also represents a developing country that is attractive to multinational firms.

Eastern Europe is appealing to the firm that is in an expansion mode. Glasnost and perestroika communist policies are opening the doors of trade and manufacturing within the boundaries of the USSR and its satellite countries. Other multinational firms plan to join the foreign firms already doing business in Hungary, Poland, Russia, and other USSR-satellite countries.

## METHODS OF ACQUIRING PROPERTY FOR CORPORATE PURPOSES

Property may be acquired directly or indirectly. A company may seek to buy the land and/or the land improvements from the owner. Or the company may buy an entire building when it wants only a portion of the building space, or it may buy the company that owns the desired property.

The direct acquisition route—purchase of the land and buildings which will be useful in total to the company—is the most straightforward and perhaps the least expensive to the company. If only part of the space is needed, say part of the ground floor space for a company's retailing outlet, the owner may be asked to sell only the needed space. If the owner does not wish to sell only part of the building, the multinational corporation may find it desirable to buy the entire building and then to dispose of the unnecessary part. Or the multinational corporation may lease out the un-needed space until it wishes to expand into the excess space later when business grows out of the initial space. If the building owner does not wish to sell the desired building, the multinational corporation may acquire the company that owns the building. This has been done in Western Europe when the building ownership was in the hands of a small company. The site was considered prime for the multinational corporation's purposes. Therefore, the corporation must remain flexible in its approach to property acquisition. The corporation may encounter all kinds of situations when the seller is approached.

## LAND ASSEMBLY AND DEVELOPMENT

To get what the company wants, it may have to acquire sufficient land and develop the desired property. A special corporate subsidiary might develop the project. If there are joint venture partners, their assistance may prove very valuable. After the project is completed, the company has the option of retaining the ownership or selling it and leasing it back. Either way the company will gain property built to its specifications.

### The Frequency of Land Assembly and Government Involvement

Public and private land assembly is common in such countries as the United States, Canada, Singapore, and Japan. In Latin America, corporate real estate executives say that private land assembly is not customarily employed for projects.

Most governments can exercise their power of eminent domain for the assembly of land. They can also use their preemptive rights—if the government reserves this right to itself—in intervening in private transactions to acquire desired property at the negotiated price. Japan and France use the government's preemptive right in real estate, for example. In the Madrid area, a major telecommunications joint venture made up of a U.S. company, a Spanish partner, and the Spanish government has used the

Spanish government's power of eminent domain to assemble a site appropriate for a major manufacturing facility.

Motorola's Japanese joint venture partner, Toshiba, helped immeasurably with the development of a manufacturing facility in a high-technology industrial community in Japan. By using the more than 200 architects of Toshiba and Toshiba's construction company, the joint venture plant was built in 1¼ to 2 years. Usually the development and construction of such a complex manufacturing facility would take much longer.

Major corporations often wait for the scarce industrial property sites in some countries. For example, one major U.S. multinational chemical company found that the Japanese owners had a long list of major corporations waiting for appropriate sites in a particular industrial park. The industrial park owners were in a position to pick and choose from the major companies on the list. Once the chemical company's plans were approved by the park owners for one of their available sites, the Japanese owners were in a position to demand that the approved development and construction plans be implemented within *three* years. Many major multinational corporations wish to warehouse sites for later development when their business expands sufficiently to fully use the site. In this instance, the U.S. chemical company had to move ahead immediately to implement the construction program approved by the Japanese park owners. They could not wait for a more favorable land development time.

The local government may have very high environmental protection standards for domestic and foreign-owned manufacturing plants. Singapore, for example, has particularly high standards that have tended to scare away some major companies. Instead of locating in Singapore, FMC Corporation, for example, has considered plant development in Australia, considered to be in the same global business sector. The Australian government might not have as high standards for environmental protection as Singapore.

Land assembly can be very difficult in Western Europe. Historically, land owners hold their properties through many generations. Property is a very desirable asset among European investors. Many local governments wish to preserve the facades of long-standing buildings because of tourism. Also, they do not want urban sprawl which increases taxation for widespread infrastructure. Tenant tenure rights also give great importance to the lessee's rights. The owner may be willing to sell, but the tenants may not wish to relocate.

Union Carbide needed a Geneva headquarters when leasable space of the desired amount and building quality were not available. Then the company considered land development, but space and time did not permit it. So they found a partially completed residential condominium building, bought it, and converted it into temporary headquarters office space. Eventually, they acquired an appropriate site and developed their own permanent office building. They had to settle for temporary accommodations until permanent ones could be arranged. This same phenomenon is now occurring for many multinational corporations in metropolitan Milan and Rome.

In Geneva, Union Carbide found sites available for development to be very scarce. In most countries outside of the United States, a major computer manufacturer has found sites for development scarce, particularly in Latin America.

Unusually high property prices may impede corporate land development. This is a major drawback to corporate expansion in Japan. Abbott Laboratories recently found exorbitant prices for scarce sites and buildings in Rome. For the time being, the company will not maintain a major presence in that market.

### Site Availability Due to the Land Redevelopment Process

Some sites are opening up because the land redevelopment process is taking place. For example, an obsolete manufacturing-warehousing center in the inner city of Frankfurt is being redeveloped. That large tract may be developed for current businesses, domestic and foreign-owned. Four large tracts in the Milan metropolitan area are being redeveloped by joint ventures or by their current owners. They include the Pirelli-Bicocca, Montecity, Garibaldi-Repubblica, and the Portello-Fairgrounds tracts. Montedison is redeveloping the area called Montecity. Their real estate subsidiaries, as well as large Italian real estate brokerage firms, are marketing the land to domestic and foreign corporations. The advantages of these redeveloped sites, according to their sponsors, are planned mixed-use developments with government planning approvals and government and developer provided infrastructure for high-technology buildings and company operations.

### Site Availability Due to Office Park Development

Office parks in the Frankfurt suburbs are being developed for marketing to both European and non-European corporations. The local real estate industry is well aware of the scarcity of high-quality office space in the central business district of Frankfurt and is trying to remedy the situation with new, possibly profitable, land development in the suburbs. The same thing is true of Rome where many multinational companies have a reason to be. Therefore, local entrepreneurs and the government are in the process of developing office parks that may serve the property needs of both domestic and foreign companies.

Since office park sites are attractive to corporate site selection teams, they may find over 7,000 business parks around the world described in the Geo-Sites Index of the December 1987 *Site Selection* journal.

### Site Availability Due to the Extension of the Urban Infrastructure

Walt Disney Productions was attracted to the Eurodisneyland site east of Paris because the local commune, provincial, and federal governments were willing to extend the necessary infrastructure to the particular sub-urban/rural site. With the property infrastructure, the mixed-use project with a European entertainment focus could be developed over a period of years. One of the most strategic factors was the decision to extend the TGV fast rail line to the site from both Paris and Calais. Therefore, the site will be accessible to the British clientele that arrive via the tunnel under the English Channel.

Anheuser Busch is developing a large tract on the east coast of Spain relatively close to Barcelona. They forecast high volumes of visitors to their planned entertainment center year round because of the mild weather on the coast and the infrastructure brought to the site by the Spanish govern-ment. The government encourages this mixed-use development and hopes that it can be ready for the 1992 Barcelona World's Fair. Many tourists to the World's Fair would also visit this spectacular theme park, which will be accompanied by industrial, residential, and commercial space. Anheuser Busch has been looking for an entry point for the production and marketing of their alcoholic beverage products in Europe. The various Busch Gardens theme parks in the United States are well patronized by U.S. and foreign tourists.

### Use of a Separate Subsidiary for Corporate Land Development

A corporation whose principal product is not real estate will often es-tablish a separate subsidiary for land development. This corporate subsid-iary may insulate the holding company from legal and financial liability associated with land development. For example, Philip Morris uses a sep-arate development company, Mission Viejo Realty, for its land develop-ment projects.

## COUNTRY SELECTION

As the corporation management with the aid of its real estate director establishes global expansion plans, it analyzes the country's environment and economic and legal setting before it moves to site selection within the selected countries. Here are some of the considerations for the global corporate management:

Status of the economy

Political stability and system

Economic growth

Place within regional economic growth patterns

Currency value patterns

Governmental system

Computer and robot usage (i.e., encouragement of high technology)

Encouragement of foreign investment

Absence or presence of unreasonable foreign investment controls

Population trends

Per capita income trends

Market conditions for the company's products

Repatriation privileges

Land redevelopment patterns and policies

Energy sources and costs

Transportation system and trends

Social and cultural patterns (i.e., languages spoken)

Climatic conditions

Labor force characteristics

Management systems

Raw materials availability

Legal system

Space availability
  competition for space and relative purchase prices
  regional variations within the country
  industrial development encouragement (i.e., industrial parks)

Financial system
  stability (i.e., exchange rates, government policies, institutional system)
  sources of funds
  mortgage lending and banking
  adequacy of public and private financing sources
  presence or absence of security exchanges for real estate securitization
  lease financing
  other real estate financing

Construction system
  construction environment
  typical building features
  sources of materials and appropriate labor

Valuation system

Title systems and fees

land registration system
title assurance system

Land use controls

environmental protection
tenant tenure
property purchase price controls
urban planning system
rent control
building codes

Brokerage/estate management sources and services

Property management sources and services

Some sketches of the country settings for multinational business development and property acquisition may be found in Appendix 2.A. The sketches cover the United Kingdom, Hong Kong, Singapore, Japan, Spain, France, and the People's Republic of China.

*Institutional Investor* magazine rates country credit on a worldwide basis in two special semiannual issues. In the September 1989 issue, the editors again rated the credit of Japan number one in the world.[1] Switzerland was second followed by, in declining order, West Germany, the United States, and the Netherlands. The next group of five, in declining credit order, consisted of the United Kingdom, Canada, France, Austria, and Sweden. At the bottom of the ratings were North Korea, Nicaragua, Uganda, Sudan, Haiti, Mozambique, and Sierra Leone.

Within a country, industrial real estate may increasingly take into account the cost of housing for the labor force. As countries are selected for industrial site location, housing costs for labor and management may also take on greater significance. In the August 23, 1989, *Financial Times* (London), living costs around the world were ranked in descending order. All country-city comparisons were made against London. On this comparison basis, Michael Dixon, a *Financial Times* staff reporter, pointed out the wide variation in living costs around the world and placed Sofia, Bulgaria, at the top of the living cost hierarchy and Prague, Czechoslovakia, at the bottom of the hierarchy.[2] A few other cities also at the top of the cost pyramid were Tokyo, Japan; N'Djamena, Chad; Brazzaville, Congo; Helsinki, Finland; and Oslo, Norway. Accompanying Prague as a low-living-cost city were New Delhi, India; Santiago, Chile; Karachi, Pakistan; and Gaborone, Botswana; and Johannesburg, South Africa.

## SITE SELECTION

Certain factors attain the greatest significance in multinational company site selection for a manufacturing facility, distribution center, or administrative office center. Here are some of the principal factors associated with industrial site selection:

Sources of materials
    raw materials location, availability, and cost
    semi-finished goods location, availability, and cost
Market for the products
Energy availability and cost
Labor supply and cost
Transportation cost and availability
Management's locational preferences
Taxation: local, national, economic development incentives
Repatriation of capital, royalties, management fees, interest, dividends
Currency exchange rates and trends
Quality of life

Some ideas about site selection trends from 1989–2000 were mentioned by Allen R. Wood in an article in the June 1989 issue of *Site Selection*. Environmental regulations will assume new significance, computer networks will speed site selection, and U.S. plants will grow smaller as labor-intensive industries go overseas. Transportation and currency exchange rates will become more important. Some of the changes that McKinley Conway, publisher of *Site Selection* magazine, foresees are:

Business parks will be established and operated on a global basis by a number of strong developer/broker firms. These will appeal to multinational firms due to their uniformity and quality of space.

Development organizations will have to maintain substantial databases with standardized format criteria that can be accessed by potential investors via telecommunication networks.

Since product life cycles are getting shorter, customized industrial buildings will have to be amortized over shorter time periods.

Multinational firms will demand more multiuse facilities with flexibility built into the architecture and design.

Portable industrial buildings will attract more attention from the industrial community.

Aesthetic factors and amenities will be desired more and more by industrial space users.[3]

Industrial site selection data banks such as SiteNet and EuroSitenet cover such factors as climatic conditions, the ecology of selected sites of various countries, city-by-city office market conditions including rental rates and space availability, business climate rankings, assessment of political climate and governmental support for economic development, tax incentives, sources of government financing for business and industry, and an inventory of research and development laboratories operated by the federal government, corporations, universities, and nonprofit foundations in the various scientific fields. A general site inspection checklist is shown in Exhibit 2.3.

A case study is presented in Appendix 2.A about site selection in Portugal by a highly diversified U.S. multinational company. It points out the importance to the firm of foreign operations, the general site selection objectives, the decision to expand European operations, the extent of the existing European operations, the nature of the location analysis, and the consulting support for the site selection.

## METHODS OF EMPLOYING REAL ESTATE, TAX, AND LEGAL ASSISTANCE FROM OUTSIDE SOURCES

Most multinational firms employ tax and legal assistance from sources outside their companies. Generally home office specialists in these areas are assisted by local tax and legal counsel. This practice avoids the dangers of home office personnel being unfamiliar with local laws, regulations, and conventional practices. But outside real estate assistance may or may not be used by multinational companies. More often than not, local and international real estate companies are asked for assistance in foreign real estate decision making and operations.

### Real Estate Assistance from Outside Sources

Some multinational companies such as AT&T do not use outside real estate consultants in making foreign real estate decisions. In contrast, a Chicago-based multinational company commonly uses international real estate companies, such as Richard Ellis, to make recommendations about local real estate companies when company real estate problems arise in various countries. The international real estate companies based in London and the international accounting firms based in the United States are particularly good sources for such recommendations.

International real estate firms, including Jones Lang Wootton, maintain offices in many countries. Some countries where multinational industrial firms locate have no international real estate companies. Therefore, local real estate firms not associated with the international real estate chains must be contacted following recommendations by trusted colleagues and consultants. For example, Jones Lang Wootton and the other international real estate companies are not yet located in the Republic of Korea (South Korea).

The multinational company may contact more than one local real estate

**Exhibit 2.3**
**Site Inspection Checklist**

**Buildings**
—Number, location, size
—Type of construction
—Age
—General condition
—Flooring materials
—Floor drains/to where
—Spill evidence/cleaned up

**Utilities**
—Electricity
—Natural gas
—Oil
—Telephone
—Sewers
—Water
—Storm Drains

**Physical Features**
—Parking areas/paved or under roof
—Roads
—Power lines
—Public Buildings
—Dwellings
—Structures/improvements
—Rights-of-way

**Security Features**
—Access roads
—Fencing and gates
—Vegetation barriers
—Bike trails
—Campfire/party remains
—Boat launching areas

**Adjacent Land Use**
—Surface water
—Roads/utilities

—Housing/industry
—Vacant land
—Vegetation types

**Waste Evidence**
—Drums, barrels, containers
—Waste materials
—Construction/demolition, debris
—Discolored soil
—Odors
—Leachate seeps
—Discolored surface water/ surface with oil sheen
—"Unnatural soil"
—Ash or blackened area

**Chemical/Fuel/Drum Storage Area**
—Type of construction
—Age
—General condition
—Security/access
—Spill control/berms
—Spill evidence

**Manholes/Catch Basins/Drains/ Fill Pipes**
—Where they are
—What they are for
—What do they look like
—Unusual appearance or odors

**Vegetation Features and Conditions**
—Type
—Maturity
—Density
—Condition (stressed)

**Water Features**
—Wells
—Springs
—Seeps
—Swamps/wetlands
—Ponds
—Streams
—Direction of runon
—Direction of runoff
—Surface erosion
—Evidence of flooding

**Geological Features**
—Topography/slope
—Soil characteristics
—Rock out-crops
—Sink holes
—Excavations
—Spoil piles
—Mining activity
—Quarries/pits
—Diversion ditches
—Soil stockpiles

**Process Tanks/Wastewater Tanks**
—Size
—Materials of construction
—Purpose/contents
—Inside/outside
—Above grade/below grade
—Lined/unlined
—Contents
—General condition
—Leaks
—Connecting piping secure
—Chemical feed/pump system
—Spill evidence

**Pits/Ponds/Lagoons**
—Size/location
—Materials of construction
—Purpose, contents
—Above/below grade
—Lined/unlined
—General condition
—Freeboard
—Leaks
—Fill/drain pipes

**Disposal Areas**
—Size
—Location
—Age
—Contents
—General condition
—Debris
—Drums
—Sludge/residue/rubble
—Discoloration
—Odors
—Monitoring wells
—Cover materials
—Vegetation
—Equipment condition
—Surface contours
—Erosion
—Leachate (analytical results)

**Chemical Transfer Points**
—Where
—What is involved
—Inside/outside
—Paved/unpaved (when)
—Spill evidence

From an article entitled "Corporate Real Estate Environmental Checklist" by William W. Falsgraf, Environmental Partner, Baker & Hostetler, Cleveland, Ohio.

source for information before deciding to use a single company for their corporate purposes. An international oil company follows this practice. An international courier company uses a checklist for various sources in overseas site selection which involves seeking out

Local economic development offices

Major construction companies in the country

Local real estate people

Local property owners in the neighborhood of the prospective site who may know about the ownership of the parcel

The local economic development office may be listed in guides maintained by such organizations as Conway Publications. The local real estate companies may be accessed through company worldwide directories such as those maintained by Jones Lang Wootton and Richard Ellis of London. The worldwide directories of the International Real Estate Institute and the International Real Estate Federation list local real estate companies for countries in which members are located. International phone books list the construction and real estate companies in the terminology of the particular country. For example, one may look under the term "real estate brokerage companies" in the United States, whereas one would look under the term "estate management companies" in the United Kingdom.

Talking with local banks will reveal the desired economic development offices, the major construction companies, and the leading local real estate companies. The banks are glad to provide service in exchange for the bank accounts and other banking fee services that the company may require. An international bank may have real estate offices within its organization. For example, Citicorp has recently established Citicorp Real Estate offices in many cities and countries which the international banking firm serves. For example, there are Citicorp Real Estate offices in Paris, Frankfurt, and Milan.

International real estate magazines, such as *World Property*, cover local real estate offices in ads and articles. The magazine has recently profiled many worldwide real estate leaders.

The multinational company may interview several local and international real estate companies before selecting one company. The company will check the real estate functions, contract terms, and fee systems of the considered company before making a decision. A large U.S.-based international oil company follows this procedure in selecting the one local real estate broker to satisfy their needs.

### Legal Assistance from Outside Sources

Good local legal advice may be even more important to the multinational firm than good local real estate advice, according to a U.S.-based multinational diversified pharmaceutical company. Normally local real estate advice supplements headquarters legal counsel. The outside legal counsel of the home country may have legal associates overseas in the project area. There are a few international legal firms that can give service in many countries through their branch offices. Baker & McKinsey, headquartered in Chicago, is said to be one of these international firms that provides legal service. Regardless of the local overseas legal advice, the headquarters legal staff usually supervises the overall legal work.

In the United States, real estate law differs by state. Real estate law also differs among countries and among the regions and local areas of a single country. For example, within the United Kingdom, England and Wales observe the common law while Scotland operates under a variation of the civil code.

### Tax Assistance from Outside Sources

The international accounting firms provide international tax assistance to multinational companies. The same firm that assists the company in its home country may give tax help overseas. Arthur Andersen and Peat Marwick have both provided valuable international assistance to Abbott Laboratories. Laventhol & Horwath offers worldwide real estate consulting and appraisal services as well as tax advice to its multinational clientele.

## PREPURCHASE AND PRESALE ANALYSIS: DUE DILIGENCE AND ENVIRONMENTAL ASSESSMENT

Due diligence and environmental assessment should precede purchase or sale of a property in almost any country today. The prospective property buyer should know the government's environmental policies and regulations. This is one part of locational analysis from the buyer's point of view. The prospective buyer should know the property's condition with respect to asbestos content of the structural features, water treatment methods typically employed, the nature of the effluent, the placement of the waste water, the extent of air and noise pollution resulting from the building's typical use, the methods used to reduce or eliminate air and noise pollution, and the typical use of contaminating chemicals in the normal operation of the plant.

When the owner prepares to sell the property, both the seller and the buyer should determine the seller's responsibility for the present condition of the property. After the performance of the due diligence process and the environmental assessment, the prospective buyer and seller are prepared to negotiate the contract for the title transfer. The seller may need to discount the normal sale price if environmental problems are present when the property is sold. The buyer might buy the property subject to the environmental defects if the listing price is reduced by the appropriate discount.

Environmental risks must be managed to reduce potential cost. A number of recent environmental disasters worldwide have been associated with multinational corporate operations. In response, many countries are reevaluating their environmental regulations and their enforcement mechanisms. As countries build up their "arsenal" against environmental disasters and environmental pollution, companies must reexamine their approaches to the management of environmental risks associated with their worldwide properties. Due diligence and environmental assessment have become significant current topics of discussion and multinational company action.

### Environmental Assessment

Generally the environmental risks may be assessed by identifying the risks present and the company activities and facility usage that contribute to the risks. The environmental regulations of the local government will guide the company in these identification programs. The country's environmental concerns become the company's concerns.

The asbestos, radon, contaminated soil and water, air pollution, and other conditions associated with the environmentally impaired property may be identified by multinational company staff that is specially trained and educated or by outside attorneys and consultants. Often internal environmental assessments are conducted by attorneys or specially trained real estate department employees. To assist them in their duties, an environmental site assessment checklist, like the one in Exhibit 2.4, may be used.

### Global Environmental Risk Management Strategy

Once the sources of environmental pollution are detected by the company or outside staff, the company must devise a plan for risk management. Management methods must identify specific actions that should be taken and controls that should be implemented within the company so that local environmental regulations will be met.

Increasingly, the company's lenders want to be assured that the company's property meets local environmental protection regulations before the lenders close the loans. Having to meet expensive antipollution requirements may force a company into bankruptcy and loan foreclosure. The lender is wise to make certain that the company is in compliance with

**Exhibit 2.4**
**Environmental Site Assessment Checklist**

**General Information**
—Owner
—Contact person
—Location
—Size of facility
—Age
—Prior uses of land
—Site plot plan
—Number of buildings/size
—Construction of buildings
—Progression of construction

**Process Operations**
—Principal products
—How much/how many
—Processes used
—Chemicals used/how
—Maintenance chemicals
—Time at present operations

**Wastewater Sources**
—What are sources
—Flow/characteristics
—How managed/treated
    (past/present)
—On-site treatment/what kind
—Where is discharge
—What happens to sludges
—Permit status
—SPCC plan
—Wetlands permits
—Spill history

—Agency contact
—Notice of violation
—Compliance schedules
—Other enforcement actions/
    citizen suits

**Air Emission Sources**
—What are sources
—Flows/characteristics
—Emission control
—Emission points
—Permit status
—Monitoring requirements
—Notices of violation
—Compliance history
—Agency contact
—Notices of violation
—Compliance schedules
—Other enforcement actions/
    citizens units

**Solid/Hazardous Waste**
—What are sources
—Quantities/characteristics
—Treatment/storage/disposal
    (past/present)
—On-site/off-site disposal
    (past/present)
—Manifests
—RCRA permits
—Corrective action/solid waste
    management units

—State solid waste permits
—Compliance reports
—Compliance history
—Agency contact
—Notices of violations
—Compliance schedules
—Other enforcement actions/
    citizens suit
—Government Superfund
    actions
—Private party Superfund
    actions

**Fuels Management**
—What is used
—How much
—Storage

**PCB Equipment**
—Location
—Size
—Type
—Test results for equipment
—Inspection reports
—Annual reports
—Disposal records

**Asbestos**
—Location
—Tests concerning its
    condition
—Disposition/disposal records

**Underground Tanks
(past/present)**
—Location
—Size
—Age
—Construction materials
—Registration
—Permits
—Contents
—Testing results (when)
—Monitoring results
—Removed when/how/by
    whom
—Inspection reports
—Closure plans

**Hazardous Communication**
—Labeling
—Training
—MSDS

**Community Right to Know
Compliance**
—§311
—§312
—§313 toxic chemical release
    reporting

From an article entitled "Corporate Real Estate Environmental Checklist" by William W. Falsgraf, Environmental Partner, Baker & Hostetler, Cleveland, Ohio.

each country's environmental laws and regulations. The benefits of a global environmental compliance strategy are presented in case form in Appendix 2.C.

## NOTES

1. "Institutional Investor's 1989 Country Credit Ratings," *Institutional Investor*, 33, no. 10, September 1989, p. 302.
2. Michael Dixon, "How Living Costs Vary Around the World," *Financial Times*, August 23, 1989, p. 10.
3. Allen R. Wood, "Site Selection Trends—1989–2000," *Site Selection*, June 1989, p. 13.

## BIBLIOGRAPHY

Bartley, William. "The Case for Pre-Purchase Property Assessments." *Building Operating Management*, July 1989, pp. 62–64.
Brown, Michael. "Bank One Deal: IBM to Take Six Floors, Equity Position in Tower." *Indianapolis Business Journal* 10, no. 17, August 7–13, 1989, pp. 1, 52.
"Buildings Ready Now!" *Site Selection*, February 1988, pp. 249 + .
European Issue, *International Real Estate Journal* 16, no. 2, 1989.
Evans, Peter. *Banking on Property 1989*. London: Debenham, Tewson & Chinnocks, 1989.
Farrell, Pia. "France's Biggest Builder Branches Out." *International Herald Tribune*, July 14, 1989, p. 11.
Finlay, Martha, Michael O'Connor, and David Gay. "Guide to Corporate Facility Planners and Major Investments." *Site Selection*, February 1988, pp. 50 + .
Gabetti, Spa. *Milan City Report: International Property Bulletin*. London: Hillier Parker May & Rowden, 1989.
"Geographic Guide to Development Organizations." *Site Selection Handbook*, April 1987, pp. 272 + .
"The Geo-Sites Index." *Site Selection Handbook*, December 1987, p. 1266.
Hines, M. A. *Global Real Estate Appraising*. Scottsdale, Ariz.: International Real Estate Institute, 1990.
———. *Handbook on International Real Estate Investment*. Westport, Conn.: Quorum Books, 1987.
———. *International Income Property Investment*. Scottsdale, Ariz.: International Real Estate, 1985.
———. *Investing in Japanese Real Estate*. Westport, Conn.: Quorum Books, 1987.
James, Canute. "Cool Wind of Divestment Blows in the Caribbean." *Financial Times*, July 26, 1989, p. 5.
Lunitz, Stanley. "Commercial Bribery Is a Hushed Up Business Danger." *The Savant* 5, no. 10, August 1, 1989, p. 4.
Manning, Christopher A. "Is Ownership of Corporate Real Property Better than Leasing?" *Site Selection Handbook*, January/February 1988, p. 8–12.

Parker, Joel R. "Characteristics of New Corporate Facility Investments." *Site Selection Handbook*, June 1988, p. 25.

*Pitfalls in Development*. Atlanta: Conway Publications, 1978.

Volhard, Rudiger, and Dolf Weber, ed. *Real Property in Germany*, 3d ed. Frankfurt am Main: Fritz Knapp Verlag, 1989.

# APPENDIX 2.A

# COUNTRY PROFILES

## UNITED KINGDOM

The economy has been very stable and expanding during the 1980s. The government has reduced its budget by continuing to privatize the large businesses which were originally government-owned. Also, to reduce the government budget, council housing was marketed to the current occupants and the general public. Some land use controls were lifted and employment in this sector was significantly reduced. Universities and other parts of the educational system have been encouraged to rely more on private financing and less on federal and local government financing. They were asked to be responsible to public needs, including the preparation of business managers for the coming decades. Historically universities leaned toward the arts and sciences and virtually ignored business management methods and practices. With the monies saved through various cost-cutting avenues, the British Treasury debt has been continuously repaid without floating more Treasury debt. Government debt is declining through this financial program.

The government of the United Kingdom is preparing to make a bid for the leadership role in the new Europe to be created by 1992. London has long been an international financial center. Now the British government would like to exert more influence over the formation and management of the European Community or the "United States of Europe," as some have labeled the phenomenon. The "capital" of the new Europe has not been designated. In the running are Brussels, the headquarters for the European Community; Frankfurt, the international financial center in West Germany that is rather centrally located; and Paris, another international business center in northern France that is rather centrally located in Western Europe. The United Kingdom already exerts an influential role over the European Community formation as do France and West Germany.

As the economy of the United Kingdom maintains its strength, the Japanese are using British locations to enter Europe. They are suggesting to the government of the United Kingdom that, in exchange for the required planning permissions for manufacturing and assembly plant establishment, their exports to the European continent will reduce the British trade deficit. In any case, the United Kingdom needs to gain a position where its exports exceed its imports. Car assembly for export could help reduce the deficit. At the same time, traditional British auto manufacturers could accomplish the same objective with production of more products that would fit overseas market demands.

The pound sterling is weaker than it once was, but it is a strong international currency. Its position as an international currency lies in the shadow of the West German deutsche mark, the Japanese yen, and the U.S. dollar, however. Britain's international financial community has been invaded by the largest overseas financial institutions including U.S. and Japanese institutions. So a multinational corporation that wishes to find the lowest cost financing may gain advice and marketing assistance from various corporate finance specialists in the London market. They can tap into international and Euro markets with many different financial instruments which might fit the corporation's purposes. The International Stock Exchange and the Unlisted Stock Market are both reorganizing and regrouping for the coming computerized competition. Since London's Big Bang of 1986, the shakeout and restructuring has continued. The Big Bang deregulated the financial markets based in London. The brokerage commission structure is no longer administered, but fees for services are fully negotiable between the servicer and the client.

The United Kingdom encourages foreign investment with industrial development, financial and other incentives and full repatriation rights for capital, profits, management fees, and royalties. Unlike in earlier decades, these are no exchange controls. There are essentially no foreign investment restraints except perhaps for the United Kingdom's vital defense industry and food sources on the island.

As the personal and business incomes of U.K. entities rise, a multinational corporation may see new markets. The country may be an attractive manufacturing location for the company's marketing of products to the new Europe. The United Kingdom may also be a good prospective assembly point for overseas marketing of goods.

Land redevelopment is encouraged by the British government. Wales, England, and Scotland—the three separate parts of the United Kingdom—have been subject to land redevelopment for centuries. When older land uses become obsolete, newer land uses are encouraged. Since the mid–1980s, for example, retail development has been taking place more in the suburbs than in the central cities. In the central cities older premises are being redeveloped for more consolidated and planned retail shopping centers which are close to existing mass transit lines. The older industrial areas of Newcastle-upon-Tyne, Liverpool, and Manchester are still undergoing land redevelopment to bring back their earlier economic prosperity, with new lines of business in new or renovated premises.

The United Kingdom has abundant oil and gas resources and coal deposits. They have nuclear power plants, but continue to experience protests against the generation of nuclear power. The protestors fear pollution of the entire environment and in the immediate vicinity of the plants. Since the North Sea oil drilling now provides ample supplies, the government and the utility companies can deemphasize the need for nuclear power for London and for industrial plants all over the country.

Since the major freeways have been improved during the mid–1980s, the road transportation system of the United Kingdom is relatively good. Some local and rural roads remain narrow for the traffic volume they have to handle. The principal roads connecting Dover with Edinburgh and Glasgow, Scotland are good for truck and passenger car traffic. The rail system connects all parts of Wales and Scotland to London. All roads "lead to London" because it is, by far, the most important urban area of the United Kingdom. Even though good air commuter service has linked all important U.K. cities, the service is being improved. The most recent addition to commuter service was the development of the Docklands International Airport for commuter service from London to important continental European cities such as Frankfurt and Paris. The tunnel under the English Channel is replacing the regular and hydrofoil ferries that have long plied the waters between Dover and Calais and other French ports. The tunnel will link the United Kingdom, France, and other Western European countries by road and rapid rail by approximately 1994. The extensive subway system of London carries a large proportion of employees between the inner-city and suburban homes and their inner-city London workplaces.

Computer and robot usage are encouraged by the government and by the competition of private enterprise. Even small businesses are encouraged to computerize their accounts and other business processes. Government and industry have long supported advancements in industrial engineering through financial support of the world-renowned schools of engineering at Oxford and Cambridge.

The United Kingdom has had relatively slow population growth. Per capita incomes are rising with increased productivity, gradually reduced personal and business taxation, and the government privatization programs which reduce the government budget. The trends may go the other way if the wishes of the current Hong Kong residents are honored by the British homeland. As 1997 approaches, Hong Kong residents are pressing the United Kingdom for passports and visas for permanent settlement in the United Kingdom to escape the reign of the mainland Chinese government over Hong Kong in 1997 and thereafter. The United Kingdom already has permitted many Indian and European nationals to immigrate and its population has grown to some extent because of this immigration.

Most U.K. citizens speak English. Employees of international U.K.-based companies also speak English as they take tours of duty in Australia, Japan, Singapore, India, France, and other countries. A few learn foreign languages in order to serve their temporary overseas posts more effectively. The English spoken by the British is somewhat different from the English spoken by U.S. citizens. Different words may describe the same asset or phenomenon. Even the real estate markets of the two countries are very different. English is the common language, but some vocabulary is dissimilar.

The climate of the United Kingdom resembles that of the northeast part of the United States and Nova Scotia. The British Isles are on about the same latitudes as these portions of North America. For example, London has a short summer and a long period of rain and fog during the winter and spring. The winter brings high winds, ice, and snow across the islands. The Scottish climate approximates that of southern Norway and Sweden—very cold, snowy, and windy.

United Kingdom citizens tend to migrate to London for employment because it offers the most jobs of a wide variety at the highest wages. London is the chief financial, entertainment, manufacturing, government, retailing, transportation, and cultural center of the country.

The labor force is generally well-educated. Training and retraining in industrial skills are provided by business and industry. Generally the labor force is trainable and willing to work a 38- to 40-hour week with reasonable vacation periods and legal holidays. In contrast to Asian employees, the British workers are accustomed to five-day work weeks. As in the United States and other countries, many "moonlight" on second jobs that require night and/or weekend work. A high proportion of British women work whether they are married, have children, or are single.

The attorneys, architects, urban planners, physicians, and other professional people are centered in London. London is the business center of the British Isles. Even the majority of tourists visit only London when they visit the United Kingdom and never venture out into other areas. Since tourism is one of the main industries of Britain, employment in tourism is found chiefly in London.

The English management system has historically been paternalistic. The Labour Party has significantly influenced labor-management relations. Until the Tory Party took office about ten years ago, Britain was a highly socialized country. The Tory Party has reintroduced capitalism to the government and private enterprise system. Company managers are now more concerned about worldwide market competition than about social welfare programs and company responsibilities for the employee. Managers of British firms are trying to raise their competitive position in world markets. The Japanese are entering the British marketplace and gaining large parts of British and world markets with goods produced in the United Kingdom. The British companies are restructuring and refinancing for future world competition.

Many raw materials and partially or totally finished products must be imported to the United Kingdom. Foodstuffs produced in the United Kingdom are inadequate for the U.K. citizens. Precious metals, minerals, lumber, wearing apparel, and many other goods must be imported to satisfy British market demands. Because Britain imports more than its exports, it's a debtor nation like the United States, in contrast to Japan which is a creditor nation.

England and Wales operate under the common law while Scotland operates under a form of civil code. U.S.-based companies find it easier to do business under the common law system with which they are familiar. The attorneys of the U.S.-based company can work easily with the U.K. attorneys on British legal matters.

Industrial space is available in special enterprise zones and other industrially designed areas across the United Kingdom. Particularly concentrated industrial zones are found in south Wales near Swansea and in the area between Edinburgh and Glasgow in Scotland. Heavy manufacturing, including auto manufacturing and assembly, is found in south Wales while the Scottish area is attractive to high-technology companies.

Industrial enterprise zones are scattered throughout the United Kingdom. Special tax, employee retraining, and other financial incentives are associated with these zones. Multinational companies tend to look to these locations with respect to raw materials, required semifinished goods, work force, and proximity to markets. The government encourages the zones partly to enhance employment in high-unemployment areas of the country. The government-associated industrial zones tend not to be around London because of the high rate of employment there. Generally the farther north one goes from London, the higher the unemployment rate.

Commercial space is also more available at more reasonable rents the farther one goes from London. Commercial space is acquired at relatively high rents and purchase prices in the London metropolitan area. High-quality commercial space for sale or rent is scarce both in the City and in Mayfair. The London Docklands are being redeveloped for front- and back-office space for financial institutions and multinational corporations. Nearby housing and waterfront recreation may also attract corporate people and offices to the Docklands redeveloped area. The international commuter airport is located in the midst of this redeveloped area east of the Tower of London down the Thames River.

Private industrial parks have existed in the United Kingdom for years. A concentration of these planned developments, located around Windsor, Reading, and Bracknell, are generally reached by the M4 motorway. They are also relatively close to Heathrow International Airport. The Reading parks particularly cater to high-tech industry.

Before and since the Big Bang in October 1986, the financial markets of London have been unstable. The pound sterling was stronger in earlier years; now it's relatively weak as compared to other international currencies. The deregulation of the London financial markets has caused bankruptcies, employee layoffs, financial institution restructuring, termination of product lines by investment and merchant bankers, and relocation to new premises where new computer systems are installed. The British financial markets have long provided full financial services, but these markets have not had the depth of U.S. financial markets. The British sources of funds were substantially supplemented by international sources of funds, particularly those of Western Europe. Now the major Japanese banks have established positions in the London market. Their ample funds lend a needed depth to the market. The U.S. commercial and investment banks have retreated somewhat from the London market because of long-term losses as the major Japanese institutions have entered the same market.

Mortgage lending in Britain has been confined in general to the "clearing" banks and building societies. Where the building societies finance residential properties, "clearing" banks finance commercial properties. Foreign investment bank subsidiaries are now competing with the banks and building societies in the financing of residential properties. The U.S.-based lenders securitize their mortgages for sale to investors in the marketplace. Since the banks have provided long-term mortgage financing for commercial property owners, the British life insurance companies have historically arranged for development and construction financing and then have purchased the entire project from the developer or have become the major partner in a joint venture with the developer. The British life insurance companies have preferred major commercial property ownership to the long-term financing of other property owners. In fact, for many years they have allocated 15 to 20 percent of their insurance assets to the real estate sector. U.S. life insurance companies and pension funds seldom commit more than six percent of their assets to real estate ownership. (Recently these U.S. financial institutions have allowed as much as 10 percent of these assets to real estate ownership.)

Public and private real estate financing sources in the United Kingdom have been inadequate for unusually strong land development periods such as the mid–1980s in London's City and West End. The maximum volume of real estate financing usually available from the shallow British financial markets has been £ 75 million. This maximum amount was adequate when the London City office buildings did not exceed 200,000 square feet. In recent years, more modern, functional office buildings of greater floor space have been built to accommodate the large trading floor needs of the domestic and foreign securities houses. At the same time, construction and development costs have risen to compete aggressively with the high property costs of Tokyo. So foreign real estate lenders and investors have stepped into the British markets to fill the gap in financing needs. Mortgage securitization has permitted release of some assets so that real estate financing in higher volume would be possible.

Due to the stringent requirements of the International Stock Exchange in London, many of the securitized mortgage issues have been listed instead on the Luxembourg Stock Exchange where the listing requirements are not as onerous. The International Stock Exchange and the unlisted security trading system are available for use in the United Kingdom, but the costs may be more than competing security marketing and rating alternatives. Once asset-backed securities receive high credit ratings from Standard & Poor's or Moody's Investors Service, they may be listed, traded in the "over-the-counter" market, or privately placed with investors. If interest is strong for private placement, the issuer of the asset-backed securities may not pay the costs of S&P or Moody credit rating.

Lease financing is commonly employed for British real estate financing. Britain is known for its layered ground and building leases. Many leasehold estates have required financing over the decades. The British financial markets are also called upon to do financing of strata-title estates. (The U.S. real estate term comparable to strata-title is condominium or cooperative.)

Many international construction firms have operated out of the United Kingdom for centuries. They are known for excellence in construction management and have access to building materials and construction labor which may be scarce in countries where they win bids to construct public and private projects. Much of the work they engage in overseas is associated with government-provided infrastructure such as airports, dams, power plants, road systems, bridges and causeways, canals, ports, and off-shore oil drilling rigs. When the Middle East terminated many of its major government projects, the British international construction companies had to turn to major domestic and worldwide commercial projects.

The valuation system of the United Kingdom is based on the standards and professional designation requirements of two real estate trade associations—the Incorporated Society of Valuers and Auctioneers and the Royal Institution of Chartered Surveyors. They train specialists in the fields of land and building surveying, estate management, cost estimation, real estate marketing, valuation, and other real estate areas. Various universities in the United Kingdom also offer courses and professional seminars to prepare prospective applicants for professional real estate designations. For example, the City University of London offers mainly evening courses for real estate designation aspirants. Wolfson College of Cambridge offers land economics courses, such as valuation, which meet the requirements of the professional real estate designations. Five approaches to the valuation of a property tend to be taught: (1) direct capital comparison, (2) investment, (3) residual, (4) profits, and (5) the cost of replacement.

The United Kingdom maintains a land registration system, but not all property documents are registered within the system. The establishment of a land registration system depends on the wishes of the local government. As the years pass, more and more local governments are establishing the registration system that assures title. Certificates of registration are given to current owners who turn in the certificates when they sell their registered properties. Then new certificates of registration are drawn up and given to the new owners.

Estate conveyance and inheritance laws have changed over the centuries. The fee tail system is no longer practiced, for example. At the death of the parent, the property title does not necessarily go to the oldest living son. Inheritance rights of this nature—fee tail—do not operate automatically. All of the living children of the deceased may inherit from the parent including the younger sons and daughters.

Comprehensive land use controls affect property ownership in the United Kingdom. Areas are zoned for specific land uses. Building codes are established and enforced, as are environmental protection regulations. Even though the current government has weakened the land planning system with large budget cuts, land planners still are respected by local and federal government officials. Generally their land use policies are focused on preservation of the property tax base and the investment viability of central business districts as opposed to suburban land development where mass transit does not converge and high land density is not preserved. They preserve green space for densely populated residential and commercial neighborhoods. They preserve the uncluttered and uncommercial motorway intersections by generally not permitting the building of auto service stations, motels and hotels, and restaurants at these locations. For example, the major traffic intersections of the M25 outer belt motorway that surrounds London are uncluttered with commercial enterprise such as regional and super-regional shopping centers. Instead, retail warehouse projects and free-standing DIY ("do-it-yourself") retail units are permitted for development at some distance from the major traffic intersections of these limited-access motorways. The land use controls do not include tenant tenure and government purchase price controls. The government does exercise the power of eminent domain when necessary for the development of worthwhile projects that benefit the general public.

Since council housing was put up for sale, the rent controls originally established for the government-owned and rented council housing have weakened. Not all of the large inventory of housing has been sold to current or prospective occupants; therefore, residential rent controls may be necessary related to family size and income, or the handicaps or advanced age of the current or prospective occupants. Commercial rent control was applied to the office building space of London in the early 1970s when rent and property prices were rising rapidly. The commercial rent control was terminated within a year or two due to its disruptive effect on the real estate market. Existing office space increased in value. New building construction which could not be justified on the basis of the capped rents showed extensive depreciation. The owners were not encouraged to maintain the existing office properties because rents could not be raised to compensate for the increased quality and functionality of the premises.

Land taxes have been used to slow down property speculation. The government participated in the capital gains from land sales. But property purchase price controls apparently have never been employed as a land use control device by the United Kingdom.

The estate management business involves hundreds of thousands of U.K. citizens. The membership of the Incorporated Society of Valuers and Auctioneers and the Royal Institution of Chartered Surveyors testify to this large industry representation. These specialized real estate people serve a financial market that is particularly geared to real estate investment and finance. The U.K. financial institutions invest a large percentage of their total assets in real estate. Other countries whose financial institutions approach this real estate investment level are the Netherlands and West Germany. Individuals, estates, and families also value real estate ownership for investment income. The growing corporate sector of the United Kingdom occupies vast amounts of commercial and industrial real estate. Corporate employees require sufficient housing with the right amenities at the right price. In the United Kingdom, corporate real estate involves renovation and land redevelopment because the nation has a long history. Many older, perhaps obsolete, commercial structures are standing on sites which are valuable for prospective corporate business. Today's computerized and robotic industries must have buildings that will accommodate these advanced systems. At the very least, older buildings must be renovated to accommodate higher electrical loads, floors that will bear the weight of modern office and plant equipment and layouts, and modern heating, cooling, and ventilation systems.

Multinational corporations may manage their own U.K. properties or they may contract with estate management companies to do the work. Many international real estate firms, headquartered in London, provide property management services along with other valuable real estate services. These firms typically manage pension fund real estate under contracts that require property and investment management. Since many of the firms, including Debenham Tewson & Chinnocks, Frank Knight & Rutley, Jones Lang Wootton, Richard Ellis, and Healey & Baker, have international offices, they can provide international services to the multinational corporation. These services may involve commercial, industrial, and residential property services. These international real estate companies are not located in every country, but they do maintain branches in industrially developed countries. The networks of worldwide offices serve countries in the various regions that are represented. For example, Singapore offices tend to represent Indonesian and Malaysian real estate. A Bahrain office may represent real estate interests in the Gulf States that include Qatar, Saudi Arabia, Kuwait, and Abu Dhabi. The Sidney or Melbourne office may represent New Zealand as well as Australian real estate interests.

## HONG KONG

Hong Kong is a vibrant English colony located on a southern peninsula of mainland China and on a few islands offshore in the South China Sea. It is one of the world's most prosperous manufacturing and distribution centers. The citizens of the densely populated colony produce a large portion of the world's electronic products, textiles, and toys. Its retailing centers in Kowloon on the mainland and in the Central District of Hong Kong Island serve customers from around the world. Administrative offices of many of the world's largest corporations—particularly the world's largest financial institutions—are located in high-rise office buildings in the Kowloon and Central business districts.

The political future of the colony is uncertain. In 1997, mainland China regains control of its Hong Kong territory from the British colonial government. The People's Republic of China (PRC) government has repeatedly said that it guarantees the continuing capitalistic freedom of the Hong Kong companies and citizens after 1997. More uncertainty was added to this picture when the PRC government clamped down on the insurgent students when they revolted during May and June of 1989 in Tiananmen Square in Beijing. The PRC government subsequently purged the top political leadership of sympathizers with the student demands for more freedom for the Chinese people. The Chinese leaders of the capitalist movement in China were ousted from power. So the Hong Kong colonists fear the consequences of a Chinese takeover of their small capitalist district which is currently separate from mainland Chinese society and politics.

Hong Kong has thrived as the center of distribution and manufacturing for southeast Asia. Its high level of productivity has led to relatively high wages and salaries for the Hong Kong employees who were willing to work and be trained for special distribution and production positions. The generally unregulated business community with its low tax rates has encouraged the vibrant economic growth. This supplier of many of the world's goods is fearful about its economic and personal future. China is planning to move into the colony in 1997 as part of its defense establishment. Other PRC regulations could threaten future worldwide distribution and production.

Even though the 1997 takeover date was established in the early 1980s, major multinational companies have continued to move into Hong Kong and the special enterprise zone in Guangzhou in the extreme southern part of mainland China. The corporations have not been discouraged by the upcoming communist takeover of Hong Kong, but have kept their sights on the vast market represented by China and its potential as a manufacturing base. Chinese labor—including Hong Kong labor—represents relatively low cost. This labor is highly trainable and motivated by higher wages and salaries and higher standards of living. Hong Kong and mainland Chinese labor are typically employed a six-day week with long daily working hours.

The Hong Kong dollar is administratively tied to the U.S. dollar. Therefore, as the U.S. dollar has declined due to deliberate U.S. government devaluation, the Hong Kong dollar has also declined in value. The United States has long been a key trading partner of the colony.

Under the current government system for Hong Kong, Queen Elizabeth of the United Kingdom appoints its governor. Hong Kong is a protectorate of the British government and has been a British colony for centuries. Since most of the government officers are not elected, the people of Hong Kong were to be guaranteed election of some of their representatives by both the colonial government and the government of mainland China. The general elections were to begin in the mid–1980s, but they have not yet taken place as the 1990s begin.

The Chinese mainland government began to infiltrate Hong Kong government, business, and society in the early 1980s. Most companies have representatives of the mainland government working alongside Hong Kong representatives, whether the workplace is an international financial institution or a manufacturing facility. Mainland Chinese businesses have bought partial or total interests in some Hong Kong companies. The Hong Kong utility companies are partially owned by mainland Chinese investors including government agencies. The Bank of China has constructed the tallest building on Hong Kong Island in competition with the new lower high-rise structure of the Hongkong and Shanghai Bank. Mainland Chinese society, business, and government are gradually moving into Hong Kong.

Large numbers of Hong Kong middle and top company managers have moved out of Hong Kong each year. Others have or are acquiring passports and permanent visas for countries overseas where they may relocate at any time. Some countries, such as Canada, accept substantial land, property, and company investments from Hong Kong residents and companies in exchange for emigration rights and permanent visas. Once the Hong Kong resident is assured of exit rights, that person may remain in Hong Kong to benefit from the profits and capital gains possible before the 1997 takeover date.

Many foreign companies have major investments in Hong Kong. For example, Citicorp has recently spent hundreds of millions of U.S. dollars on its Hong Kong computer installation. This is a big regional office for the bank which wishes to serve both Hong Kong and mainland China. If its major computer installation is taken over by China, corporate management expects compensation from the Chinese government. Since the company would continue to operate, it could more easily serve mainland China after 1997. Many other multinational companies appear to be thinking the same way as they continue to invest large sums in Hong Kong operations.

The Hong Kong government has enthusiastically encouraged foreign investment. The government seeks a net positive trade balance with more foreign companies exporting more goods abroad. There are essentially no controls restraining foreign investment in Hong Kong. The government fully cooperates in finding appropriate production, distribution, and administrative properties in Hong Kong for prospective multinational firms. Many government incentives are associated, in particular, with locations in the New Territories on the mainland peninsula.

Land has been developed in the New Territories by the government for all highrise configurations. High-rise manufacturing facilities are expected to exist near high-rise residential and commercial buildings. The employees travel less distance on the rail system if they live very close to their places of work. Retail facilities have been developed within the residential and industrial areas, and several kinds of sports facilities have been constructed on New Territories land. The Chinese University of Hong Kong is located there also. The educational facilities are intermingled in urban space with the residential, commercial, and industrial buildings. Most of this redeveloped land is where low-rise obsolete buildings once existed. New industrial growth is the impetus for the continuing development of Hong Kong's New Territories.

In contrast, Hong Kong Island is primarily mountainous land with coastal highrise building development that is situated on reclaimed land. The Central District is the administrative office center of Hong Kong where the highest quality retail space is located. Retailing, manufacturing, and entertainment centers are located in other parts of Hong Kong Island. New and older high-rise apartment buildings are found primarily between the Central District and Victoria Peak at the northeast corner of the island in newly developed communities around new rail stations.

The power plants of Hong Kong serve both Hong Kong and the nearby portion of mainland China. They provide electric power to the mass transit subway system that is the colony's principal transportation. Recently the rail lines have been extended to the east side of Hong Kong Island from the main terminal in the Central District. The road system of the island and the peninsula carries a small part of the traffic. Many Hong Kong citizens cannot afford a private passenger car, and parking accommodations are now insufficient for the current car volume. More high-rise parking structures are needed to accommodate the current inventory of cars. A second tunnel under the bay between the island and the peninsula has been recently completed. This provides two routes to the international airport on the peninsula for residents and visitors to the island. Ferries constantly traverse the bay, supplementing the subway line and the two channel tunnels for cars. In addition, privately owned boats are tied up at harbors for water transportation across the bay and to other destinations including Macau Island.

Manufacturing costs are contained by use of low-cost manual labor. Computer and robotic manufacturing is little used in the colony. The work week covers six days of the seven, and the free day is staggered across the work force. Not everyone has a Sunday free from work. The labor force is very willing to work these long hours because the Hong Kong people strive to improve their standards of living. When they receive opportunities, they are willing to work. Many arrived earlier from mainland China, and they realize the opportunities for improved living standards in Hong Kong in contrast to the low standard of living on the mainland. Recently boatloads of Vietnamese people have arrived at Hong Kong also seeking a quality of life unrestrained by communist governments. The Chinese population of Hong Kong continues to rise, so that the densely populated colony can barely accommodate its own citizens without offering refuge to hopeful immigrants from nearby countries.

The population of Hong Kong continues to grow because of immigration from Vietnam and normal population growth. A third source of the growth is immigration from the People's Republic of China. Whenever Chinese people from the PRC are allowed to immigrate to Hong Kong, they do so. Many of the mainland citizens have relatives in Hong Kong whom they visit during vacations. The vacations in Hong Kong and other locations are approved by the PRC government as a reward for productive and faithful service to the government and its companies. However, many mainland people want to move permanently to Hong Kong to obtain higher wages and salaries, better housing conditions, more varied foodstuffs, better working conditions and job responsibilities, and freedom from government work assignment. Hong Kong's society and culture are associated with the atmosphere of capitalism. People living in the southern part of the PRC speak Cantonese which is spoken in Hong Kong. The Mandarin-speaking residents of northern China may have more difficulty getting accustomed to Cantonese-speaking Hong Kong.

Little working and living space is provided for each Hong Kong citizen, including the expatriate foreign residents. The leasehold purchase prices that result from leasehold auctions reflect the scarcity of space. Since the cost of leasehold land is so high, only high-rise buildings can justify their development cost. Both public and private housing is built for prospective owners and tenants. Hong Kong residents constantly try to "trade up" to larger and better equipped housing with increases in their incomes.

Toward the PRC border and in the New Territories more space per person is found in residential, commercial, and industrial buildings. This area, which is located quite distant from the central business district of the island and the peninsula, also accommodates the agricultural sector of Hong Kong. Toward the PRC border, buildings are wedged in among the rice paddies and the lotus ponds. The New Territories to the northeast of Kowloon are generally not committed to agriculture, but to residential, commercial, and industrial space. Industrial development—foreign and domestic—is encouraged there, by financial and other incentives from the Hong Kong government.

Because of the British occupation of Hong Kong, its legal system is based on the English common law. As Chinese from the PRC continue to enter the colony before 1997, the legal and political system continues to take on more of the characteristics of communist party controlled mainland.

Construction and land development face obstacles in Hong Kong for several reasons. Land use controls are stringent, the density of the population inhibits construction progress, and most of the building materials for high-quality construction projects must be imported. Even management of international construction companies are imported temporarily, at least for major projects such as the second tunnel under the bay. The construction companies winning the bids on major structures often help finance the projects. For example, Japanese often win the bids because their offers finance the projects. The international companies may bid lower due to home government provision of lower-than-market-rate loans for company financing.

The high-rise buildings needed for densely populated Hong Kong must have firm foundations within the reclaimed land. The foundations must support concrete and steel buildings with numerous floor partitions for relatively small offices, apartments, and workplaces. Glass, marble, granite, and other exterior cladding provide the usual facades in the two central districts of Kowloon and Central District on the island.

Condominium and strata-title space is common to apartment and commercial buildings in Hong Kong. The financial system accommodates the financing of this individually and company-owned space. Since the life insurance and pension fund industries are not well developed in Hong Kong, most of the real estate financing is derived from commercial and merchant banks. The government and financial institution policies are relatively stable since they administer the colony's real estate finance needs. Because of the presence of the major banks of the world in the Central District, the colony usually has adequate funds for financing most real estate projects. Large loans are syndicated among the numerous foreign and domestic banks, including the Bank of China, and Hongkong and Shanghai Bank. Long-term mortgage loans are usually extended over a period of 12 to 15 years with floating interest rates. The base for the floating bank mortgage rates is usually the Hong Kong prime rate which is compiled among the few leading Hong Kong banks. The recently consolidated Hong Kong security exchange may accommodate any securitized real estate loans. In the past, the colony's investors have subscribed to a variety of real estate trusts whose advisors were the major banks and property companies located in Southeast Asia. The plunge of property and property trust prices in the 1970s radically weakened the demand for property trusts today. Most developers request leasehold mortgage loans for their projects on leased land, and they are accommodated by the Hong Kong financial institutions who are accustomed to leasehold mortgage financing.

Property interests are valued by foreign and domestic real estate appraisers. Their methods of appraisal and the content of written reports to clients are guided by two major real estate appraisal associations, one that is linked to the Royal Institution of Chartered Surveyors of London and one that was recently organized by Hong Kong appraisers. Generally, the rapid movement of Hong Kong purchase prices and rents dictates the use of the market comparison analysis. The written appraisal report may reflect the appraiser's use of this method primarily. The appraisers with the international real estate firms who perform a large volume of the Hong Kong appraisals are well acquainted with the five methods of British real estate appraisal. Many of the appraisers with foreign-based companies maintain professional designations from the Royal Institution of Chartered Surveyors which require in-depth knowledge of the five basic methods. Jones Lang Wootton, Richard Ellis, and Ballieu Knight Frank provide a large portion of the appraisal and other real estate services for the Hong Kong community and prospective foreign investors in commercial and industrial property. The leading appraisal firms tend to use computer methods for information storage and retrieval and report generation.

Hong Kong has a land registration system that is regarded by Hong Kong real estate professional people as quite comprehensive and reliable. Title assurance is generally provided through this land registration system.

Land use is thoroughly controlled. Urban planning commands respect from the investment and real estate community. As part of the comprehensive planning system with its continual set of reports, property prices and rents are tracked in the numerous urban and rural areas of Hong Kong. Plans are made for land use into the future and are coordinated with the government transportation departments and with private companies for the rail and roadway systems. Housing plans are closely related to the provision of transportation services and to the locations of the main arteries and stations. Planning includes taking precautions against the monsoon season and its threats to property and persons. Rent controls affect primarily the public sector housing. There are no government-instigated property purchase price controls.

Advance deposits are required for valuable leasehold site purchase. These advance deposits resemble the key money payments of Japan and Western Europe. They are derived from the heavy demand for prime commercial space that is extremely scarce on Hong Kong Island and the Kowloon peninsula. These advance deposits and the total property prices are generally established by an auction method of sale.

Real estate brokerage and estate management services are provided mainly by Hong Kong appraisers who are living permanently in the colony. Some expatriate British and other nationality employees serve British estate management firms, either permanently or on a tour of duty basis. The British citizens retain their British passports for possible eventual return to the United Kingdom. A few American real estate brokers operate in Hong Kong where they primarily serve Hong Kong clients who wish to invest in property in the United States or Canada. If a company needs property management services, it may employ the services of a domestic- or foreign-based real estate firm for this particular function. Some major Hong Kong property companies, such as the Hongkong Land Company, manage their properties through company-owned subsidiaries rather than use outside, independent real estate companies.

## SINGAPORE

The economy of Singapore is stable because it is controlled by the government. It is a planned society where the citizens feel that they benefit measurably from the government's benevolence. The goals of the government include lifting the standard of living of its people and protecting the environment from adverse pollution from various industrial sources. The government plans to replace all low value-added industries with high value-added industries that will employ the highly educated and skilled personnel that have been developed by the Singapore educational system. These personnel will be well compensated for their educational and skilled backgrounds. The transfer of technology from the advanced countries will lead to the high value-added society. Pursuing these goals, the government has replaced most of the substandard housing with modern, well-built standard housing. The political stability of the country and its steady progress toward a high value-added society has supported the major expenditures for new housing and improvement of the educational system.

Since Singapore has reached a high level of economic development already, it is a role model, in part, for the emerging nations of Indonesia and Malaysia. Malaysia lies on the other side of a river which forms the boundary between the Singapore peninsula and the Malaysian mainland. Indonesia is located across a wide waterway to the south and west of Singapore. Indonesia and Malaysia, like Singapore, are populated mainly by Chinese people who relocated from mainland China many decades ago.

Since the British colonized Singapore long ago, most of the English-speaking people are British. Most of the leading world banks that are located in Singapore are managed by English-speaking people, many of them British. The American minority are generally associated with the American bank branches and multinational corporations that are based in the United States. The English language is studied by native Singaporeans in their public schools. English is spoken in the Singapore business and tourism communities about as fluently as the Chinese language.

The Singapore dollar, though not an international currency, is stable and remains valued at approximately U.S. $0.50. Its value reflects the strong government control of the economy and of Singapore's society.

Foreign investment is encouraged by the strong, stable currency and government incentives. Full repatriation of profits, management fees, royalties, and capital is permitted by the government. But foreign purchase of land is generally not permitted by foreign entities other than companies for their operations and personnel housing. Singapore covers very little land, so what it has must serve primarily the growing Singaporean population.

A good market may exist for products manufactured by a foreign or domestic company. Many foreign joint ventures with Singapore companies operate plants in designated industrial areas and zones in Singapore. The marketing of such imported or domestically produced goods is controlled by the government since they approve or disapprove the content of the newspapers and other printed literature.

The government strongly supports land redevelopment. Most of the central business district land is owned by the government and leased to the highest bidders of approved land uses. Generally, old buildings are considered ripe for redevelopment even though the tourist trade may prefer the historic facades. The society approves only new or recently built structures for any land use. Therefore, the buildings used in the earlier British colonial days have essentially been removed and replaced by modern structures. The new buildings are set in the lush green environment of well tended lawns and gardens.

Singapore is one of the most beautiful and modern countries of the world. Since it lies within 100 miles of the equator in Southeast Asia, it receives rain almost every day of the year, and it is never cold.

Singapore's economic base has long been oil refining and ship drydocking for repair and maintenance. It is located on a widely used waterway which caters to the oil supertanker traffic from the Middle East as it moves to eastern delivery ports. As oil prices declined, so did the economy of Singapore. Ship maintenance also declined as oil shipments from the Middle East declined. Part of the oil refined on an island offshore from the Singapore mainland came from Borneo to the east. But most of the oil came from the Middle East. Only a small portion of the oil has been derived from Indonesian sources to the south and west of Singapore.

The roadway system of the small peninsula called Singapore serves well its population, business, and industry. Recently a subway system has been extended to the north so that even better mass transit is available to residents of locations more distantly removed from the central business and shopping districts. Much of the retail and hotel district is located along the Scott and Orchard Roads and not in the central business district which thrives on banking and corporate business. A Japanese-built international airport serves as a connector to other southeast Asian nations and other parts of the world. Singapore Airlines, continuously ranked as one of the best in the world, is headquartered in Singapore. The government owns the airline and strives to retain its reputation.

As the government seeks to promote high value-added production, it encourages technology transfer which includes computerized and robotic processing and manufacturing. It promotes the education and training of its labor force so that local labor will be well utilized in industries using advanced technology. Per capita incomes tend to increase with time. Part of the income increase is associated with this government policy and with technology promotion.

Few raw materials are available in the small country, but raw materials may be acquired from sources of the Southeast and South Pacific regions. Australia, not too distant, offers a wide variety of natural resources for Singapore's importation. High-quality building materials, as well as construction management, are often imported from Japan.

Since Singapore was once a British colony, its legal system is based on the English common law. Its private clubs and sports are also associated with its earlier British history.

Ample vacant space is available for most land uses. The government and the banking system encouraged construction as the tourism and oil industries went into decline. Tourism was vitally affected by the exit taxes that neighboring countries imposed on their traveling citizens. Singapore was once the retailing center of Southeast Asia. A large volume of customers were drawn from Indonesia, Malaysia, and other nearby countries. Singapore maintained a good assortment of goods and services for this regional clientele, but the departure taxes slowed down this outside retail trade measurably. The multinational corporations and financial institutions that relied at least partly on the lucrative oil business declined with oil prices. Many banks and multinational corporations fled to Hong Kong, Japan, and other countries where profits might be generated. So Singapore became "overbuilt" in the hotel, apartment, retail, and other sectors in the mid–1980s.

To accommodate all kinds of high-quality structures and high value-added businesses on the small peninsula, industrial buildings were designed as mid-rise buildings. This architectural pattern fostered high-tech industry. Environmental controls also promote high-technology businesses that do not create air, noise, and water pollution. Full-incentive industrial packages have long been offered to the industries that can be housed in compact, mid-rise structures. Land is scarce for all land uses.

The government, its central bank, and the state-owned financial institutions create financial stability. The international currency used in the local market is the "acu," the Asian currency unit. It is an artificially created basket of southeast Asian currencies in which many Singapore financial transactions are denominated. A number of multinational corporate shares are traded on the relatively small Singapore Stock Exchange. Its system provides the basis for operations in financial options and futures. The position of Singapore on the world globe promotes its use in round-the-clock security trading. It is spaced between the Hong Kong and Japanese security exchanges and those of India, the Middle East, and Europe. This financial center is located not far from the Australian security exchanges to the south and east of the peninsula.

Turning to real estate investment and financing by local institutions, we find that the Development Bank of Singapore, a state-owned financial institution, is engaged in real estate investment in Singapore and overseas. The postal savings system and the domestic and foreign commercial banks provide a great deal of the mortgage lending. Many mortgagors borrow from their pension funds entrusted to the community pension fund as a low-cost source for home financing. Since the residential properties of Singapore tend to be priced relatively high, a home buyer needs to accumulate substantial equity before mortgage funds can be located. Many buy condominium units, since few detached single-family dwellings are available for domestic and foreign residents.

Leasehold mortgage loans are desired by many investors in commercial structures. Much of the commercially zoned land of the central business district is available only from the Urban Redevelopment Corporation on long-term ground leases. The auctioning of the commercially zoned land in this area is of primary importance in the commercial real estate market. Some wealthy Chinese persons and families do not need financing for the development and construction of high-rise downtown commercial buildings, often built for regional banks, but some investors need some leasehold mortgage financing. If the leasehold loans surpass the financial limits of a single bank, loans are commonly syndicated among the numerous banks of the Singapore financial district.

Singapore has historically lacked sufficient construction management and skilled construction labor. Project bids have often been requested from international construction companies headquartered in Japan and South Korea. Then skilled construction labor may be acquired from other countries such as Taiwan. The government has been forced to regulate the permanent immigration of construction labor to Singapore after the workers labor for two or three years there. Many foreign workers get acquainted with Singaporeans and want to marry and stay in Singapore after the projects are finished. The government has established firm immigration policies due to its small land area and its population and industrial growth requirements.

The land use controls in Singapore are exacting. Environmental controls are fully enforced and government-sanctioned. Rent controls generally cover the older residential structures for which there is great demand due to the reasonable rents. Building codes must be met by the numerous developers.

Real estate brokerage and property management services are provided by domestic and international real estate companies. These services are part of a full-service component offered by such international companies as Richard Ellis and Jones Lang Wootton.

## JAPAN

The economy of Japan is robust. While a high-level of foreign trade continues, the domestic economy has been stimulated by government action in the last two years. The government with its figurehead emperor and Diet Parliament is very stable. The same political organization has controlled the Diet for many years. An opposition party is gathering strength for the first time due to public disclosure of personal scandals involving the government leaders. The Allied Forces at the end of World War II helped form the current form of government. The Japanese economic growth continues on a high level worldwide. The principal Japanese trading companies and financial institutions are positioned for continued economic expansion in all the world, including Africa and Central and South America. The Japanese yen is quite strong and is fast becoming an international currency. Japan's federal government controls business abroad. Before any significant action is taken by a Japanese private enterprise, it must gain the approval of government organizations such as the Ministry of International Trade and Industry. Foreign investment in Japan in encouraged to some extent. The government still may review and approve proposals from foreign entities seeking to do business in Japan. Generally this approval system is only a formality with little obstructionist power. But the high cost of entering certain industries, such as stock and bond brokerage, investment banking, and commercial banking, tends to exclude all but the major international companies. The Japanese companies will not work closely with their potential foreign competitors; in daily business activity, they tend to exclude foreign company participants from their group activities.

Japan permits complete repatriation privileges for capital, dividends, royalties, management fees, and other payments to overseas parties. The yen is fully convertible into other currencies. Recently the yen has become an international currency like the U.S. dollar and the German Deutsche mark.

Japanese companies and consumers tend to prefer imported products in many areas of business, particularly U.S. and European products of a superior quality. This preference is shown in their many advertisements that use Caucasian models. But the retailing and wholesaling networks of Japan have historically excluded imported products that might diminish the profitability of competitive Japanese products. Therefore, the U.S. and Japanese governments continue to discuss the lowering of the trade barriers to imports into the Japanese markets. If the products are made in Japan, their marketing tends to be more successful. Most of the

Japanese production of foreign-derived products involves Japanese joint venture partners.

Land redevelopment is crucial in Japan. Their expanding domestic and global business requires more building space at home. With an extreme scarcity of vacant land for development, land redevelopment takes on more than normal significance. Reassessment of space use is a continuing task for the government and private enterprise. If an industry such as shipbuilding goes into a permanent decline in world markets, the space released from shipbuilding operation is immediately considered for allocation to other more pressing land uses. When a military base is phased out, that space is reallocated to other land uses. Otherwise, land reclamation from the ocean and bays is an expensive alternative. Land reclamation must continue because it complements the reallocation of redevelopment land. More land is needed for the growing population, business, and industry which rests on earthquake-prone land.

Energy for industry in Japan comes primarily from nuclear plants and imported gas and oil. Nuclear plants tend to be more costly than fossil fuel power plants. Imported gas and oil means higher cost energy sources. The Japanese islands have no oil and gas reserves or coal deposits. They have timberland that is generally protected as park land and green areas for the urban communities and the tourism industry.

When Japanese consumers and companies buy even more cars as their personal and business incomes grow, they enter roadways that are already clogged with vehicles. Traffic jams inside and outside of Tokyo are a constant nuisance. The toll roads, freeways, and other traffic arteries need redevelopment for greater capacity. The bullet train system is supplemented by the regular train system, but not all areas are well served by train service. The best service lies between Fukuoka and Tokyo.

The international airlines transportation is improving with the construction of the international airport at Osaka. This should take some of the pressure off Narita International Airport which is located quite a few miles east of Tokyo in Chiba Prefecture. There is another general aviation airport to the southwest of Tokyo between Tokyo and Yokohama. International courier service employs these airports for their overseas flights.

Robotic and computer equipment are developed and manufactured in Japan. Japanese industry and business use computer and robotic systems to aid information analysis and retrieval, and to aid in cost cutting in manufacturing and distribution processes. Several global companies based in Japan offer robotic and computer equipment.

The population of Japan is growing slowly, as it is in the United States and the United Kingdom, due to birth control devices and the desire for higher standards of living which result from higher household incomes and fewer children. The government is concerned about its aging population as are the governments of the United States and Europe. More retirement communities are being developed, along with better retirement plans for public and private organizations. Multiple generation households are disappearing with greater retiree independence and financial resources.

Per capita incomes are increasing in Japan, but the prices of standard housing at a reasonable distance from workplaces are increasing even faster. One of the reasons the earlier zaibatsu's were so profitable was the lower labor costs of the Japanese personnel. Since the foreign companies, recently located in Japan, have offered higher salaries to desirable Japanese employees to entice them from their "lifetime" Japanese employers, the competition for Japanese labor has tended to increase personal incomes. The low unemployment rate also causes wage rates to be higher than might be with higher unemployment rates. The unemployment rate of Japan approximates 2.5 percent while that of the United States approximates 5.25 percent. The United States considers 5.25 percent a relatively low unemployment rate.

The Japanese business culture has been based on consensus of group opinion and on lifetime employment with a single employer. Both of these cultural patterns may be breaking up. Foreign companies are hiring Japanese people from Japanese companies, many times with the promise of much higher salaries. The use of quality circles for employee discussion of important business matters to arrive at consensus decisions may be dissipating. Individualism, American and European style, may be cutting into the cultural environment with the strong Japanese-American-European business competition.

Only one language is generally spoken in Japan—Japanese. Business people readily learn other foreign languages when their business responsibilities require it. The Japanese top corporate and government management tend to speak English, for example. As the Japanese companies "invade" Europe, they, of course, will learn the European languages for ease of communication and negotiation. Of course, English is the international language of finance and of business.

The climatic conditions of Japan vary from the extremely hot and cold temperatures of the western slopes of the mountain ranges on the west side of the island chain to the more temperate weather of the Kanto plain in which Tokyo lies. Hokkaido Prefecture on the island of the same name has cooler temperatures year round since it lies on the north end of the island chain. The shorelines are buffetted part of the year by typhoons probably associated with the typhoons of south Asia. The islands are subject to continuous earthquakes of various magnitudes on the Richter Scale. Since the earlier wooden buildings of the Japanese cities are being replaced by steel and concrete buildings, the threat of fast-expanding city fires is lessening. Dense populations in wooden buildings were once a fire hazard of tremendous magnitude.

Most Japanese citizens live on the plains and not in the mountains. They generally prefer to live as close as possible to their workplaces as do most working populations of the world. Close residential proximity to the workplace is generally not possible. Therefore, a high proportion of Japan's working population live an hour or hour and a half commute from their workplace.

The labor force is characterized by docility and respect for authority. Company unions are pervasive, but the industrial labor unions of the United States and Europe are generally not found in Japan. Employees are readily trainable. Many start to work for their "lifetime" employer upon graduation from a Japanese or foreign university. The corporate hierarchy is readily observed by the company employees. They work long hours and at least five and a half days a week on average. Recently the government asked companies to allow their employees Saturday off once or twice a month. Otherwise, the Japanese worker tends to work all day Saturday or only Saturday morning. Six-day work weeks are characteristic of Asia, in general. Company employees may enjoy the benefits of company-owned recreation centers, golf courses, baseball teams, and continuing education facilities.

A high percentage of single women work until they are married. Most Japanese women do not attain positions beyond clerical levels. Until recent Japanese elections, they had not attained any political power to enhance their employment status.

Japanese citizens have been encouraged recently by their government to take their offered one- and two-week annual vacations. Such recreational time has created a need for free-time recreational development in Japan and abroad. Many Japanese citizens are traveling the world for the first time. In previous decades, the Japanese employee stayed on the job dedicated to his or her work even though annual vacation time came and went.

Japanese global company management expects many of its employees to take tours of duty overseas on corporate assignments. The employee is expected to acquiesce to such overseas assignments. After an overseas tour of duty of two or three years, the employee may expect to be reassigned back to the Japanese home office. The employee may or may not take his spouse and children to the foreign post for the relatively brief tour of duty on corporate business. The farflung Japanese corporate locations are maintained by this management-employee system.

Very few raw materials are native to Japan, so most raw materials, including food, must be imported. The raw materials may then be processed with other semifinished goods into finished products which are principally exported. Rice must be imported from the People's Republic of China and other nearby countries. Minerals and lumber are imported from Australia; lumber also is imported from Canada, but seldom from the United States. Minerals of various types are also imported from South America and Africa. To speed this importation of vital foreign goods, Japan is thinking about building a canal across Nicaragua so that ships can reach eastern South American ports and African ports more easily in less time than currently possible.

Adoption of the civil code by Japan means that contract law there is similar to that of Western Europe. Businesses that normally do business under the English common law must adapt to the civil code system. These foreign companies need the assistance of the fifteen thousand Japanese attorneys who serve the 130 million population of the country. There are legal assistants for the minimal number of attorneys who may help the multinational firms in areas that do not require important legal advice.

According to the Building Owners and Managers Association International of Japan, little space of any kind is available for multinational corporations entering the Japanese market with their expatriate employees. The competition for the small amount of space available—residential, commercial, and industrial—comes from both the domestic and the foreign sectors. Japanese companies and households desire more working and living space as the Japanese standard of living and working rises. The highest pressure for good space is felt in the central business district of Tokyo. There continues to be migration from other parts of Japan to Tokyo for work, entertainment, and schooling. Tokyo is the center of Japanese culture, the arts, business, government, education, transportation, and every other facet of Japanese life. Since Japanese wages and salaries are highest in Tokyo, there is a natural migration toward this workplace. Some companies are headquartered in Osaka or other cities, but most are headquartered in Tokyo.

Property prices continue to climb due to scarcity of residential, commercial, and industrial space. The highest property prices are found in Tokyo, Osaka, Kyoto, Nagoya, and Kobe. The bullet and regular trains link these high-valued areas together. Property values in the other urban and rural areas of Japan fall significantly lower than the property values of these key urban places.

When a foreign company seeks manufacturing, distribution, and research and development space in Japan, the government encourages the foreign company to locate in outlying areas such as Hokkaido where fewer people reside and where employment rates are lower due to fewer work opportunities. Kyushu prefecture and the large area north of Tokyo are also less populated. The government seeks to steer foreign companies away from the already overcrowded Tokyo and the other high-valued urban areas. Thus a foreign company can enter the Japanese market for less total cost because the outlying areas offer lower property prices and a labor supply at lower cost. Manufacturing plants are steered away from Tokyo to reduce air, water, and noise pollution. The transportation system of Tokyo is already overcrowded during rush hours.

The government would like to encourage resettlement from the principal urban areas into other regions of Japan. The west coast is lightly inhabited due to the extremes in temperatures and the mountainous terrain. The island off Osaka in the Shikoku prefecture is being developed for industry, business, resort recreation, and permanent housing since space on the island has historically been underutilized. New roadways, bridges, and infrastructure are being built to encourage the resettlement to the island community.

The government has encouraged, through several means, the development of industrial parks in many areas of Japan. Generally they are placed in less populated areas where pollution from manufacturing will not harm the environment as it might in a highly populated area. Many of the industrial parks are located along the coastline to permit the use of water power. The Japanese nuclear power plants may also be closeby. The coastal locations also may serve the ocean shipping needs of the manufacturers.

The Japanese yen has developed recently into a strong, international currency. Two or three years ago the Japanese government decided to permit the yen to become an international currency, influenced by international monetary conditions. The Japanese government can no longer fully control its value and use. The yen is now used in international business and finance as the U.S. dollar, the German Deutsche mark, and the Swiss franc are used. The respective national governments can only partially control the values of these international currencies. The Group of Seven coordinates its efforts in controlling the values of all the international currencies.

The institutional system of finance in Japan is changing, albeit in a deliberate, gradual manner. The Bank of Japan and the regulators of the securities markets have permitted only slow changes in their institutional system. For example, only a few foreign investment banking houses have been permitted to become full members of the Tokyo Stock Exchange each year. The membership costs remain high. Smaller foreign financial institutions cannot bear the cost even if the Japanese financial regulators authorized their memberships. Membership attainment does not guarantee profits from investment banking activities.

The listing requirements are stringent as they are in New York for the New York

Stock Exchange. Then the listed security does not necessarily trade in high volume on the Tokyo Exchange. In the latest edition of *Euromoney* magazine, the trading activity of stocks listed on the Tokyo Stock Exchange was analyzed. Not all of the 50 or so listed stocks of major foreign corporations have traded in high volume. Market activity in a single stock depends on demand and supply in that security marketplace.

The relatively high savings rate of the Japanese individual and household provides funds for the Japanese economy. Individuals place their funds with a well-defined set of financial institutions which invest in a variety of loans, securities, and other assets depending on expected profitability for the shareholders and the depositors. Until recently, the investment returns from the Japanese postal savings system were tax free. From historically low interest rate payments on commercial and special bank deposits, yields have increased a little for the depositors who now have their investment returns taxed.

The ten largest banks in the world are headquartered in Japan, according to the latest issue of *Euromoney*. Therefore, one of the largest sources of funds is these ten banks. They each invest in a multitude of investment instruments and other investment opportunities. Their offices are spread worldwide to serve a global banking clientele. Therefore, they are a major source of funds for the world's business enterprises. Mortgage lending and mortgage banking are part of their functions.

Since Japan is encouraging employees to use their deserved vacations and to work a shorter week, Japanese households are being encouraged to spend more money on consumption. If consumption increases from increased personal income, perhaps the high Japanese household savings rate will not decline. Otherwise, the increased domestic and foreign consumption may result in a lower savings rate overall.

Asset securitization is increasing among the Japanese financial institutions. The same thing is true for financial institutions around the world wherever active security exchanges are present. Most financial institutions are adding to their reserves to satisfy international capital requirements, as encouraged by the Bank for International Settlements and other international institutions. Through asset securitization, loans of all types may be securitized and marketed to institutional, company, and individual investors worldwide. Mortgage securitization, initiated in the United States, is catching on in financial markets worldwide. In like manner, a multinational corporation may securitize its liabilities and market them to investors with the aid of investment bankers.

The Japanese financial institutions finance properties in many ways. In mortgage financing, they have historically made company loans on the basis of the company credit and then taken offered collateral as an additional inducement to make the loan on good terms. Nonrecourse mortgage loans have not appealed to Japanese real estate lenders. But Japanese financial institutions have entered into joint ventures with real estate developers and investors to finance major real estate projects. The banks can take equity positions in the financing of real estate. The banks, particularly, finance associated Japanese companies in this way. Even though the earlier "zaibatsu's" were dismantled by the Allied Forces after World War II, there remained interlocking directorates that involve many companies associated with each city and trust bank. They seek to financially accommodate their closely related companies.

International construction companies are based in Japan. They compete with international construction companies from Turkey, South Korea, the United Kingdom, the United States, France, and West Germany. In the past, Japanese international construction companies have been able to undercut much of their competition with scientific management methods and low cost funds from the Japanese headquarters and the federal government. Part of the Japanese construction company success is also based on qualified and experienced construction managers, high-quality building equipment manufactured by Japanese firms, and the willingness of the Japanese construction manager to work abroad for extended periods. If a Japanese company wants an employee to work abroad for a tour of duty, the employee does so without complaint. The workers are obedient to company requests and are loyal to their "lifetime" employers.

Commercial buildings in Japan are designed for little space per employee. The average Japanese person is small of bone structure and relatively short in height. Smaller employees require less building space for their work than the larger employees in Europe and North America. Also, the working space per employee is lower for Japanese employees than for most American and European employees who work for major multinational companies. Even though Japan excels in robotic and computerized systems, many office tenants are not completely or even partially computerized. However, Japanese companies are gradually computerizing their work forces, as are companies in Europe and the United States. Therefore, most new buildings must incorporate space designed for computer work stations even though not all companies are fully computerized.

High-quality building materials are manufactured in Japan. Mitsubishi elevator systems are used around the world in high-quality, high-rise office buildings. The raw materials and semi-finished goods needed for high-quality finished products must be acquired from abroad. Japan manufactures steel, but it must import iron and other raw materials. It has no natural resources upon which it may draw other than labor, management, and research and development findings. Japan does not import, even temporarily, construction labor from overseas. Local workers are trained to perform the construction jobs needed. When the international Japanese construction companies work abroad, they tend to take only management to the site and then hire local personnel for construction labor. Japanese workers have generally been highly trainable for jobs that need to be done. The cost of construction in Japan is rising due to the scarcity of construction labor and the gradually rising wages and salaries in the real estate sector.

The government has devised an appraisal system that samples market values every six months. The many licensed appraisers and their appraisal associates use the results of the six-month samples to derive their market values for specific properties. License exams are given periodically. Preparation for the expected license exam questions is given by the Japan Real Estate Appraisal Institute and the various trust banks. As well as providing real estate appraisal education, the Japan Real Estate Appraisal Institute publishes the trends in property values by land use and geographic areas. A key parcel within each subject site is selected for valuation. From the value of this key property, the total property value is drawn. Cost, market, and income approaches to the valuation of the single property may be used. The written report of the licensed appraiser gives complete details about the methods used in arriving at the final estimate of value. By reading the report thoroughly, the client may be led by the appraiser through the framework of appraisal analysis to the final conclusion about the value of the property. In general, the methodology of the book, *The Appraisal of Real Estate*, by the American Institute of Real Estate Appraisers, is adopted by the Japanese appraisers. But the real estate systems and land use controls of Japan have a number of unique features.

Japan maintains a land registration system that is considered by the Japanese real estate community to be accurate and reliable. When a person wants to check the title to a property, he or she checks the records with little fanfare. An attorney is generally not needed to verify the title holder, the liens against the property, and the marketability status of the title. The Japanese Ministry of Justice can enforce the requirements for accurate information on the records.

Details about the land use controls of Japan can be read in this author's recent book, *Investing in Japanese Real Estate* (Westport, Conn.: Quorum Books, 1987). In summary, three general categories exist for land use districts across Japan. One category does not permit land development, another permits land development in approved and exceptional circumstances, and third category permits land development of the approved types. Before a retailing project such as a shopping center may be built, the citizens and business people of the immediate community may give their approval of the proposed retail land development. Generally the government preserves the competitive status of the small retail outlets which saturate the Japanese landscape.

Stringent environmental regulations are imposed on building owners and developers. The federal land planning system is very sophisticated with high-level research and policy making. The federal land planners convey their recommendations to the prefectural and urban planning authorities who tend to carry out their wishes. Adjustments are made to federal land plans for unique local conditions.

Rent control covers residential space that was built prior to the Second World War. Commercial rent control is applied to shopping centers, office buildings, and other commercial structures. Rents that are considered exorbitant may be set aside by the government agency in charge of rent control enforcement. Since rents may be reviewed frequently, a constant upward adjustment of rents may be scrutinized by the rent control enforcement agency. Central city Tokyo office leases generally run two years before renewal and rent review time.

Tenant tenure allows the tenant to stay in a rented space as long as the tenant abides by lease terms. The landlord cannot evict the tenant for insufficient retail sales per square meter or tsubo (3.3 square meters) or nonconformance with the desired shopping center tenant mix. The landlord must persuade the tenant that it is in the tenant's best interests to vacate the space for other space more desirable for the tenant's business. Through negotiation with the tenant, the landowner may be able to terminate the lease and find a better tenant for the space.

The Japanese government has the right to approve negotiated property purchase prices. It may or may not exercise this authority. When property prices are rising more rapidly than the government feels is good for the Japanese society, the government may exercise its powers. It can set aside what it considers an exorbitant price and ask the seller to accept a lower price. The seller or vendor may agree to the lower price for the property, but the vendor may realize that the higher price is payable under the economic laws of supply and demand. The vendor is tempted to receive "under the counter" payments to compensate for the higher market price which the buyer is willing to pay. Supplementary payments of this type are received by vendors according to market information.

Building codes in Japan generally call for earthquake-resistant construction systems, particularly for high-rise buildings. Adherence to the stringent codes has gradually upgraded the quality of the high-rise buildings. Fires and floods from earthquakes and typhoons are less a threat with the enactment and enforcement of land use planning districts and modern building codes.

The irrigation and reclamation programs of Japan have long been important to land development and the health and safety of Japanese citizens. The water control systems throughout Japan protect the populace and their buildings from flood and the damaging waves of hurricanes. Healthy environments with clean and sanitary drinking water are partly the result of water control systems.

Large real estate brokerage firms operate throughout Japan. They complement the many local real estate firms. Computer systems aid the marketing of available properties and of land development projects. Some of the Japanese real estate firms have global operations, such as Mitsui Real Estate Co. and Mitsubishi Estate Co.

The global real estate firms headquartered in Japan may invest and develop in one or more countries outside of Japan's boundaries. A number of these companies have invested in properties in the United States for their own account and for investor groups based in Japan. The extent of the foreign property investment and development depends on the policies of the real estate company's top management, the amount of funds available for overseas investment, the investment policy position of the Japan Ministry of International Trade and Industry, and the personnel available for overseas assignment. Mitsui Real Estate and Mitsubishi Estate Companies each have numerous diversified global firms associated with their real estate operations. In some instances, the associated real estate company assists a subsidiary company in developing overseas property for the company's use. For example, expatriate housing may be needed by the associated company. The associated construction or real estate development company can assist with the property requirement.

The reader may want to refer to four recent books by this author for more detail: *Investing in Japanese Real Estate* (Westport, Conn.: Quorum Books, 1987); *Japanese Shopping Centers: Financial and Investment Features* (Scottsdale, Ariz.: International Real Estate Institute, 1985); *Guide to International Real Estate Investment* (Westport, Conn.: Quorum Books, 1988); and *International Income Property Investment* (Scottsdale, Ariz.: International Real Estate Institute, 1985).

## SPAIN

The Spanish economy is thriving. Higher levels of productivity for higher profits are associated with Spanish and foreign joint venture companies. The Spanish people are willing to work to reach higher standards of living. With Spain's entry into the Common Market, the market of Europe is open to their products and services. They see a bright horizon of endless business opportunities.

Madrid has been the center of Spanish business opportunity since the mid–1980s.

Foreign companies have purchased Spanish financial institutions and industrial companies or have formed joint ventures with them when outright purchase was not possible because of Spanish company resistance or lack of sufficient capital. Europeans, Japanese, Americans, and others are represented in the new company involvement. Policies and regulations concerning foreign direct investment were changed by the Spanish government in the mid–1980s, and today they encourage foreign investment.

The government of Prime Minister Gonzalez seems quite stable even though union agitators and Basque separatists sometimes terrorize the Spanish community. The rapid advancement of the economy and the standard of living might generate more uncertainty than would occur in a mature economy. The economic growth is exemplary for a country that earlier languished under a military dictatorship for an extended period. During the rule of Generalissimo Franco, the economy of Spain suffered.

Both Spain and Portugal on the Iberian Peninsula are entering the business life of Western Europe. Spain, though, is far more advanced than Portugal. The communist party has never attained in Spain the same strong influence it has in Portugal. Both societies reached a peak in global trade and colonization in earlier centuries and then faded in modern times. Now they are both seeking again to attain economic and political prominence within a New Europe.

The Spanish peseta is considered a weak currency in world terms. It is not an international currency that is widely used in international trade.

The government permits the repatriation of capital, profits, management fees, royalties, and other such corporate payments to the corporate headquarters and other company locations. Generally this is a characteristic of the members of the European Community.

Corporate products may have a large, growing market in Spain. The growth of the community is accompanied by a growth in demand for domestic and foreign goods and services. Even foreign life insurance companies have recently established branch offices in Spain to gain greater policy sales among the companies, individuals, and households that are receiving higher incomes.

Spain's land use control and planning policies encourage land development and redevelopment. The Crown Estates of the Franco era have been confiscated by the government, and new land developments have been planned and executed on some of the immense tracts of land. Since land for development remains scarce at prime locations in Madrid, obsolete buildings there are demolished or renovated for new tenancy at higher rents. The government has also encouraged redevelopment of the existing produce markets into food-focusing shopping centers with modern facilities. Older structures that once housed the fresh produce marketplaces are being redeveloped into modern shopping centers.

Much of Europe lacks energy sources, and most of its natural gas is piped in from Russia; most oil is shipped in from northern Africa or the Middle East. Without local gas and oil sources, energy costs tend to be relatively high.

Spain is improving its highway and rail systems. New transportation systems are planned to link Seville to Madrid. Barcelona wants to get new transportation systems in place to serve its metropolitan area before it hosts the 1992 World's Fair. For some years, new rail lines have been considered for the east coast to link the Marbella resort area of the south to Barcelona and other European cities to the north. Iberia Airlines continues to link the principal Spanish cities to other Western European cities.

High technology is being introduced to Spanish manufacturing through technology transfer that is sometimes linked to foreign joint ventures with Spanish partners. The use of computers and robots is encouraged by the leadership in order to improve the productivity of Spanish workers. They are anxious to produce more readily marketable products for the European market in particular. Computer and robotic manufacturing represent to them cost-cutting mechanization that leads to higher profits, wages, and salaries from the higher productivity and sales.

Spain's population growth was rapid earlier because its relatively poor and uneducated society had low economic and social aspirations. Catholicism, the principal religion of the country, traditionally promoted large families for the glory of God and for the financial security of the elderly. The Spanish population characteristics now resemble those of the typical European family—smaller households with older heads of household and higher per capita incomes. The Spanish language is widely spoken while English is generally taught in school along with Spanish.

Most parts of Spain have a temperate climate. The east coast attracts tourists from other parts of Spain and Western Europe because of its warm climate. The highlands of the interior of the country tend to have cooler temperatures.

The labor force of Spain is highly trainable and anxious to work, generally speaking. They want "to get ahead." Many foresee opportunities resulting from Spain's entry into the mainstream of Western Europe's economic prosperity.

Spanish industry and business are increasingly run by foreigners. Therefore, the management systems of the United States, West Germany, France, Sweden, the United Kingdom, and other countries are being assimilated into Spanish business. Since the Japanese have begun to invest in Spain, the Japanese management systems should become well known in the near future.

Raw materials for business operations and construction materials tend to be scarce in this Iberian country. They are not known for large timber reserves, iron ore, oil and gas reserves, industrial diamonds, gypsum, or other valuable natural resources. Therefore, they must import many of their raw materials and semifinished goods for their production and assembly plants. But oil and gas reserves are found closeby in the northern African countries. Other countries of Africa, including South Africa, have generous reserves of valuable minerals and other raw materials. The proximity of such large natural resource reserves may reduce importation costs.

Spain, along with the other Western European countries on the continent, operates under the civil code. The Napoleonic code, which was transmitted to other parts of the world in the era of the great Spanish empire, was known to be a mixture of the civil codes of Spain and France. Napoleon conquered that area of Western Europe, and the Iberian Peninsula became a part of the Napoleonic empire.

Space for commercial development is scarce in the heart of Madrid. Industrial space may be found in the fringe suburban areas of Madrid, but the stringent land use controls increase the scarcity because permissions for building development take a long time. The combination of stringent land use controls and a scarcity of development sites have forced property prices higher. But the economic development of Spain began on a large scale only in the early 1980s. Therefore, property prices are considered relatively low and yields from property investment relatively high in comparison with the rest of Europe. Since the demand for commercial and industrial space is high in Spain, the divestiture of corporate space should meet high demand.

There are two major metropolitan areas in Spain: Madrid and Barcelona. On a worldwide scale, these cities are relatively small. Spain is not a densely populated, highly industrialized country. The east coast's population increases significantly with the influx of tourists from northern European countries during most of the year.

Industrial development is encouraged by the government and by private organizations. Numerous incentives are offered to domestic and foreign prospective investors. The government takes an active role in providing land, trained labor, and tax and financial incentives to those considering industrial development within the country's boundaries. The Spanish government and its private sector is now in competition with the other governments and private enterprises of the European Community, Asia, and North and South America in attracting industry.

The financial system of Spain is based on commercial and merchant banking. Insurance companies from Spain and abroad market policies and invest in Spain and wherever else competitive investment yields may be found. Mortgage companies provide real estate financing as do the other financial institutions. A number of cross-border mergers and acquisitions involving domestic and foreign banks has strengthened the banking sector since the early 1980s. Large retail banking networks are supported by these large banking institutions. But the security exchanges are not highly developed. The Spanish currency is relatively weak and not used as an international currency. The banking system accommodates point-of-sale financing through demand deposit accounts at leading retail stores.

International real estate firms have operated in Madrid and Barcelona for a number of years. Their offices were established in high-quality office buildings along the Avenue Castellano in Madrid in the early and mid–1980s. They entered the real estate market to compete with local real estate firms as foreign real estate investment in Spain was gaining momentum. Jones Lang Wootton and an affiliate of Hillier Parker May & Rowden handle much of the international and domestic real estate business as brokers or estate managers.

Rent control has plagued residential space. Many landlords have not had financial incentives to maintain and redevelop their residential buildings as physical depreciation and functional and economic obsolescence have taken a toll on the existing buildings. Even though many residential communities have been built with high-rise architecture, the older housing accommodations still need to be replaced with more spacious, modern units. Parking in residential areas continues to be a problem. Many employees must drive to their places of employment because of the dispersal of business and industry locations and the lack of adequate public transit.

## FRANCE

With the continued government of President François Mitterrand, the economy of France prospers. One of the chief goals of his administration is to place France at the center of the emerging unified Europe. The French offer Paris as the capital of the new Europe in competition with London, the established international center for European affairs, and Brussels, the headquarters city for the emerging European Community.

The agitation of the labor unions of France, which support the Mitterrand position, continually stirs up the process of economic growth. Mitterrand's government has tried to raise wages and salaries, lift regulations by privatizing major French companies, lower taxes through the reduction of the government budget, increase investment through the lifting of exchange and investment controls, and promote industrial growth through cross-border joint-venture approval and industrial payment of subsidies.

France is part of the emerging "United States of Europe." The recent head of the European Community was a French political leader. France is one of the leading countries of the new economic union, along with West Germany and the United Kingdom. Of the three countries, West Germany has the strongest economic position. The United Kingdom is historically the center of international finance and commerce. West Germany's economy is splintered due to the reorganization of the capitalistic part of Germany by the Allied forces after World War II. France is an important partner in the Group of Seven that coordinates world financial policies. West Germany and the United Kingdom also take their rightful place in this significant financial group.

Generally the French franc is not considered an international currency due to its weakness and the weakness of the French economy. Since the U.S. dollar has been devalued during the 1980s, the French franc has gathered relative strength in the world marketplace.

Like the other European countries, the government of France is based on coalitions of several political parties. Since a number of political parties including the communist party exert influence over national and domestic affairs, it takes a coalition of parties to gain the government leadership. Therefore, the current Mitterrand government, a coalition government, is considered liberal, but its financial affairs tend to be conservative.

Foreign investment is encouraged, but investment from European Community sources is generally encouraged more than investment from non-European Community sources. If the foreign investment adds to the economic growth and prosperity of French business and its citizens, that investment is encouraged no matter what the source of funds. For example, the French celebrated in mid–1989 the establishment of a Japanese Nissan plant outside of Paris. Foreign investment and foreign exchange controls have been liberalized in recent years. Repatriation of corporate profits, interest, royalties, and service fees are still subject to proper authorizations, approved license agreements, and transmission through approved banking intermediaries. Only a few of the state-owned banks and industrial companies have been privatized, and those have been privatized since 1985. The French now impose few controls on capital and profit repatriation in comparison with earlier governments.

Since the French economy is thriving and incomes are rising, the market for many foreign-based and domestic products is expanding. The government is extending computer technology down to the grass roots level. It is seeking higher productivity since it has reduced French inflation to very reasonable levels, approximately 5.5 percent in recent years. Earlier inflation in France was 25 percent or more on an annual basis.

There are two principal regions in relation to economic and land development: (1) Paris and its environs and (2) areas and provinces outside of the Paris region. Urban planners have designed and redesigned Paris over the centuries. Their planning policies have been politically motivated and politically administered. Generally land redevelopment for the center of Paris has been encouraged over any new land development. The ambiance of the "world's most beautiful city" is a factor to be preserved from the viewpoint of land planning policy. Redevelopment policies tend to preserve the original historic facades of buildings, the wide, tree-lined boulevards including the Champs Elysees, the mid-rise architecture of commercial buildings, and a low degree of commercial signage that might block historic views which attract tourists. The land development policy of the federal government is directed toward new land development in new towns on the Paris periphery and in the provincial cities. Employment rates and wage and salary levels tend to be the highest in the Paris metropolitan area. Economic development in outlying areas is thought to better equalize the disparity between the Paris and the provincial city employment conditions. Therefore, the designated industrial and commercial redevelopment areas where the government offers packages of financial and other incentives are located outside of Ile de France.

France receives its natural gas supplies mainly from a pipeline from Russia. Its oil is derived from northern African countries and the Middle East. Because France does not have sufficient natural power sources, such as oil and gas, it must depend on such outside sources. Since it is an industrial nation with a relatively large population, it uses large amounts of power continuously. It is dependent on foreign trade for energy sources and other products.

The transportation system is steadily improving. New fast trains will link various parts of France to other parts of Western Europe, including the United Kingdom via the rails of the tunnel under the English Channel. The subway system of Paris carries a heavy load at rush hours because it is efficient and economical. Taxis are plentiful, but somewhat expensive as in London. Orly and Charles de Gaulle airports handle a high volume of commuter and international flights. Air France airline serves many destinations including the United States with frequent flight schedules.

Population growth is relatively low. Per capita income is rising with the slow growth in population and with the payment of higher wages and salaries. Most French citizens speak French but also learn English in their public and private school systems. There is a high degree of national consciousness. Unlike Spain, France maintains regular 8 to 5 or 9 to 5 working hours during weekdays. Some Spaniards honor the historic pattern of midday siestas; the French take no siestas from noon to 2 o'clock. The work week approximates 38 to 40 hours.

France has a northern temperate climate with four seasons and a range from rather stifling heat in the summer to cold, snow, and ice in the depths of the winter. This description characterizes the Ile de France and the central and northern parts of France, while the southern part of France along the Riviera has a warmer year round climate. In the Nice-Monte Carlo coastal area, winter temperatures still drop into the 30 to 40 degree Fahrenheit range. But the summer season lasts longer with warm temperatures for boating, sunbathing, and other beach activities. France has mountainous regions to the east toward Switzerland and to the south toward Nice and Monte Carlo. The mountains of France, near the Swiss Alps, are snow clad much of the year.

The French industrial worker is usually unionized. The unions strike, perhaps frequently during the year, to attain union objectives. A combination of union and company management representatives run the many state-owned companies in France. The labor strikes tend to be very disruptive to commerce.

The top management of the leading corporations of France are often political appointees as well as major stockholders—if the company is privately owned—and leading public figures. A few French universities prepare young people for corporate management positions, particularly high-level positions in multinational corporations. The chief international business school is INSEAD, located in Fontainbleau, France, a western suburb of Paris which also houses one of the large royal palaces.

One of the chief occupations of France is farming. But France has few natural resources that may serve as raw materials for French manufacturers. Agriculture is a principal industry in most of the provinces outside the Ile de France, the Paris region.

Since Napoleon reigned with his military conquests and maintained his head-quarters in Paris, the civil code of France became known as the Napoleonic code when it was transmitted to distant countries including the United States. The state of Louisiana has adopted the Napoleonic code for its legal system.

High-quality commercial space is scarce in the central business district of Paris, and vacancy rates are very low. The city planners liberalized their building regulations in the mid–1980s so more new construction and building renovation is now encouraged. But few sites become available for new construction. Building renovation is still encouraged more than new construction. In the center of Paris, usable building space is small by United States standards. Space for foreign corporate headquarters was provided by the City of Paris in the La Defense redevelopment area across the Seine to the west of the central city. Now that office building community is almost completely built up while more corporate headquarters space is needed. Other office parks in other parts of the Paris suburbs provide outlying office space that foreign corporations may or may not like.

Paris real estate analysts are fearful that, when the current office building construction and renovation is finished, the market may be overbuilt. In light of the formation of the new Europe in the early 1990s, an "overbuilt" condition will probably never occur. More corporations wish to enter the European Community "before the door is closed" to the new "European fortress." Only four cities compete for these corporations wishing new European administrative headquarters—Paris, London, Brussels, and Frankfurt. Some foreign companies still want major offices in all of these European capitals. Many major multinational companies are already located in the four capital cities. Most multinational corporations do not wish to be located in the outlying provincial cities of France. In contrast, multinational manufacturers may find the designated industrial parks of the French provinces to be attractive, where reasonably priced workers with appropriate industrial skills are available.

With the reelection of President Mitterrand, the French government and its exchange rates are relatively stable. Since the U.S. dollar has low value, building land, labor, and equipment costs in France are relatively high. As the U.S. dollar has increased in value during the summer and fall of 1989, these French costs are declining for U.S. corporate investors. France has sources of capital that may be tapped by multinational corporations. Commercial and mortgage loans are available from both privately and publicly owned financial institutions. The Paris Bourse is available for flotation of stock and bond issues, though this particular security exchange handles a low volume in comparison with the International Stock Exchange of London. Merchant banks and foreign investment banking houses can privately place corporate issues with various worldwide investment sources. Lease financing for French properties is available from banks and finance companies located in France and other parts of Europe.

France houses international construction companies. This sophisticated construction management may be applied to large corporate projects in any location in France. These international companies have access to various construction materials worldwide. Since French architecture is wide ranging in design and materials, the corporations may build any type of structures. France represents architecture that ranges from the traditional and historic to the avant garde and controversial. The Grand Arch of the La Defense corporate office district is an example of the French acceptance of the avant garde in architecture.

The valuation system is characterized as a governmental and a private sector system. Small one- and two-member appraisal companies tend to serve government valuation purposes. The private international and domestic real estate firms with valuation staffs primarily serve the private sector. The appraisal fees are more negotiable in the private sector.

The numerous land use controls keep prices high on existing structures of international quality. They also keep land prices high; increased corporate demand keeps the building and land prices rising. They inhibit new construction in areas of Paris which multinational corporations would prefer for their national and regional headquarters.

Environmental protection is a theme of the French populace. France's Green Party lets itself be heard.

Tenant tenure and rent control affect the residential and commercial property inventory. Building codes are a part of the urban land use controls. But the government does not exert property purchase price controls. French government agencies do exercise their rights of preemption in order to acquire space for government-directed land redevelopment.

Property management is usually performed by a subsidiary of the building investment company or by the owner's employees. Some property management is conducted under contract with local and international real estate companies such as the Paris-located, British-chartered surveyor firms. These international real estate companies perform many real estate functions for French clients including property management and brokerage. If a corporation wishes to acquire or divest itself of corporate property, the many local and international real estate firms can offer full brokerage services. The international firms are usually multi-lingual to enhance personal negotiation of real estate transactions.

## CHINA

After the student revolts of May and June 1989, the government of the People's Republic of China (PRC) replaced the leadership with less liberal advocates of domestic entrepreneurship. The student leadership was jailed, executed, or reassigned to rural jobs rather than university positions and urban jobs. The new leadership still espouses domestic elements of capitalism and fosters foreign investment, particularly for the export of products. Financial reserves and foreign hard currencies are still needed. Without hard currencies, the government cannot borrow and pay its debts to foreign sources and cannot permit repatriation of capital and profits to foreign investors that serve the economic objectives of the PRC. Tourism is fostered because it brings in foreign hard currencies.

The economic growth of China continues on a steady path. The increased foreign investment in the country by multinational industrial corporations means the transfer of technology to the developing country. Industrial development that promises the transfer of technology is particularly favored by the Chinese and Communist party leaderships. On the other hand, multinational companies seek the Chinese advantages of lower cost labor that is trainable and willing to work and the expanding Chinese market for consumer and business goods.

The 1989 student revolt set back the progress of the Chinese economy for a short period. Multinational companies withdrew their personnel in threatened positions. They hoped to ask their personnel to return to their Chinese homes and companies when the political reprisals were over and the economic stability restored. The multinational companies found new leadership in China to work with in operating and expanding their companies.

In Asia two very populous countries have developing economies. One, the People's Republic of China, has a population that exceeds one billion people. The other, India, has projected growth to one billion people in approximately five years. Pakistan, Burma, and Sri Lanka are also populous countries with growing low-income populations. Since China is a natural antagonist of the USSR, the large country is a buffer for capitalistic Japan, the Republic of Korea, the Republic of China, North America, and Europe. The Communist party of China is independent of the Communist party of the USSR and its Eastern European satellites. China wants to develop its economy, defense establishment, and standard of living without interference from the USSR which lies to the north and west of China.

China utilizes two currency systems simultaneously, one for transactions with foreign entities, the other for internal transactions. Since the two currencies are controlled by the central government, the report of approximately 15 percent inflation for the country is subject to question. Recently foreign workers and companies operating in China have reported actual inflation much higher than the government-reported level.

Even though the Communist party membership in China approximates only 15 percent of the Chinese population, it controls the government. It has generally been a diplomatic and economic friend of the United States since the early 1970s, but Japan has proven to be its principal supplier of borrowed funds and its chief trading partner. Japan is dependent on food supplies from this large neighbor with its immense agricultural south. The "rice bowl" of southern China serves Japan as well as its domestic market. Japan has room and the topography for very little cultivatable land.

Even though China encourages foreign investment and the transfer of technology, its foreign investment controls are formidable. It approves only joint Chinese-foreign investment where foreign currency is attracted and where foreign firms produce in China products mainly for export. China is anxious to once again have a positive trade balance. In the 1980s China, like the United States, had become a debtor nation. Both countries had large trade surpluses in prior decades. Repatriation of profits, royalties, management fees, and capital are generally not permitted in China due to the minimal level of hard currency reserves and a negative balance of trade with most countries.

The government has promoted land redevelopment in its major cities including Beijing, the capital city. Through development and construction of high-rise residential and commercial buildings, it has raised the living and working standards for those companies and individuals who can afford the new premises. These modern buildings have replaced low-rise buildings with minimal sanitation, heating, and cooling facilities. Much of the land redevelopment of Beijing has catered to the foreign community. Many of the new buildings are affordable only by foreign companies who must house their domestic and expatriate staffs in standard quality office and residential buildings. Part of the land redevelopment has been devoted to high-rise luxury hotels to serve the expanding transient foreign community. Foreign company personnel and tourists are housed in these large, luxury facilities. For example, major hotel chains and management companies have been permitted to build large hotels in midtown Beijing and outlying urban areas of Beijing and Shanghai.

Much of China's energy is produced along the Yangtze River in the central part of China. The water source is used for fossil-fuel power plants. China has some nuclear capability that it uses mostly for defense production. The coal deposits of northwest China have been difficult to exploit because of the lack of appropriate mechanized equipment and adequate roadways for transporting workers, management, and materials. The rail system of China permits the transportation of bulky, low unit value products such as coal over long distances.

Recently China has purchased more foreign-manufactured commercial aircraft for their China Airlines fleet. Intercity flights over long distances are part of the modern Chinese transportation system. Airline terminals and associated services at the airports need to be developed further. Since the road system amounts to narrow, poorly maintained surfaces for heavy and light trucks and a few passenger vehicles, the rail system is the mainstay of the Chinese transportation system. Some automobiles are being manufactured in China, but most personal incomes are not high enough to afford private passenger cars. Since commune governments assign workers to jobs within the respective communes, little commuting to workplaces is necessary. Less need exists for private passenger automobiles. But trucking and rail systems are needed for the distribution of products across the vast country where production occurs in specific districts. For example, food products and silk thread are produced in the south and the food products, at least, are needed in all parts of China. The urban labor of Beijing and northern cities produces silk fabric from the silk thread of the south.

The Chinese government has fostered birth control to restrain the population growth. Each couple is permitted to have one child. Additional children are discouraged by the government, which does not provide full services to any additional children. The communes reprimand and otherwise sanction their members with two or more children per household. As the leadership strives to raise the standard of living for the Chinese, it realizes that a population explosion counteracts advances in economic productivity.

Per capita income has been rising in China. Part of this growth has come from the entrepreneurial system that was introduced to the economic system by Deng Xiaoping in the early 1980s. Once a person has produced the government allotment, that person may produce goods and services that may be sold to raise the personal income of the person and his or her household. Factory managers may increase their incomes by manufacturing the state allotment of products and then producing more for entrepreneurial sale. The profits from the surplus goods manufactured may be distributed among the management and the workers as bonuses. With the bonus money additional necessities and some luxury goods may be purchased, if they are available in the marketplace from domestic or imported sources.

Chinese employees work a six-day week. They speak the Mandarin dialect in the northern part of China around Beijing and Cantonese in the southern part around Hong Kong. English is spoken at the numerous universities where visiting professors in most academic fields come and go on academic tours of duty. The management systems of Japan and the United States are taught to aspiring young Chinese business people. The Chinese do not shirk their work responsibilities and duties. They are a hard-working, industrious people. But the government assignment of workers to the numerous jobs that need to be done often results in untrained workers assigned to jobs that need skilled workers.

China has a temperate climate. For example, Beijing gets very cold in the winter and very hot in the summer. The year round temperatures of southern China are said to be milder than the extreme temperatures of the four seasons that affect Beijing. Annual monsoons batter the coastline along the South China Sea.

Repeated explorations for natural resources have uncovered most of them in this large country. But bringing out the minerals and other natural resources is a problem due to the poor transportation and industrial mechanization in the areas of the reserves. Also the distribution system for all products and services is generally inadequate. Most of the natural resources are found in the northwest quadrant where the citizens are less economically advanced. They have been isolated from the mainstream of Chinese economic and social activity that centers in Beijing and Shanghai. While Beijing has long been the government center, Shanghai has been the center of commerce, finance, and law.

The legal system of China is slowly developing. The business joint venture agreements and their enforcement have been one of the major catalysts for legal change. The Chinese government has asked for foreign participation in the development of their legal system and the legal education of future attorneys.

The mortgage law of Hong Kong adopted in the mid–1980s was based on the English common law. Contract law of the mainland may be a mixture of both common law and the civil code.

The new buildings of Beijing reportedly have high vacancy rates due to the political unrest, the decline in tourism that resulted from the political unrest, and the decline of foreign entry into a market that has not produced reasonable profits over a reasonable period of time. The rents for the high-quality residential and commercial properties of Beijing have scared away prospective tenants. These rents are competitive with the high rents of Tokyo and London. Perhaps the high vacancy rates will force a decline in rents as owners seek to fill their premises. The overbuilding of Beijing has not been accompanied by overbuilding in Shanghai. Reported vacancy rates in Shanghai, the historic business center of China, have been substantially lower than in Hong Kong.

The Canton area special development zone continues to develop. Ground leases are extended to desired manufacturing companies with many corporate commitments to immediate land development and business operation. The development incentives are linked to the Chinese need for employment, the training and education of workers in modern methods, transfer of technology, and industrial development for export. The Chinese government assumes full ownership of the land and buildings after the specified date in the contractual agreement. From the foreign company's point of view, the Gangzhou special development zone provides an opportunity for profits within a brief 10- to 20-year period. Then China takes over all assets left by the foreign companies.

The reminbi, the official government currency of China, is fully controlled. Exchange rates are administered by the communist government as part of their economic policies. The finance ministers have sought the advice of financial leaders across the globe. Two of the principal financial goals at present are reduction of the inflation rate and reduction and eventual elimination of the national trade deficit with most countries. On the general credit rating of the country, China continues to float bond issues in the international and Euro markets. They tend to get better than prime rates on these securities. Generally Japanese investment bankers arrange for and market the issues. Then consortia from worldwide sources subscribe to the large issues. Some of the government's funding comes from domestic sources. In recent years, China has developed commercial banks with mortgage lending functions. These are deposit-taking banks whose funds may be drawn from the banks by the government. Both the private and public sector financial institutions do not have the capacity for the projected economic development of the country.

During the 1980s, stock exchanges were established in six to eight major cities. These institutions will mobilize domestic capital to finance business and industry. Business has been permitted the right to incorporate. The sale of stock is made possible by the presence of the new security exchanges.

Because of the major building programs in China in the 1980s, many workers have been trained in construction technology. Often the projects have been managed by Japanese and other international construction companies who offer management expertise, sources of project financing, and access to scarce high-quality building materials. Few quality building materials are available in China. Any available would come from recently established foreign joint-venture companies who have brought with them the technology to produce high quality building components.

The international real estate companies that maintain offices in Beijing offer a full line of real estate services including valuation and brokerage. Since Chinese land is not sold to foreigners, most appraising deals with ground leases and building ownership of foreign-domestic joint ventures. The building ownership may extend only for the period of the land development contract with the Chinese government. Most foreign-owned properties revert to Chinese ownership after an established period.

The forerunner of a title registration and assurance system is the government survey of land use and ownership that has been conducted in the mid–1980s. With this valuable information, a well-organized land registry may be established.

Extensive land use controls affect foreign use and temporary ownership of Chinese buildings. On the domestic level, the commune government assigns land and buildings to the commune members. On a foreign level, government bureaucrats in Beijing allocate valuable urban land to various competing foreign land developers and multinational industrial corporations. The government controls rents and regulates business activities with production quotas, taxes on profits, and worker assignment.

# SITE SELECTION IN EUROPE—A CASE STUDY

## Terry L. Rees

In this paper I will describe a site selection recently undertaken by United Technologies Corp. (UTC), which culminated in the location of a manufacturing plant in Valongo, Portugal.

### The Importance of United Technologies' Foreign Operations

Since the 1970s, a major diversification and growth has transformed UTC from a $2 billion aerospace company to a $17 billion-plus, broadly based manufacturing concern which operates over of 300 plants in 26 countries. Additionally, we maintain sales and service offices in virtually every nation of the world.

We operate from the corporate headquarters in Hartford, Conn., commonly known as the Gold Building. Some of UTC's better known divisions are: Pratt & Whitney, Carrier Air Conditioning, Otis Elevator, Hamilton Standard, Norden Systems and Sikorsky. These divisions maintain either the number one or two market-share positions (in revenues) worldwide in over 80 percent of our total product lines.

As an example of UTC's international presence, Otis, with 1987 worldwide sales of $2.5 billion, is the world's largest manufacturer of elevators and escalators, as well as the largest servicer of such products. That world-wide presence is both a source of great strength and a challenge to UTC. With Otis' 42,000 employees in 569 district and branch offices and 1,700 service locations in 143 countries around the world, the differences in language, culture and politics can be staggering.

Global expansion by UTC has increased its international sales to approximately 40 percent of total sales. In 1987, international sales amounted to $7 billion. Of the company's 190,000 employees, 75,000 are located outside of the U.S. In 1987, approximately $2 billion of sales came from direct exports from U.S. operations generated primarily by the Connecticut-based aerospace companies.

In 1987, UTC ranked as the 21st largest manufacturing company worldwide and as the 16th largest U.S. company in sales by foreign operations. We are ranked number 15 on the Fortune 500 list. United Technologies has significant international assets.

### General Objectives

With the foregoing background in mind, we will examine a site-selection project recently undertaken by United Technologies' Automotive Products Division (APD), which manufactures wire assemblies, plastic trim and com-

ponents, electric motors and electromechanical products for the automobile industry. The primary domestic customers for these products are the auto makers Ford and Chrysler.

> *‘*
> *This siting study deals with the site search and selection of a 146,000-sq.-ft. building on 11.4 acres on the outskirts of Porto, Portugal.*
> *’*

Europe accounts for approximately 25 percent of APD's total revenues, which in 1987 were approximately $1.3 billion. The division's European products consist of wire harness assemblies, electric motors for power windows, seats, door locks, electric switches for headlights, windshield wipers, cruise-control mechanisms, plastic interior components and automotive air-conditioning systems.

This siting study deals with the site search and selection of a 146,000-sq.-ft. building on 11.4 acres on the outskirts of Porto, Portugal. The facility was purchased to provide additional wire harness assembly capacity for the 1989 model years and beyond as APD continues to grow in Europe. The facility was needed to enable the firm to maintain a competitive manufacturing-cost position, as Portugal has very reasonable labor costs and corporate tax rates in relation to other western European countries.

The facility will produce Ford Escort wire harnesses

*Terry L. Rees is manager, international real estate, for United Technologies Corp. This article is taken from Rees' presentation to a workshop of IDRC's Chicago World Congress.*

Reproduced from *Site Selection*, September/October 1988, by permission of the publisher, Conway Data, Inc., Atlanta. No further reproduction is permitted.

presently made in the United Kingdom. This change will allow the UK facility to commence manufacturing the Ford BE13 (Fiesta's replacement) harnesses for the new car's introduction in January 1989, so no jobs were eliminated. The change of products should, in fact, allow the UK plant to expand in the future due to an improved product mix.

> **'**
>
> *The facility was needed to enable the firm to maintain a competitive manufacturing-cost position, as Portugal has very reasonable labor costs and corporate tax rates in relation to other western Europe countries.*
>
> **'**

The new plant will be headed by a general manager who will report directly to the vice president of European operations in Cologne, Federal Republic of Germany. Directly responsible to the new plant's general manager will be the following functions: production, manufacturing, engineering, production and material control, finance and personnel.

### The Decision to Expand

After five successive years of growth and sales expansion in Europe, Automotive Products Division's European operations are an established leading supplier of wiring harnesses. The greatest share of this expansion has been through APD's operations in Spain (MAISA) and the United Kingdom (UTA UK Ltd.). These two organizations required more factory space by the end of 1988 and APD felt pressure to provide more low-cost manufacturing space due to the fact that major competitors — Yazaki, Reinshagen and Bergmann — had completed or were in the process of completing new manufacturing facilities in Portugal.

In order to meet projected sales volume over the next four years, APD had to implement phase one of its expansion plan, which required a minimum of 75,000 sq. ft. and the employment of 500 additional people by 1990. If sales dictated, and APD anticipated that they would, a second phase with an additional shift of 500 employees is planned within the same building. The phase-two plans call for expansion into the non-utilized portion of the existing building.

### Existing European Operations

Current European wire harness assembly operations serve the following European customers: BMW, Audi, Porsche, Ford of Europe, Rover Sterling, Volvo, Saab, Renault, Peugeot, Fiat, PSA, Talbot, Citroen and Maserati. These automobile manufacturers are served from locations in Spain, West Germany and the United Kingdom.

### The Location Analysis

Because of the locations and requirements of these varied customers, adequate transportation throughout Europe was critical to the venture's success. Therefore, transportation by land and air were extremely important to this new operation.

> **'**
>
> *. . . adequate transportation throughout Europe was critical to the venture's success.*
>
> **'**

Initially, we considered several low-cost labor areas, among which were: Morocco, Portugal, Tunisia and Yugoslavia. Each of the countries was rated on such factors as industrial environment, labor costs, employment policy, employee absenteeism, labor productivity, direct labor skills, customs facilities, investment incentives, ease of capital and profit repatriation and economic climate. We also evaluated the political stability, social stability, cultures, the extent of municipal red tape, geographic considerations and internal and external communications, including telephone, telex and facsimile services.

### The Site Selection

Portugal was the very evident first choice among the countries considered. In addition to the aforementioned reasons, Portugal was chosen due to the fact that it has the lowest labor costs in western Europe. A member of the European Economic Community, it has shown a stable economic and political environment, and its social and cultural ethos are easily understood. There is manufacturing and engineering talent available, and it will be possible to hire and relocate management as needed.

> **'**
>
> *We decided, based on transportation considerations, to locate in or near Porto, Portugal's second largest city.*
>
> **'**

In most industries in Portugal, unions and employers enter into binding agreements, usually one year long, which cover working conditions and pay. For pay purposes, workers are divided into categories, and an agreed minimum pay scale is designed for each category. The country's average working week is 42 hours, and the minimum holidays are 13 national days and 22 working days. Portugal observes equal pay for men and women. Wages are paid monthly in 14 payments. The extra two installments are paid in July prior to the summer holidays and in December prior to Christmas.

Once Portugal was decided upon, we had to determine where to locate the facility. We decided, based on transportation considerations, to locate in or near Porto, Portugal's second largest city. We selected Porto, located in northern Portugal, due to its excellent access to APD's Spanish operations and the rest of Europe.

APD was seeking a site with the following characteristics:

- Located near an established population center — adequate labor,
- Adequate highway and airport access — transportation,
- Adequate land/building space for future expansion needs,
- Adequate industrial infrastructure,
- Progressive and cooperative municipal officials,
- Adequate ingress and egress to the facility's grounds,
- Reasonable cost of land and improvements and
- Adequate schools, housing and amenities.

Due to timing constraints, we preferred an existing facility to constructing one from scratch on an undeveloped site. We examined three areas near Porto that had acceptable land and facilities; the locations included: Serem, Ilhavo and Valongo. Detailed investigations of the three areas were made and Serem, which is a small industrial area approximately 40 miles south of Porto, was eventually eliminated as unsatisfactory due to its more rural location and limited labor availability. Only 1,100 people were employed within a five-mile radius of Serem, and we anticipated needing 1,000 within three years. The risk was too great that not enough labor would be available when needed.

> **'**
> *Due to timing constraints, we preferred an existing facility to constructing one from scratch on an undeveloped site.*
> **,**

The next area, Ilhavo, was located about 50 miles south of Porto near the coast in an industrial area. The location appeared satisfactory, but in the end the only acceptable building was old, and renovation costs proved to be too high for a marginal facility. We were also concerned that Ilhavo might be too far from Porto, where our managerial and professional employees would likely live, and commuting times were deemed to be unacceptably long. The subsequent elimination of Ilhavo left us with a preference for Valongo.

Valongo is about five miles from Porto and was the nearest to the airport of any of the three locations considered. That, too, was an important consideration. Valongo is a city

of 91,000 people, with roughly 28,000 men and 30,000 employable women over the age of 18. Additionally, the entire Porto area could also be utilized to supply labor for the Valongo site. The building under consideration consisted of only a shell without floors and utilities. The large amount of construction finish required gave APD an excellent opportunity to complete approximately one-half of the building in phase one. In phase two, we plan to expand into the balance of the building.

The Valongo site had adequate access, and cooperation from municipal officials was excellent. The site is adjacent to a new expressway scheduled to open in 1990. In fact, a very small portion of the plant's property was scheduled to be taken for the off-ramp to the freeway. We were able to negotiate a swap to provide some additional parking area at the side of our facility in return for the land designated for the off-ramp.

The city agreed to extend the necessary utilities to the facility at no cost.

### Consulting Support

This location decision was aided by several parties that acted as consultants during the process. First, the real estate firm of Fenalu, SA, which belongs to the European Commercial Property Assn., assisted UTC with feasibility and valuation studies. Second, we received support from the Portuguese Investment Institute, which assists industry to locate in Portugal and which administers this nation's economic incentive program.

### Conclusions

In review, United Technologies' Automotive Products Division feels that they have located an excellent facility in a prime location for transportation throughout Europe. The location offers an abundance of well-qualified workers who will welcome having good jobs close to home. The land and building were purchased in April of 1988. We are currently finishing the facility and preparing to install the necessary equipment in order to be operational by year-end 1988.

### SUGGESTED READING

1 MacDermott, Richard C. "Recent Trends in Location Analysis." *Industrial Development,* September/October 1986, vol. 155, no. 5, pp. 21-22.

2 Wilson, Reece C. "Exploring the Corporate Site Selection Framework." *Industrial Development,* September/October 1987, vol. 156, no. 5, pp. 15-19.

3 Wheeler, Dale D. "Key Site Selection Issues for the Corporate Fixed Assets Manager." *Industrial Development,* vol. 157, no. 2, pp. 6-7.

# THE BENEFITS OF A GLOBAL ENVIRONMENTAL COMPLIANCE STRATEGY

## Paul Cullen Beatley

Companies operating multinational industrial facilities are challenged today with a growing array of government regulations designed to protect human health and the environment. Many policy experts believe that the 1990s will bring tougher rules and even global harmonization of some environmental laws and policies. What began in developed countries in the late 1960s and early 1970s as an effort to mitigate the effects of industrial pollution has spread to newly industrializing countries and even to many less-developed countries. Not only has the scope broadened from cleanup to reducing end-of-pipe pollution, but initiatives to prevent pollution in the first place are steadily progressing in many countries.

The next decade of environmental action is bound to have profound impacts on virtually every aspect of global business — from what and where a company produces, to the design of processes and facilities, to the final disposition of its products and industrial by-products, especially wastes. Environmental due-diligence studies will play an increasing role in global mergers and acquisitions also as more governments adopt policies requiring plant owners to assume the burden of site remediation. Companies with well-developed and executed environmental compliance strategies will not only minimize their risks, but may even improve their competitive positions by incorporating environmental issues into their long-range strategic planning processes.

Most business leaders have long since disabused themselves of the idea that the "fad" of environmental protection would go the way of the hula hoop. Public sensitivity to environmental issues is as strong as ever in most countries today and is expected only to increase. This concern has been fed by a chronology of environmental disasters. The failure of traditional political parties to adequately address these concerns saw the advent of "green" parties in a number of western democracies. The relative decline of these political movements in recent elections is only proof of growing public concern, as the mainstream parties incorporate these issues into their programs. In the meantime, such movements have sprouted up in less-developed countries, with similar impacts on the policies of mainline parties.

Today, not even the governments of eastern Europe and other communist countries can entirely resist the mounting pressure to respond to these issues.

| Diary of Environmental Disasters | | |
|---|---|---|
| 1945-1967 | Minimata, Japan | Mercury poisoning |
| 1974 | Love Canal, N.Y. | Toxic chemicals discharge |
| 1976 | Seveso, Italy | Massive dioxin contamination |
| 1984 | Bhopal, India | Toxic gas release |
| 1986 | Chernobyl, USSR | Radioactive contamination |
| 1986 | Basel, Switzerland | Chemical pollution of the Rhine |
| 1987 | Kotka, Finland | Chemical spill in harbor |
| 1988 | Pittsburgh, Penn. | Oil spill in the Monongahela River |
| 1989 | Valdez, Alaska | Massive crude oil spill |

In addition to popular demands, cumulative pressure has built up from another quarter to force governments to forge ahead with new programs. Twenty years of developing environmental regulations and programs have created an entirely new, multibillion-dollar global environmental industry with a vested interest in ever tighter regulations and technological requirements. The success of this industry has suggested to the authorities in many countries that it is not shortcomings in the technological field which con-

*Paul Cullen Beatley is an environmental consultant with A.T. Kearney, Inc., in Alexandria, Va.*

Reproduced from *Site Selection*, May/June 1989, by permission of the publisher, Conway Data, Inc., Atlanta. No further reproduction is permitted.

strain policy choices, but the choice of policy which limits technological innovation.

## Managing Environmental Risks Overseas

Effective management of the risks associated with environmental liabilities requires a plan encompassing four essential points:

- risk identification,
- identification of activities contributing to risks,
- identification of specific actions and controls to manage the risks and
- the development of a quality assurance program to monitor risk management plan performance.[1]

Development of such a plan, while no simple matter in any case, is made easier when the laws and regulations are codified and effective institutions exist for their enforcement and compliance monitoring. This situation is true in virtually all of the industrialized, developed countries. The risks which are difficult to gauge are those associated with future, and as yet undefined, policies, legislation, regulations and judicial interpretations. However, reasonably accurate projections of these new requirements can be made, at least in the short term, by monitoring the activities of the regulatory agencies and following developments in the legislative process.

Some newly industrializing countries, for example, Brazil and Mexico, have begun to spell out specific regulatory requirements and to develop effective institutions for their implementation. However, the majority of developing countries, especially in the less-developed Third World, generally lack the legal and institutional framework for environmental protection. Where limited standards exist, they are often poorly enforced if at all. It is this regulatory void which poses the most serious threat to companies operating overseas. In the absence of regulatory guidelines, local plant managers and their staffs may not be sufficiently sensitive to environmental risks and liabilities in their drive to improve output and profitability. Often, it is only after an environmental incident occurs that the local authorities take action against a plant or company. A proactive environmental management program, based on the "pollution-prevention-pays" principle, can help a company avoid or minimize these problems.

## The Direction of Environmental Programs in the Industrialized World

Most countries in the three main trading blocs began developing tough environmental protection programs in the middle to late 1960s. These programs are continuing to evolve and expand in scope, placing ever more responsibility on industry for the costs of cleanup and prevention. In some cases, such as the London Dumping Convention and the Montreal Protocol, governments have recognized that action in one country alone is insufficient and concerted international efforts are required to resolve air and water pollution problems. International trans-shipments of hazardous and toxic wastes is another area gaining increasing attention from a number of governments and international bodies.

The United States took the lead in applying a regulatory rod to polluting industries by imposing air emission standards and water effluent limitations and by developing a "cradle-to-grave" approach to hazardous waste management with the passage of the Resource Conservation and Recovery Act (RCRA). Superfund provided the government with an enforcement mechanism to compel those responsi-

ble for the thousands of uncontrolled and abandoned hazardous waste disposal sites to assume the burden of remediation. In addition, virtually every state has enacted its own environmental regulations, some of which are more stringent than the federal requirements. Several states have either enacted or are considering laws requiring sites to undergo environmental integrity assessments and have a clean bill of health before they can be transferred to a new owner. In some cases, even lending institutions can be held liable for site remediation.

> ‘
> *Where limited standards exist, they are often poorly enforced if at all. It is this regulatory void which poses the most serious threat to companies operating overseas.*
> ’

Congress has tightened requirements and increased the criminal penalties in amendments to all major environmental legislation, and the Justice Department has stepped up civil and criminal prosecutions for violations of these acts. A ban on land disposal of untreated hazardous wastes, as stipulated in the 1984 amendments to RCRA, is due to take effect in early 1989. This law combined with the NIMBY (not in my backyard) syndrome, which has prevented the siting of new commercial hazardous waste management facilities in many parts of the country, will certainly add to the rising costs of waste disposal. The shipment of troublesome wastes abroad has also come under heavy criticism lately; the possible banning of this practice will also contribute to mounting costs.

While the U.S. has led the world in the stringency of its environmental laws and the liabilities associated with contamination, many European countries have been leaders in the field of waste minimization. Long recognized as an important part of good housekeeping, waste reduction and the promotion of "clean technologies" (*i.e.,* low- and non-polluting industrial processes) have become priorities in the environmental programs of several western European countries. The French government, for example, pays up to 50 percent of the cost for research into widely applicable waste-minimizing technologies and offers investment subsidies of 10 percent for demonstrations of pollution prevention techniques.

The Dutch government spends about $8 million per year on research and development (R&D) of clean technology, including the potential role of biotechnology in curbing waste generation. A pilot program in West Germany funded at the level of $8.1 million per year for two years was instituted in 1986 by the Ministry for Research and Technology to help develop waste minimization R&D projects. To give a strong economic incentive to companies to reduce waste streams, the Bundestag (the West German parliament) also enacted a law to tighten treatment and disposal requirements which is expected to double or triple the costs of waste disposal.

The reasons for this emphasis are not hard to see. Europe is one of the most densely populated regions of the world. A circle with a 644 mile (400 kilometer) diameter centered on Lille in northeastern France would encompass the industrial heartland of Europe — the Ruhr and Rhine valleys, Antwerp, Brussels, northern France, Randstad (Holland), greater London and the Midlands, the industrial heart of the U.K. This high concentration of industry and population means heavy pollution, and all indicators suggest that current growth will increase at faster rates in the future. At the same time, shipping Europe's wastes abroad is becoming less of an alternative in view of protests from the countries which once received them.

Recognizing that national action was insufficient, the European Community (EC) heads of state or government[2] determined in 1972 to establish a European Community environmental policy. Moreover, the Single Act, which amended the Treaty of Rome, devoted an entire chapter to environmental policy, bringing it henceforth within the European Community's competence. The Community has implemented four environmental action programs since 1973.

The first two such programs dealt essentially with remediating existing problems, while the third represented an overall preventive strategy for safeguarding the environment and natural resources. The fourth action program, begun concurrently with the European Year of the Environment in 1987, confirms the preventive strategy, but also seeks to make environmental protection an essential element of all economic and social policies. The rationale behind this is that differing national policies and the resultant disparities could have a negative effect on the functioning of the common market.

---

**COMPARATIVE HAZARDOUS WASTE PROGRAMS**
**MAJOR INDUSTRIAL COUNTRIES**
*Summary of National Programs*

|  | D | F | GB | I | NL | USA | Japan |
|---|---|---|---|---|---|---|---|
| Registration/Licensing |  |  |  |  |  |  |  |
| -Transporters | Yes | Yes | No | Yes | No | Yes | Yes |
| -TSD Facilities | Yes | Yes | No | No | Yes | Yes | Yes |
| Transport Controls |  |  |  |  |  |  |  |
| -Manifest | Yes | Yes | Yes | Yes | Yes | Yes | No |
| -Import/Export Control | Yes | Yes | Yes | Yes | Yes | Yes | Yes |
| TSD Facility Permitting | Yes | Yes | Yes | Yes | Yes | Yes | Yes |
| All Operating Sites |  |  |  |  |  |  |  |
| Permitted | Yes | Yes | Yes | No | Yes | No | Yes |
| National Strategy/Plan |  |  |  |  |  |  |  |
| to Establish Facilities | No | No | No | No | Yes | No | No |
| Old or Abandoned Sites |  |  |  |  |  |  |  |
| -National Inventory | Yes | Yes | No | No | Yes | Yes | No |
| -Cleanup program | No+ | No+ | No | No | Yes | Yes | No |

+ = No plan, but cleanup occurring
D = West Germany; F - France; GB - United Kingdom; I - Italy;
NL = The Netherlands; USA - United States;
TSD = treatment, storage and disposal

---

As the European Communities[3] move closer to the goal of a single, unified market by the end of 1992, companies can expect closer coordination and harmonization of the environmental laws of the 12 member states.[4] Under the original terms of the Treaty of Rome, member states were allowed a certain degree of derogation from the rules governing the customs union in order to protect the environment and health and safety. These exceptions have, in recent years,

become the rule as numerous governments have used environmental or health and safety standards as a means to erect new non-tariff barriers (NTBs) to intra-Community trade.

While all of the member states have implemented environmental protection policies, their complexity and the severity with which they are enforced varies widely from country to country. West Germany, Denmark and the Netherlands have adopted the toughest approach in this respect. Some of West Germany's larger chemical firms, however, have expressed concern that these legal disparities cause them to be unfairly penalized. Their complaint is that the high costs associated with compliance with West German antipollution laws puts them at a disadvantage to competitors in member states with similar but less stringent laws.

> ❛
> *. . . the direction of European Community environmental legislation in the context of 1992 will be towards harmonization, based not on the lowest common denominator, but somewhere toward the higher end of the scale.*
> ❜

The Commission of the European Communities recognized early on that a certain degree of harmonization of environmental and health and safety rules would be necessary for the completion of the internal market. Hence, specific mention of these was made in the Single Act, which amended the Treaty of Rome. However, a recent ruling by the European Court of Justice on the Danish beverage container case gave new impetus to act on this. In its decision, the court determined that until environmental laws are harmonized, individual member states would be free to implement their own rules, even if these contravened the EC's free trade policy. Already the government of the Netherlands is using this as a precedent to introduce new measures which the Commission claims will restrain trade.

Thus, environmental issues are rising to the top of the agenda in the EC with respect to 1992. The appointment of Italy's Carlo Ripa di Mena as commissioner with specific oversight of the EC's Environment Directorate General (DG XI), the expansion of DG XI's staff and Commission President Jacques Delors' call for the establishment of an EC environmental agency, all reflect the new level of concern in Europe for environmental protection.

Apart from purely environmental considerations, the Commission feels that adaptation to higher standards demanded worldwide will have a positive impact on European industry's ability to compete successfully in the global market. As well, strengthening environmental policy is expected to generate new investment in infrastructure and in the manufacture of new quality-oriented products, which should in turn have favorable consequences for employment.

Thus, the direction of European Community environmental legislation in the context of 1992 will be towards harmonization, based not on the lowest common denominator, but somewhere toward the higher end of the scale. Several countries, particularly Britain and Italy, would not welcome standards based on West German or Dutch regulations. The Commission will try to find a compromise position, aided by financial assistance in the form of soft loans through the European Investment Bank and aid through the European Regional Development Fund. The eventual result will be a Community-wide floor of environmental rules, below which member states will not be permitted to go, but above which they will be free to legislate.

Japan responded to a series of environmental crises by passage of a comprehensive set of laws covering air, water, noise, soil and other forms of pollution. Known in the 1960s as the most polluted country in the world, Japan has today become a role model in pollution control in many areas. Japan's air pollution-control laws, for example, are among the strictest in the world. And the country has become a leader in the area of technology stimulation in which strict environmental policies have led to rapid technological innovation. An example of this is the development of a new type of waste incinerator, which produces minimal atmospheric pollution and which is used for energy co-generation.

Japan's extensive legislation governing hazardous waste follows the principle that the waste generator is ultimately responsible for insuring adequate treatment and disposal. In addition, by stressing waste management strategies based on waste minimization and recycling, the government has been relatively successful in reducing overall levels of industrial and hazardous wastes.

The Japanese Environment Agency has responsibility for the coordination of national environmental policies. Several other agencies are also charged with pollution control. While these agencies interact freely, the lack of centralization has made the Japanese regulatory system overly complicated and piecemeal. Because social sanctions are based on shame rather than guilt, the government had little cause to resort to legal sanctions in prior years. However, criminal prosecutions for more serious violations of the environmental laws have become more frequent recently.

Under the Environmental Pollution Offense Law, both a company's management and its employees can be imprisoned and fined for violations. Some areas of environmental protection being considered by the government for future action and with significant implications for the cost of waste disposal and industrial liability include:

- manufacturer responsibility for disposal of wastes posing particular treatment and disposal problems,
- effective monitoring to prevent illegal dumping,
- increasing waste-handling charges to promote waste reduction,
- safe management for the transport of hazardous wastes,
- techniques for reducing environmental loading through more effective waste-management requirements,
- removal of obstacles to promote regional waste disposal,
- reclassification of some wastes in view of the manner in which they are managed and
- new guidelines for the treatment of certain organic wastes.

## Pollution Control in Newly Industrializing Countries

Only a few years ago, multinational companies were encouraged to site their most environmentally offensive facilities in developing countries. Fifteen years ago the Brazilian state of Goias ran newspaper ads declaring, "We want your pollution." This was only one of the most blatant examples of a common practice in many parts of the developing world to take advantage of popular fears in developed countries in order to promote their own industrial development. The prevailing attitude was that environmental protection was a luxury that "rich" countries could afford but not an issue of importance to countries struggling with poverty and economic backwardness.

Times have changed. Economic development and environmental protection are no longer viewed as mutually exclusive, competing goals. Many newly industrializing countries have recognized that, while they are generating growing volumes of hazardous waste, they have not developed effective laws and institutions to control the environmental impacts of it. Nor do the nations possess the technologies needed to do so adequately. Studies have shown that the most serious environmental contamination in the world occurs in rapidly growing urban areas, such as Mexico City, Sao Paulo, Jakarta, Lima and Calcutta, as well as in other countries that have recently experienced rapid industrial development and urban growth.

Several Latin American countries have already taken advanced steps to rectify this situation. Brazil has enacted some 30 environmental laws, decrees and regulations stipulating the permissible limits to air, water and soil contamination. In addition, the Brazilian National Economic Development Bank has refused to provide financing to any project which has not received approval of the environmental secretariat, SEMA.

The new Brazilian constitution includes one of the most comprehensive chapters on environmental protection in the world. It charges the government with the task of regulating industry and development to prevent risks to health and the environment and to preserve and restore the genetic integrity and diversity of the country. The state of Sao Paulo has used a 1976 statute to shut down a number of polluting plants. The state is the home of Cubatao, once described as the "Valley of Death," but now the greatest environmental success story in Brazil. Today, only 93 points of toxic emission from local factories remain of the 320 identified in 1984 when CETESB, the state environmental agency, launched its pollution-control program.

> '
> *The new Brazilian constitution includes one of the most comprehensive chapters on environmental protection in the world.*
> '

Private and state-run industries in Sao Paulo, as well as the multinational companies, have installed pollution-control equipment and are complying with the strict laws. No new polluting plants have located in the state since the program began. Several companies are in a legal battle over paying for the cleanup, but most of the region's industries are actively cooperating in the cleanup efforts.

Other Latin American countries are also taking a more serious approach to industrial pollution. Mexico recently passed a general environmental protection law to pull together all previous legislation in order to strengthen enforcement. The penalties for violations have been stiffened and include fines, jail sentences and liability for remediation costs. In Argentina, Santa Fe Province used the criminal code to jail the crews of two ships for fuel spills and for cleaning their fuel tanks in the Parana River. The province also added stiff fines and gave factories, which were discharging toxic substances to the river, six months to build and use waste treatment facilities. Waste minimization efforts have also registered successes. Venezuela takes pride in a new solvent recovery unit at the Du Pont plant in Valencia, which saves some $200,000 per year in recycled solvents.

Environmental cleanup and institution building have also been boosted in Asia and the Pacific Rim. Over the next decade, several Asian countries, including Hong Kong, Taiwan, the Philippines, Thailand, India, Indonesia and China, are expected to implement stricter pollution-control regulations and to spend heavily to clean up their environments. Many of these countries are expected to develop U.S.-style programs. These new initiatives are being assisted by the U.S. Dept. of State's Trade and Development Program (TDP), which has budgeted more than $2 million for seminars and feasibility studies to be conducted by American companies on behalf of these governments.

For the first time, many of these countries have incorporated strategies for environmental protection into their five-year development plans. China, for example, has embarked on an ambitious program of developing industrial waste management facilities in every province in the country. Thailand's sixth development plan (1987-91) aims at developing and implementing a national toxic and hazardous waste management plan.

Companies operating plants in these newly industrializing countries can expect tougher pollution-control laws in the near future as well as increasing pressure to clean up contaminated sites.

## The Pollution Control Dilemma in the Third World

While the movement toward industrial pollution control has been slow in the newly industrializing countries, it has been largely nonexistent in much of the less-developed world. Environmental issues in these countries generally have revolved around the destruction of tropical forests, desertification and resource depletion rather than industrial pollution. However, an abrupt refocusing has recently occurred as revelations concerning the dumping of European and American hazardous wastes in Africa and in Caribbean countries have evoked cries of "toxic terrorism." Reactions have ranged from a threat by Nigerian officials to shoot those responsible to a unanimous resolution from the Organization of African Unity (OAU) condemning the practice.

In response to growing demand from developing countries, the United Nations Environment Programme (UNEP) has initiated talks aimed at the drafting of a treaty to regulate international shipments of hazardous wastes. In fact, negotiations for such a treaty have been under way since 1985. Now, however, for the first time more than half of the countries participating are developing nations.

Currently the United States requires waste exporters to inform the receiving country's government of shipments and contents. European Community rules require informed prior consent from the receiving country before wastes can be exported. Virtually all wastes sent to developing countries are disposed of in landfills, with a resulting increasing danger that toxic chemicals will leach into the soil or groundwater. Most of the receiving countries have neither the technology to dispose of such wastes in an environmentally sound manner nor the legal framework to adequately regulate the practice.

> '
> *In response to growing demand from developing countries, the United Nations Environment Programme (UNEP) has initiated talks aimed at the drafting of a treaty to regulate international shipments of hazardous wastes.*
> ,

UNEP's draft treaty would impose a strict system prohibiting exports of toxic wastes unless the importing country first agrees in writing. UNEP also would require notification at four stages of each shipment, from the time the shipment is planned until its final disposition in the importing country. The goal is to make it exceedingly difficult to obtain approval for the movement of hazardous wastes. The effects of such a treaty, combined with stricter regulations in the U.S. and other industrialized nations making landfills increasingly rare in those countries, will almost certainly result in more difficulties and higher costs for toxic waste disposal.

This new focusing of attention on industrial pollutants in developing countries may also pose important difficulties for multinational companies. Those operating industrial facilities in the Third World may find that the new attitude toward pollution will make disposal of their wastes more problematic. Despite the fact that most multinational companies are far more conscientious about pollution control than most domestic operators, many nonetheless found the lack of rigid environmental regulations an asset and a clear attraction for setting up operations in developing countries. However, the lack of control regulations will not excuse a company from liabilities resulting from an accidental discharge of toxic materials. In this climate, the lack of a regulatory framework to use as a guideline for safe plant operation may leave local plant mangers without an effective tool for risk management. It is precisely in this regulatory void that most international companies face their most serious challenge.

Where a proactive environmental regulatory compliance strategy based on local government regulations is not possible, top management must take the necessary steps to ensure that foreign operations are conducted according to the same high standards as exist in their home country. This is true not only of existing facilities, but of new facilities and those obtained through mergers and acquisitions.

The multilateral development banks have begun to scrutinize environmental factors in their lending and project-funding decisions. The World Bank, for example, requires more stringent safety and pollution-control measures on some Bank-financed projects than are required in many industrialized countries. Thus a few companies have been forced to incorporate more expensive design features in plants partly financed with World Bank money than would have been the case back home.

In addition, as companies scramble to favorably position themselves in Europe, for example, through strategic mergers, they should not lose sight of the fact that many European companies have important operations in Africa and in other parts of the developing world which may not necessarily be operated according to U.S., or even European Community standards.

## Help Is at Hand

Operating environmentally sound facilities overseas, and particularly in the developing world, will require an active commitment on the part of top management. In the last few years several organizations have stepped up their activities to assist in this. UNEP, in collaboration with other United Nations organizations, has recently begun to focus on the problems of industrial pollution in less-developed countries. UNEP's Industry and Environment Office (IEO) can help companies with information concerning pollution control in the Third World. The IEO's emphasis has recently shifted from end-of-pipe mitigation to waste minimization or elimination. The IEO is concentrating on applying to developing countries cost-effective, low- and non-waste technologies, developed in the industrialized countries. The IEO has also developed guidelines on low- and non-waste technologies, environmental impact assessments and the siting of industries in developing countries.

In collaboration with the World Bank and the World Health Organization, the IEO is producing a manual for developing countries on the safe disposal of hazardous wastes as well as publishing the quarterly, *Industry and Environment,* distributed in 167 countries. UNEP also has an agreement with the French government to provide experts on request to developing countries to advise on issues such as pollution control, hazardous waste disposal and non-polluting technologies. A similar agreement exists with Japan, and other industrialized countries are expected to join in such programs.

Other initiatives include:

- the establishment in Geneva of an International Environmental Bureau by the International Chamber of Commerce;
- the World Health Organization's Collaborating Center for Environmental Pollution Control;
- the International Program on Chemical Safety (IPCS), which promotes international harmonization of chemical assessments and improvements in laboratory techniques;
- the OECD Environment Committee's promotion of harmonization of pollution-control regulations, a system to track trans-boundary shipments of hazardous wastes and safety and regulation in biotechnology; and
- the World Environment Centre (WEC), a nonprofit

organization which serves as a bridge between industry and governments by sending volunteers to Third World countries to assist in solving industrial pollution problems.

These world bodies, as well as many non-governmental organizations, are currently building the framework for pollution control in the Third World in collaboration with governments of developing and industrialized countries. No doubt, it will be many years before serious environmental protection programs come into force in most of these countries. However, companies can better manage their environmental risks by carefully monitoring the activities of these organizations and incorporating their more important recommendations into the management of their facilities. Also, by adopting UNEP's theme that "pollution prevention pays" and drawing on the wealth of information these programs have to offer, waste minimization can be a financially as well as an environmentally sound proposition.

## Know before You Go

Firms contemplating the development of overseas manufacturing operations would be well-advised to study carefully the local pollution-control laws and regulations in force where new plants are contemplated. Companies that already have overseas operations should, at the very least, institute the same management oversight programs for environmental compliance which they use in their home countries. Failure to do so may, at the very least, result in adverse publicity, or worse, stiff penalties ranging from heavy fines to plant closures. Many of the environmental disasters that have occurred were not so much accidents as the direct result of a failure to manage environmental affairs adequately.

## ENDNOTES

1 See Deets, Lee A., "Environmental Risk Management," in *Industrial Development,* March/April 1988, Conway Data, Inc., Norcross, Ga.

2 Now called the European Council.

3 The European Communities include the European Economic Community (EEC), the European Coal and Steel Community (ECSC) and the European Atomic Energy Community (Euratom).

4 France, Italy, West Germany, Belgium, the Netherlands, Luxembourg, the United Kingdom, Ireland, Denmark, Greece, Spain, and Portugal.

# 3

# *LEASING SPACE*

Multinational corporations lease space for their use. They also lease excess space to tenants. The excess space might be located in company-owned premises or within leased space. A company may reduce its labor force during a lease, so with its landlord's permission, the company can sublet the excess space.

A company may lease land and then construct buildings on it or merely lease building space. Or the company may own the land, build on it, and then sell both land and buildings to an investor and lease them back. These sale-leasebacks are common worldwide. At the termination of the lease, there is usually a purchase option for the current occupant.

## THE NATURE OF THE LEASE

A lease is a contract in which the lessor, the owner, gives the right of property occupancy to the lessee, the tenant, in exchange for rental payments and other contractual terms. Under common law, leasehold estates are classified as (1) estates for years, (2) periodic estates, (3) estates at will, and (4) estates at sufferance. The leasehold estate that runs for years is a contract with a starting and an ending date. The period of time may be a month, five years, or an extended period of time such as 49 years. The landlord and tenant may negotiate renewal options. The periodic leasehold estate is a contract that gives an automatic renewal option at the end of successive, defined lease periods. If the lessee does not give appropriate notice of vacation of the premises and occupies the premises beyond the termination date and time, the lessor assumes renewal of the lease by the lessee. The lessee is obligated to honor the lease terms for another period of time, perhaps the same term as the original lease period. For example, a one-year lease "rolls over" to another one-year lease period if the lessee abides by the lease terms and remains in the premises beyond the original termination date and time. The one-year lease may be terminated by the lessee giving the landlord notice more than one month before its termination date. The notice period depends on the lease agreement, and the "roll over" period may or may not be the same length as the original lease period. The leasehold estate at will gives the lessee or the lessor the right to terminate the lease with appropriate legal notice. The leasehold estate at sufferance gives only the lessee the right to terminate the lease with appropriate legal notice. The original lease may have run out, but the landlord's interests are served by having a lessee in the space until the lessee finds new premises at affordable rent. The landlord might not have found a replacement tenant either.

The landlord usually assumes financial responsibility for exterior property maintenance and at least part of the insurance and property tax expense under an operating lease. The landlord also manages the maintenance of common areas while the tenants pay the common area maintenance on an equitable basis. Under a capital lease, the tenant pays the interior and exterior maintenance costs, the property and liability insurance premiums, and the property taxes on the land, land improvement, and buildings. The landlord-investor merely finances the land and building development costs. The other expenses related to the property are responsibilities of the tenant under the lease agreement. A sale-leaseback usually describes a capital lease, while a lease of office space describes an operating lease. A lease agreement with an option to purchase, where the payments are applied in part or totally to the purchase price, may be labeled a capital lease. The government's tax authority may differentiate between capital and operating leases for business income tax purposes.

The lease merely gives rights of possession and use to the lessee. The lessor regains possession at the end of the lease. The leasehold rights are merged back into the lessor freehold estate at the termination of the lease.

The lease specifies the amount of each lease payment, the place of payment, the timing of the payments (i.e., once a month, once a quarter, once a year), the legal use of the premises by the lessee, the nature of the rights of subleasing to sublessees, the starting date, the ending date and time, the indexing provisions, the provisions for rent reviews, and the options to renew the lease. Other clauses depend on the type of building and the nature of the space use. For example, shopping center leases differ from office building leases. Office building leases differ less radically from industrial leases than they do from shopping center leases. Residential leases are usually quite different from commercial and industrial leases because of the land use conditions.

## LEASING SPACE FOR CORPORATE USE

Some reasons for corporate leasing of space are related to multinational operations; some are appropriate for both multinational and national operations. Let us look first at the rationale in general for corporate leasing of space whether the company is involved in multinational operations or not.

### General Reasons for Corporate Leasing of Space

The corporation may temporarily need space, or the space available for purchase may not appear appropriate for company operations. If permanent premises are being acquired or developed, leasing may be a temporary situation. Leasing also conserves corporate cash and permits off-balance sheet financing. Finally, the company may be expanding rapidly and may not be able to take the time to develop premises on unimproved land.

### Reasons for Corporate Space Leasing Overseas

When a company is expanding into a new country, it may want leased space while it evaluates the market potential for its products. It stays flexible in its property acquisition by leasing rather than purchasing. If market predictions prove to be true, major properties may be needed. Otherwise, the initial space may be adequate for the near future. If the market for the company products increases gradually, additional space can be leased. For example, Campbell Soup is expanding gradually into world markets, and it faces tremendous competition from other food products companies, including CPC International and Unilever Corporation. Recently it has experienced losses in the global marketplace that have caused the rethinking and restructuring of its global operations. When a company is uncertain about the market prospects in specific countries and urban areas, it might lease space—at least office space—before moving forward. Since Campbell Soup's food manufacturing is automated, it may have to purchase or develop manufacturing premises to guarantee specially designed operating facilities. For flexibility, its office and warehouse space could be leased.

If the company policy states a preference for property ownership and appropriate space is not available for purchase, the company may wait in leased premises while it develops or acquires space for its operations. Abbott Laboratories found that in Rome many companies start out in small leased apartments that were partially offices. As the company expanded in the Rome market, it finally found larger premises to fit its needs. Office space in Rome has been very scarce in terms of multinational corporate preferences. At present, outlying suburban sites are finally being developed for adequate corporate space.

AT&T is expanding into London even though appropriate space is not available. They are leasing as they acquire a British networking company and make plans for permanent premises. Other companies are expanding rapidly overseas and consider leasing space before permanent premises are acquired or built. United Parcel Service is one of those fast-expanding global corporations.

A multinational company may wish to conserve cash. Rapid global expansion of company manufacturing, distribution, and company administration might prompt leasing rather than purchasing. The conserved cash can be placed in production, inventory, and distribution. At present Xerox's global policy reflects this viewpoint; Dow Italia is engaging in sale-leasebacks in Italy, probably for the same reason. Union Carbide, as part of its major restructuring, has recently engaged in office building and warehouse leasing. The restructuring may indicate rapid global expansion by the three separate corporation entities under the new Union Carbide holding company. That expansion may require massive amounts of cash or further financing.

Companies that continually finance in the world marketplace must retain their credit ratings with balance sheets exhibiting the required financial ratios. Leasing of property reduces balance sheet liabilities because the lease obligations are often shown off the balance sheet. Leasing, rather than buying or building, prompts higher equity ratios and lower debt ratios. Only the current lease obligations show on the profit and loss statements. Off-balance-sheet financing is a powerful motive for some companies that pursue property leasing.

Some governments do not approve foreign property purchases. The Middle Eastern countries generally restrict them. At the same time, they restrict foreign purchase of domestic companies except under certain conditions. In Eastern Europe, Russia, and other communist-controlled countries, foreign entities cannot purchase properties. In southeast Asia, Singapore does not generally approve foreign property purchase even though it, like the Middle Eastern countries, is not a communist-controlled country. Leasing property is the approved alternative. The DuPont corporation has faced the problem in Singapore and Moscow. From the American Embassy in Moscow, they are moving to new premises being built as a joint venture between their company, a Russian government entity, and a U.S. land developer from Atlanta.

Branch offices that are subject to changed locations are often leased. IBM France has leased space, for example, for several French branch offices. In contrast, IBM in the United States has entered into a number of joint ventures where IBM becomes a tenant-owner of the building. Since its credit is used by the developer for lower cost, high-ratio financing, IBM wishes to share in the entrepreneurial proceeds from the building operation and eventual sale.

### Joint Ventures with Corporate Lease Agreements

In the past five years many multinational corporations—as well as domestic U.S.-based corporations—have entered into joint-venture agreements with corporate lease agreements. As mentioned above, IBM has enjoyed the benefits of such agreements. In the Chicago Loop, AT&T is benefitting from such an agreement in the development of a major office building. Union Carbide has entered a joint venture agreement with a German investor for the financing of its distinctive headquarters building in Danbury, Connecticut. Like DuPont, McDonald's entered a joint venture with a lease agreement for its new locations in Moscow.

## LEASING COMPANY-OWNED SPACE TO TENANTS

There are various reasons why multinational companies lease some of their space to outside companies. Excess space may exist due to a policy of building for future needs. The company is expected to eventually expand its operations into all of the space, but in the meantime, the excess space is leased to outsiders. Many companies warehouse land for future purposes. That land may be put to a secondary use to derive income from it. When a company restructures, it might create excess space in some locations. Morton, Thiokol, and the three principal divisions of Union Carbide may encounter excess space after their major reorganizations.

A corporation benefits from additional income from owned real estate which may supplement the income from its main lines of business. A diversified tobacco company derives investment income from investment property and a land development subsidiary. Sometimes the investment income benefits a real estate fund managed by the multinational corporation. The company's properties may be transferred to a real estate fund it manages and the properties may be leased back from the fund. The investors in the real estate fund benefit from the income.

## SALE-LEASEBACKS WITH PURCHASE AGREEMENTS

While long-term sale-leasebacks are commonly employed in the United States, shorter lease purchase agreements may become common in other parts of the world. Some of the shorter lease purchase agreements of Europe and Latin America have similar characteristics to the long-term sale-leasebacks of the United States.

### The Typical U.S. Sale-Leaseback

The investor purchases the land and/or building from its occupant-owner in return for a long-term lease. The property has usually been built to the occupant's specifications. Before the structures are built, the agreement may be reached between the investor and the operating company property occupant. As soon as the construction is completed, the investor takes title. Any money invested in the premises by the operating company will be repaid through the purchase arrangement with the investor. The investor may depreciate the buildings for tax purposes. If the investor finances the transactions, the investor may deduct the interest paid on the borrowed funds as the owner of the financed property. The operating company which occupies and leases the property will normally pay all expenses related to the use of the property including lease payments to the investor, property taxes, property insurance premiums, and exterior and interior maintenance. This "capital" or "finance" type lease usually gives the lessee an option to purchase. The lessee may be able to purchase the property on a declining scale as the years pass. By the end of the lease, the purchase price may be current fair market value of the property or another negotiated figure.

### The Shorter Lease Purchase Agreements of Europe and Latin America

Latin American investors may enter into five-year lease purchase plans with multinational companies. A multinational company leases the building from a Mexican investor and deducts the lease payments for Mexican federal income tax purposes. At the end of the lease, the majority of the lease payments may be applied to the purchase price and the title transferred to the lessee. This is one way to finance property acquisition and still have tax-deductible lease payments under the laws of a Latin American country.

In France, a domestic or foreign-based multinational company may negotiate a nine-year lease purchase agreement. At the end of the nine-year period, the lessee can apply the lease payments to the purchase price and take title to the property. Under French law, the lease payments of this property financing method are tax deductible.

Perhaps more common in France is the credit bail, a lease purchase plan with tax-deductible payments that extend over a 15-year period. It reduces the company's need for capital. This method of financing may compete with the other methods of property financing available to the major multinational company. U.S.-based multinational firms, without special tax structuring, are not entitled to the tax deductibility of the capital lease payments under the regulations of the Internal Revenue Service. The United States permits tax deductibility of *operating* leases that have reasonable purchase price options at the termination of the lease.

In Europe, finance and other companies offer 30- to 40-year lease purchase plans to domestic and foreign-based companies. They may be negotiated as operating or capital leases depending on the nature of the terms and the preferences of the company. The long-term operating leases may be similar to the typical U.S. long-term operating leases or sale-leasebacks.

## LEASING IN A SPECIAL INDUSTRIAL ENTERPRISE ZONE

Many countries offer, as a part of their industrial development incentive programs, special leasing arrangements for land and buildings in industrial enterprise zones. A government or economic development subsidiary may build structures to attract industrial firms. Buildings are constructed to the specifications of the firm or built as general purpose structures. The lease could be financed with government funds which may be at a lower cost than the market interest rate to even prime credit-rated industrial firms. The payments, therefore, may be lower than normally financed lease payments. In the Dominican Republic, Abbott Laboratories was attracted to the space offered in an industrial development zone. But Abbott Labs pays a market rent determined by the developers who received the development incentives from the Dominican Republic government. The space is ample, and the payments are not lower than market-level payments in this instance. The ground lease payments of special enterprise zones in the People's Republic of China are reportedly lower than market-level. But the ground leases run out within twenty years. The People's Republic of China reassumes the ownership of the land and buildings within a period of 10 to 20 years under the enterprise zone leases in effect today. In most countries the industrial development zone ground and building leases run for extended periods, and the local government does not deliberately take over ownership within a short period. Communist governments may prefer only short-term foreign company occupancy of their land. It is a way of developing their industrial enterprises without long-term foreign interference.

## U.S. MULTINATIONAL LEASE PREFERENCES OVERSEAS

Most U.S.-based multinational companies prefer leasing arrangements overseas that are similar to what they are accustomed to in the United States. They generally prefer 3- to 5-year office leases. A secondary preference is usually a 5- to 10-year office lease with options to vacate in 3- to 5-years, with obligations to pay only unamortized tenant improvement costs. To exercise the early option to vacate, they might even agree to pay all the costs of the tenant improvements.

Since the civil code leases of most other countries are unfamiliar to them, U.S. companies prefer to deal with U.S. and other property owners and developers who draw up fully documented net leases. A U.S.-based major oil company particularly has expressed this preference.

Most U.S. companies do not want to pay key money deposits for various reasons. The Internal Revenue Service might consider the advance deposits for acquisition of the space to be bribes or illegal gratuities. When a company pays key money, it receives no interest or return on that money which violates corporate profit objectives. When the landlord pays some interest after ten years or so, the rate of interest is usually less than the market rate. That interest is payable when the key money deposit is gradually returned to the company over a ten-year period. This is not good financial practice for a typical U.S.-based multinational company. These payments are particularly common in Japan and Europe where appropriate corporate property in desirable locations is quite scarce.

## VARIATIONS IN WORLDWIDE LEASES

Just as the lease purchase agreements differ widely among countries, the leasing terms for office, industrial, and residential space also vary widely. Here are some of the leasing terms in which there is variability:

Period or length of the lease

Basis for the lease, i.e., square meter, tsubo, square foot

Lessee and lessor obligations for exterior and structural repairs and maintenance

Options to renew

Rent control provisions

The nature of the index used in the lease

The application of the index, i.e., necessary change in the index

Subletting and assignment provisions

Required notice for vacation of premises

Use of premises

Required obligation to build improvements on leased land

Required declaration for lease renewal

Service charges and their payment provisions

Required security deposit

Required rent guarantee

Application of tenant tenure

Lessee financial responsibility for property taxes and property hazard insurance premiums

Insurance coverage of property by lessor

Insurance coverage of interior assets by lessee

Application of value-added tax to rent payments

Let us observe the varied leasing relationships in a few countries.

### The People's Republic of China

The ground leases to foreign entities seldom exceed twenty years and may be as short as ten years. Renewal provisions may be considered, but usually are not. The Chinese government assumes the full title to the land and leasehold improvements at the end of the lease. By contract with the Chinese government, the foreign company usually must build industrial or commercial premises, established by approved architectural plan, within two or three years after the signing of the ground lease. The space may be described in square feet or square meters. The lessee usually has full financial responsibility for the interior and exterior, including structural repairs and maintenance. All service charges are payable by the lessee. The lessor, usually a Chinese government entity, provides the site with utilities including energy sources, as well as the transportation network, such as roadways and rail lines. The ground leases are usually not indexed. The Chinese government requires advance notice of intended company vacation of the premises. The lessee is financially responsible for any property taxes or property hazard insurance premiums that are normally attributed to the landlord. Land in approved locations is usually leased to foreign companies (1) to gain the transfer of technology, (2) to increase local employment, (3) to foster manufacturing for exportation of products (to gain foreign currency reserves), (4) to promote tourism with hotel development (to attract foreign currency reserves and profits), and (5) to tap domestic natural resources with foreign investment, machinery, and equipment, technology, and experienced management. The reader may consult the author's books, *Guide to International Real Estate Investment* (Westport, Conn.: Quorum Books, 1988) and *International Income Property Investment* (Scottsdale, Ariz.: International Real Estate Institute, 1985) for greater detail.

### Hong Kong

Most land is leased and subleased. The British government leases most of the land from the government of the People's Republic of China under terms established many decades ago. These ground leases according to current agreements will run out fifty years after the turnover of Hong Kong by the British government to the Chinese government in 1997. Since it is a communist-controlled government without a fully developed legal system and contract enforcement powers, China could with little repercussion declare the agreement null and void at any time.

Office building ground leases may run for long periods. Office building space leases often run for five to ten years, perhaps with renewal options. These leases are usually subject to rent reviews at relatively frequent intervals. Service charges are assessed against the tenant on a prorationed basis. The estimated service charges are paid in advance along with the rent payments once a month. Security deposits are normally required, payable in advance when the lease is signed. There is no tenant tenure or rent control in Hong Kong, except for public housing. The landlord of retail space usually must approve subletting or lease assignment and the party (prospective sublessee) involved in the transaction with the lessee. The use of the space is part of all leases—retail, office, or industrial. The lessee on a ground lease with the British government usually pledges to assume full financial responsibility for costs associated with the premises, such as property tax and property hazard insurance premiums. This lessee must insure and maintain the premises. The sublessee who actually occupies the premises usually has the obligation to insure the interior equipment and furnishings. The ground lease usually conveys an obligation to the lessee to construct approved buildings on the premises within a designated period. The reader may consult the author's books, *Guide to International Real Estate Investment* (Westport, Conn.: Quorum Books, 1988) and *International Income Property Investment* (Scottsdale, Ariz.: International Real Estate Institute, 1985) for greater detail.

### Japan

Commercial space is subject to rent control as is residential space that has existed since the time of the Second World War or even before. Therefore, office building and shopping center leases are subject to general rent control provisions.

If the landlord wishes to raise the rent an unusual amount upon lease renewal, the tenant may appeal to rent control authorities to reduce it to more reasonable levels. So from one lease period to another many rents increase approximately ten percent, which is approved by the government.

All property leases are subject to tenant tenure. As long as the tenant meets all the conditions of the lease, the tenant may continue to occupy the leased premises. Only through negotiations between the landlord and the tenant will the space be vacated by the tenant prior to the lease termination date. To attain the highest possible sales productivity in a Japanese shopping center, the landlord sometimes discusses early termination of the retail tenant's occupancy because of less than optimal sales per square meter or tsubo. (A tsubo is 3 square meters.)

Office building leases may run for twenty years subject to rent reviews every two years. Before each two-year period, the rent may be payable in advance for the coming two-year period. The low vacancy rate of prime office space leads to this advance payment condition.

A security deposit for the lease of office space may amount to payment of three to five years' rent in advance. The deposit may be used to pay the last month's rent at the end of the lease.

In addition to a security deposit and the rent payment in advance, key money may be paid to secure the office space. The key money amount also amounts to three to five years' rent payable in advance. Sometimes the landlord builds the structures or demolishes the existing premises and rebuilds with the key money provided by the prospective building occupants. The lessor owes the lessee no interest on the key money until perhaps ten years have elapsed on the lease. Then some interest may be paid as the key money is gradually returned to the lessee over another eight- to ten-year period. These lease conditions reflect the scarcity of well-located, well-appointed and equipped building space. The central business district of Tokyo, in particular the Marunouchi financial district, experiences the most pressure for up-to-date office space.

The office space may be described in square meters or tsubos. There may be options to renew at the end of the 20-year lease with its 2-year segments. The office and residential leases are usually not indexed. The landlord has the right of approval or disapproval of lease subletting and assignment. Advance notice is required for lease renewal and space vacation. The lease normally restricts the use of premises. The service charge includes property tax and a hazard insurance premium prorated among the building tenants. The service charge also includes the prorated costs of building repair and maintenance, energy costs, and property management. In the case of industrial leased land within a defined industrial park or development area, the lease obligates the lessee to build approved premises on the site within a specified period, perhaps three years. The lessee, therefore, cannot speculate on the value of the ground lease.

Japanese law is based on the civil code. The civil code lease assumptions are put into effect unless exceptions are written into the lease. Under the common law, all lease assumptions are written into a single lease.

The reader may wish to consult the author's books, *Investing in Japanese Real Estate* (Westport, Conn.: Quorum Books, 1987), *Japanese Shopping Centers: Financial and Investment Features* (Scottsdale, Ariz.: International Real Estate Institute, 1985), and *Guide to International Real Estate Investment* (Westport, Conn.: Quorum Books, 1988) for more details about Japanese leasing and real estate investment.

### United Kingdom

Commercial leases and most residential leases are not subject to rent control. Only older residential structures built under council housing programs are subject to rent control and tenant tenure, which do not apply to commercial or industrial building leases. In industrial enterprise zones, the rent may be lowered because of tax or other financial incentives given to the developer and because industrial space is built by the development authority with lower-than-market-rate financing.

The lease period for office buildings may be 20 to 25 years, and rent reviews may occur every three to five years. Leased space is normally described in square footage. Because the United Kingdom is one of the

12-member nations of the New Europe to be formed in 1992, the measurement of building space and land must be converted from square footage to square meters. (A meter is approximately 39 inches long, and a square meter approximates ten square feet.) A lessee may be responsible for both exterior and interior repairs and maintenance, including structural repairs and maintenance. The lessee may, upon signing the lease agreement, assume the normal financial responsibilities of the lessor which includes hazard insurance coverage of the premises and payment of rates (a British term for property ad valorem taxes). There may be options to renew in the lease. Advance notice is required for lease renewal and vacation of the premises. Also a security deposit is usually required, and rents are normally paid in advance. Unlike many European leases, United Kingdom leases are usually not indexed. Rather frequent rent reviews accomplish the same financial objectives. Subletting and assignment considerations must be approved by the lessor before they can be finalized between the lessee and a sublessee or assignee. The use of the premises is restricted to specified land uses. In an industrial enterprise zone, the industrial company leasing the land may be required to build on the leased land within a specified period of time, perhaps two or three years.

Layers of leases on office buildings in London's City and West End districts are common. They reduce the incidence of strata title or condominium office buildings. Strata title accommodations may be considered by new office building owners. It would be difficult to impose strata title or condominium ownership on some space of an existing rented building.

### France

Credit bail is a familiar lease purchase plan for industrial and commercial premises. The 15-year lease payments are applied to the purchase of the property. Under the French civil code, when property is leased, the lease payments are tax deductible for federal income tax purposes. Other longer and shorter lease purchase plans may be negotiated with finance companies and other financial sources.

The French government will finance buildings and land in special industrial enterprise zones in the provinces located away from the Ile de France whose center is Paris, so that industrial company rents may be established at below-market amounts. With incentives, France has long encouraged provincial industrial development by domestic and foreign companies.

French office and retail building leases are characterized by 3–3–3 leases. The tenant may move from the premises after the termination of the first 3-year term or the second 3-year term. After the nine-year period passes, the tenant attains tenant tenure in the space. If the tenant meets all of the terms of the lease, including the timely and full payment of rent, the tenant may stay in the premises until giving proper legal notice of space vacation. The lessor cannot evict the lessee unless there is a violation of the lease terms or good cause. The lessor must negotiate with the lessee to leave the space before the termination of the lease. Many retail landlords negotiate with tenants who are producing less sales per square meter than the typical shopping center tenant in the particular line of business. Landlords want a good mixture of goods and services presented in their retail centers and they want high productivity tenants in each space. Highly productive retail tenants generate high volumes of indexed and percentage rents for the landlord.

Rent control exists for residential and commercial space. Older residential space that is publicly financed is particularly subject to rent control, but not newer, privately financed housing. When the index for the commercial lease exceeds 25 percent in three years, the tenant may apply to the courts for open market rent reviews or equity on the basis of a lower increase in sales volume and profits than the increase in rent. Commercial rents are indexed each year or at least every third year. A commonly used indexing base is the French Construction Cost Index. The French Consumer Price Index or other government-generated index may be used in the lease agreement. This is a negotiable point between the prospective lessee and the lessor.

Because of tenant tenure after the ninth year of the 3–3–3 lease, there is an automatic right of lease renewal. Security and key money deposits may be charged. Modern shopping center and up-to-date office building spaces in good locations are difficult to find for lease. Therefore, key money payments may be required by the landlords. Since France has long been a tax-avoidance society, a landlord may expect under-the-counter payments from the prospective tenant who wants to acquire space under the conditions of high space demand. The strong retail chain stores willingly pay key money to acquire well-located and managed space in the new shopping centers that have recently been built across France.

### Belgium

Like France, Belgium's commercial leases usually run for nine years including three three-year lease periods where the lessee can leave after each period. After the nine-year lease, the office building tenant has no right to renew the lease, but the retail tenant does. The retail tenant may renew for another three nine-year lease terms. Generally leases are indexed each year. A rent review occurs, through the lease terms, every three years. Security deposits are required, and service charges in addition to the rent cover prorated property insurance and local and state taxes associated with the property. The tenant is financially responsible for internal repairs and maintenance and insurance on furnishings, equipment, and bodily injury within the premises.

Because of the extreme pressure for good, up-to-date space in the present European Community headquarters city of Brussels, the prospective tenant should be prepared to pay key money for acquisition of the premises desired. Most governments and multinational corporations have already or are establishing European offices in this city. They must monitor the administrative and technical standard changes taking place within the European Council and Parliament.

### Singapore

The Singapore government restricts the ownership of its scarce land when foreign companies and individuals are involved. It wants to preserve its land for Singaporeans and their companies. The government also controls land use since it leases land in the central business district. Many hectares of central business district land have been cleared by the Urban Redevelopment Authority (URA). This land is gradually auctioned off to the highest qualifying bidders as the URA progresses in land redevelopment. The investors winning the bids must develop the land using plans approved by the URA. Much of Singapore's land has been subject to redevelopment since the Second World War. There was little fighting on the peninsula during the war, but the modernization of the country started at the close of the war. Now Singapore honors everything new and modern; traditional architecture and historic structures are not honored or preserved.

Industrial and residential space is leased to foreign companies and households. Commercial space is both leased and sold to foreign companies and other investors. Shopping centers are usually developed and operated under strata-title regimes where the individual storerooms are sold to merchants, trading companies, or other investors. One of the prominent shopping centers on Orchard Road is partly sold and partly rented to storeroom occupants. Centralized shopping center management is difficult to achieve when the storerooms are completely or partially sold to merchants and other investors. The center is less attractive to consumers because the merchandising and center advertising are not coordinated.

Houses and apartments are usually rented to foreign persons due to the property ownership restrictions. Rented apartment towers often rise from commercial podiums on the principal streets of Singapore.

### West Germany

Leases in West Germany are contracts, not estates. Since German contractual rights cannot exceed 30 years, leases are restricted to 30 years or less. Only leases for terms of more than one year must be in writing. Most standard-form leases for residential and commercial space do not involve attorneys. But leases covering large properties and leases with more detailed clauses preserving lessor interests are covered by written agreement rather than standard forms and thus necessitate the use of attorneys. The provisions of the civil code favor the interests of the lessees; therefore, the lessor often likes to take exception to the assumptions of the civil code through negotiation of the detailed lease terms.

Rent controls and tenant tenure may apply to residential contracts. The government reserves certain rights for residential tenants. Most of the residential accommodations are leased rather than owned. Homes are costly and require substantial household saving for the equity portion of house financing. The accumulation of adequate savings takes years. The savings banks of West Germany have special prospective homeowners saving plans. Part of the high cost of housing is derived from unionized construction labor costs. Also, the building codes of West Germany are stringent. High health and safety standards in construction and housing development create higher than normal housing costs. To counteract the high housing costs, the mortgage terms tend to be liberal. Personal income tax rates are relatively high in West Germany, so fewer savings are possible from less-than-normal take-home pay. The average German pays for a lot of government services. Many people speak of the cradle-to-grave public services that are expected by most Western Europeans.

Commercial leases usually run for five to ten years with possible renewal options. Sometimes they run up to twenty years. The rent is normally paid in advance as well as a cash security deposit or a bank guarantee of the rent payment. The value-added tax of 14 percent is payable on the lease payments. Commercial rents are normally indexed. A change of ten points or ten percent of the cost of living index either up or down will normally trigger a change in the lease payment. These automatic rent indexation clauses in commercial leases must be approved by the Landeszentralbank (State Central Bank). Approval is gained if the lease is binding on the lessor for at least ten years and if the indexation clause operates for the benefits of both parties. The adjustment of the rent must be both upward and downward as the cost of living index changes. The statutory notice period is three months, but most contracts call for notice of termination within three to six months of the termination date of the lease. The payment of the landlord's insurance premiums, property tax, and managing agent fees are negotiable between lessee and lessor. The responsibility for the payment depends on the market conditions at the time of lease negotiations. German landlords usually retain responsibility for major structural repairs. A sample commercial lease form may be found in Appendix 3.A.

The lessee might agree only to a partial cost of living index adjustment. If market rents are rising less rapidly than cost of living index increases, the lease may provide for automatic adjustments of less than 100 percent of the index. If the parties are unable to agree upon a market rent for a specific period, an expert adjudicator can be called in to settle the dispute.

As mentioned earlier, financial lease agreements are increasingly available in West Germany. The tax deductibility of the lease payments is attractive while the purchase price option is favorable to the lessee. They have become popular in West Germany since 1962.

Registered leases may exceed a period of 30 years. The registered lessee may transfer the title of the registered lease and sublet the premises. The parties to a registered lease may provide for an immediate reversion of all property rights upon the occurrence of certain defined events. The amount of damages to be paid in the event of the reversion may be set at the negotiation of the contract. Rent reviews for registered leases are the same as those for normal leases. A registered lease can be pledged to a creditor of the registered lessee, but the lease cannot be mortgaged.

Most apartment rental agreements are relatively short term. Young, single people in the large German cities tend to live in rented apartments. Landlords are allowed to raise the rent only to comparative levels for similar premises and only at specified intervals after completing a complicated procedure. Rent contracts with progressive increases are now permitted, but the interval between rent increases and the size of the increases are still limited by law.

## BIBLIOGRAPHY

Cohen, Gerald S. "Sale/Leasebacks: How They Can Benefit the Corporation." *Site Selection*, December 1988, pp. 18–20.

Hines, Mary Alice. *Financing Real Estate with Securities*. New York: Wiley, 1988.

———. *International Income Property Investment*. Scottsdale, Ariz.: International Real Estate Institute, 1985.

———. *Marketing Real Estate Internationally*. Westport, Conn.: Quorum Books, 1988.

———. *Overview of Global Real Estate Finance*. Scottsdale, Ariz.: International Real Estate Institute, 1989.

———. *Real Estate Debt Financing*. New York: Wiley, 1987.

*International Property Bulletin*. London: Hillier Parker May & Rowden, 1989.

# *SAMPLE LEASE*

Between: ...

> – hereinafter called "the Lessor" –

and: ...

> – hereinafter called "the Lessee" –

§ 1

**The Property**

1.  The Lessor owns the land specified hereinafter:

2.  The following buildings have been erected on the land:

3.  The Lessor grants to the Lessee a lease in the above- mentioned building of:

    a) On the ... floor
       marked in red on
       the plan annexed as Appendix...
       for use as....

    b) In the underground car park
       a total of ... parking spaces
       marked with the numbers ... to ...
       on the plan annexed as Appendix....

    c) A total of ... outdoor parking spaces
       marked with the numbers ... to ...
       on the plan annexed as Appendix....

    d) The following areas used by all Lessees jointly in proportion to the net total floor area of the building: ....

4.  a) The leased premises may be used for purposes other than those provided for under para 3 only with the Lessor's written consent.

    b) Any consent by the Lessor, even if not explicitly stated, shall always be granted subject to all official authorizations as may be required for the

Reprinted from Rudiger Volhard and Dolf Weber, *Real Property in Germany*, 3d ed. (1989), by permission of the publisher, Fritz Knapp Verlag.

envisaged change of use of the leased premises; such official authorization shall be obtained by the Lessee at his own cost.

c) Before actual use of the leased premises for purposes other than those provided for in para 3, the Lessee, having obtained the Lessor's consent, shall provide the Lessor with proof that all necessary official authorization has been duly granted or that no such authorization is required.

5. Before the leased premises are handed over to the Lessee, the Lessor shall have the following alterations carried out at the Lessee's/Lessor's expense:
. . . . . . . . . . . .

§ 2

**Rent**

1. The rent shall amount to
   a) DM ... under § 1. para 3. a)
   b) DM ... under § 1. para 3. b)
   c) DM ... under § 1. para 3. c)
   d) DM ... under § 1. para 3. d)

   Total:     DM . . . .

   plus value-added tax at the statutory rate.

2. The Lessee, having inspected the premises, is aware of their size. The Lessor therefore assumes no liability for the correctness of the present contract as to the area in square metres of the premises. The premises shall be leased as inspected.

3. The rent shall be adjusted automatically if the cost-of-living index for the Federal Republic of Germany (based on an employee-household consisting of 4 persons and with an average income 1980 = 100) as determined by the Federal Statistics Office changes by more than 10 points in either direction from the time the present agreement was concluded or from the time the rent was last adjusted.

4. The rent shall be adjusted in proportion to the change in the cost-of-living index. The adjusted rent shall be payable for the month for which the index changed as described above in para 3.

5. The above automatic adjustment clause must be approved by the relevant Landeszentralbank. This approval shall be applied for by the Lessor. Should this approval be refused, the parties shall agree on a new, admissible clause, which shall correspond as closely as possible to their purpose.

6. The monthly rent shall be paid in advance by the fifth working day of each month into an account to be specified by the Lessor.

   At the Lessor's request, the Lessee shall issue him a direct debit order.

## § 3

**Ancillary Charges**

1. All running expenses as well as the costs of management of the property shall be borne by the lessees. Ancillary charges are defined as all costs listed in Appendix 3 to § 27, para 1 of the Second Computation Order (see the appendix to the agreement) if and to the extent that such costs are incurred for the leased property; as well as all running expenses which may be incurred in the future; and all rates, taxes, and charges which may be payable in the future for the leased property.

2. To the extent that they are not paid directly by the Lessee or determined by reference to the Lessee's consumption, all costs referred to in para 1 above shall be borne by all lessees, each in proportion to the area leased by him, each underground parking space being deemed to correspond to . . . square metres and outdoor parking spaces being disregarded.

   In the absence of statutory provisions, the Lessor shall determine which running expenses shall be assessed according to consumption.

3. The lessees of premises situated exclusively on the ground floor shall not be required to contribute to the operating costs of the lift.

4. The costs referred to in para 1 shall be invoiced annually. The computation period shall be the calendar year.

5. A monthly advance payment amounting to DM . . . /square meter shall be payable for all costs mentioned in para 1. This payment is due at the same time as the monthly rent.

   Any claims arising from the annual statement of account shall be payable one month after receipt of the said statement.

6. In accordance with § 315 BGB, the Lessor shall adjust the monthly advance payment if circumstances affecting such payments should change. This adjusted advance payment shall become payable for the month following receipt of the relevant notice.

7. No interim invoice shall be issued should the tenancy be terminated during a computation period. Rather, an invoice shall only be issued at the time that the annual accounts are settled.

8. Value-added tax at the statutory rate shall be added to all costs prescribed in para 1.

## § 4

**Security**

1. The Lessee shall give security for the fulfillment of all contractual obligations on or before the transfer of the premises. This security shall be given in the form of an irrevocable, indefinite guarantee by a major German bank making it principal debtor and shall amount to . . . times the amount of the monthly rent provided for in § 2 plus . . . times the amount of the monthly advance payment of the running expenses provided for in § 3 both including VAT. The

guarantor must undertake in the deed of guarantee to effect payment upon the first request.

2. Should the monthly rent, the monthly advance payments of the running expenses, or the value-added tax be adjusted, the amount of the security shall be adjusted accordingly within one month after such adjustment has become effective.

3. Should the security be drawn upon by the Lessor during the term of the lease, the Lessee shall be obliged to restore it to its original amount.

§ 5

**Beginning and Term of Tenancy**

1. The tenancy shall commence on the day the premises are transferred in accordance with para 2. This shall also apply if, for reasons for which the Lessor is not responsible, the Lessee does not take possession of the premises on that day.

2. a) The leased premises shall be transferred on........

   b) The leased premises may, however, be transferred at a later date if, due to strikes, force majeure, or other reasons for which the Lessor is not responsible, the alterations provided for in § 1. para 5 could not be carried out.

3. Transfer of the premises shall not be postponed due to minor defects which do not adversely affect the Lessee's business activities and which can be remedied without disturbing these activities. Such defects shall, however, be rectified forthwith.

4. The tenancy shall end five years after December 31 of the year in which it began.

5. The Lessee shall have the right to demand that the lease be renewed once for a further period of five years. Such demand shall be submitted to the Lessor in writing no later than March 31 of the year at the end of which the term of tenancy ends as provided for in para 4. In this event, the lease shall be automatically extended for five years.

6. Should the Lessee not exercise his right under para 5, or after an extension of the lease under this provision, the lease shall be automatically extended by additional periods of one year unless it is terminated with no less than nine months notice before the end of its term.

7. The date of receipt of notices given hereunder shall determine compliance with all time-limits under this contract.

§ 6

**Termination for Serious Cause**

The statutory provisions shall apply if the lease is terminated for serious cause. Furthermore, the Lessor may terminate the lease without notice if bankruptcy or composition proceedings are instituted against the Lessee or if a petition in bankruptcy filed by the Lessee is dismissed for lack of assets.

## § 7

**Structural Changes by the Lessee**

1. The Lessor's written consent shall be required for structural changes to the leased premises as well as for the installation of any fixtures and fittings which might be required for the Lessee's business. All costs thereby incurred shall be borne by the Lessee. Para 4. b) and c) of § 1 shall apply mutatis mutandis.

2. Upon termination of the tenancy, the Lessee shall return the leased premises to their original condition unless the Lessor, having been offered, has agreed to take over objects installed or modifications made by the Lessee.

   Should the Lessor agree to take over installations in or modifications of the leased premises made by the Lessee, their current market value shall be payable by the Lessor. Should no agreement on their current market value be reached by the parties, this value shall be determined by an expert acting as an adjudicator and nominated by the appropriate Chamber of Industry and Commerce.

3. Gas and electrical appliances may only be connected to the existing mains in accordance with their capacity, of which the Lessee shall inform himself, and which shall not be exceeded. Additional appliances may only be installed with the Lessor's written consent. The Lessee shall bear the costs of any necessary alterations to the mains.

## § 8

**Liability for the Condition of the Premises**

**I.   Liability of the Lessor**

1. The premises shall be well maintained by the Lessor to the extent that the Lessee has not assumed the duty to carry out the necessary maintenance and repair works.

2. The Lessee shall only have a claim to damages or a reduction in rent due to defects in the lease premises or to disturbances in the operation of the premises or its technical installations if the Lessor is responsible for the defect or disturbance by reason of wilful intent or gross negligence or if the Lessor delays in correcting the defect by reason or wilful intent or gross negligence.

3. The restriction of liability provided for under para 2. shall not apply to damage covered by the occupier's liability insurance of the Lessor. However, the liability for such damage shall in each individual case be restricted to the sums insured (DM ... for property damage and DM ... for injury to persons). The Lessor shall only be liable for damages exceeding the amounts covered by the insurance policy if he has caused the damage wilfully or through gross negligence.

4. Reduction in rent or claims to damages by the Lessee due to immissions or impairment of access to the building for which the Lessor is not responsible, or due to building work by third parties outside the building, is excluded.

## II.  Liability of the Lessee

1. The Lessee shall treat the leased premises with due care and clean them regularly.

2. The Lessee shall, at his own cost, carry out all decorative repairs at regular intervals in all rooms used exclusively by the Lessee. The same shall apply to necessary maintenance and repair work to the rooms occupied and all fittings and installations situated therein (including all pipes and cables leading to and from the supply installations up to the point where they join the mains supply, roller blinds, window frames, and doors to the premises).

3. As to those rooms of the premises which are used by several or all lessees jointly (see in particular § 1. para 3. b) and d)), the Lessor shall carry out the work described in para 2. and shall apportion the resulting costs to the lessees pursuant to § 3.

4. Broken window panes in the rooms used exclusively by the Lessee shall be replaced by the Lessee unless the Lessor is responsible for such damage. As to those located in the parts of the leased premises described in para 3., the provisions contained in para 3. shall apply accordingly.

5. Blocked sewage pipes shall be cleared by the Lessee who has caused the blockage. The Lessee shall also be liable for consequential damage. Should it be impossible to ascertain which Lessee has caused the blockage, the Lessor shall undertake the necessary remedial work. The costs thereby incurred as well as any consequential costs shall be borne on a pro rata basis by all Lessees whose premises are connected to the sewage pipe in question except those Lessees who can prove that they cannot have caused the obstruction.

6. On termination of the lease, the Lessee shall surrender the premises used exclusively by him properly renovated and repaired. This shall include: renewal of the floor coverings and wallpaper, painting of radiators and heating pipes, as well as of doors, window frames and door frames, all to the same standard as when the premises were transferred to the Lessee.

7. Should the Lessee surrender the premises without having carried out the work described in para 6., the Lessor may carry out all necessary work at the Lessee's expense. The Lessor's claims in respect of the costs thereby incurred shall also subsist if these works are carried out by the subsequent lessee, and the Lessor shall in such event be entitled to compensation in respect of any damage thereby suffered.

8. Before installing any heavy objects (machines, safes, etc.), the Lessee shall ascertain from the Lessor the bearing capacity of the floors. The authorized bearing capacity may not be exceeded, otherwise the Lessee shall be liable for all damages and consequential damage caused thereby and shall reimburse the Lessor in respect of any claims of third parties.

9. The Lessee shall be liable for all damage occurring on the leased premises, whether caused by him or by relatives, employees, members of staff, subtenants, visitors, suppliers, or workmen.

Any damage to or pollution of the land or buildings other than the leased premises which the Lessee, his relatives, employees, members of staff, subtenants, visitors, suppliers, or workmen have caused and for which they are responsible, shall be rectified by the Lessee immediately and without his being requested to do so.

### III. Provisons Governing I. and II.

The parties shall have the repair and maintenance work for which they are responsible carried out within a reasonable period. If, in spite of a warning and extension of the original term allowed, one of the parties does not comply with his obligations within the specified time, the other party shall be entitled to have urgent work carried out at the expense of the party in default.

In the event of imminent danger, each party shall immediately take the necessary steps to eliminate such danger.

### § 9

### Access to the Premises

The Lessor, his agents, or representatives shall, upon giving prior notice, be entitled to inspect the leased premises during the Lessee's normal business hours. In cases of emergency, the Lessor shall be enabled to enter the leased premises at any time.

### § 10

### Structural Changes by the Lessor

1. The Lessor may, even without the Lessee's consent, carry out any improvements or structural changes necessary or expedient to maintain, preserve, or expand the building or the leased premises, or in order to eliminate imminent danger, or repair defects. The Lessee shall allow the Lessor access to the appropriate rooms and shall not obstruct or delay the execution of the work.

2. The Lessor is entitled to carry out modernization work on or in the building at any time.

3. The Lessee shall only be entitled to make claims against the Lessor based on work provided for in para 1. and 2. if the Lessee's activities have been considerably impaired thereby for more than one week.

## § 11

### Signs and Advertisements

1. All signs of both individuals and firms shall be designed and affixed in a uniform manner. The Lessor shall be entitled to give appropriate directions but shall, to the extent that this does not detract from such uniformity, take the Lessee's wishes into account.

   The costs of such signs and their erection shall be borne by the Lessee.

2. To the extent that advertising surfaces have been let, their design, which shall also be uniform, shall be subject to the Lessor's prior consent. Other Lessees must not be disturbed or impaired in their activities by such advertising.

3. § 1. para 4. b) and c) shall apply to advertising.

## § 12

### Subletting

1. The premises may only be sublet with the prior, written consent of the Lessor.

2. § 549, para 1, sentence 2 BGB shall not apply.

3. Should the premises have been sublet without proper consent, the Lessor may require the Lessee to terminate the sublease at the earliest possible date, but within one month's notice at the latest. Should this not be carried out, the Lessor may terminate the present lease without notice.

4. The Lessor shall be entitled to make his consent for a sublease dependant on agreement to an extra charge of up to . . .%.

5. In the event of subletting, the Lessee shall be absolutely liable for all acts and omissions of the sublessee.

6. In the event of subletting, the Lessee hereby and as of now assigns to the Lessor as security all claims, including any accompanying liens, which he may have against the sublessee.

7. Any form of transfer of use other than temporary shall be considered as subletting.

## § 13

### Sale of the Leased Property

§ 571, para 2 BGB shall not apply in the event of the property being sold.

§ 14

**Keys**

The Lessee shall be given the following keys when the premises are transferred to him: . . . .

These keys as well as all duplicates thereof which the Lessee may have had made shall be returned upon termination of the lease.

Should the keys not be returned in spite of a warning and an extension of the deadline, the Lessor shall be entitled to replace the locks at the Lessee's expense.

§ 15

**Death of the Lessee**

The Lessee in the names of his heirs waives the right to premature termination provided for in § 569 BGB.

§ 16

**Term of the Lease**

§ 568 BGB shall not apply upon expiry of the term of the lease.

§ 17

**Several Lessees**

Where several persons lease the property together, they hereby authorize each other to accept and deliver all declarations concerning the present agreement. In granting this authority, they exempt each other from the restrictions provided for in § 181 BGB. This power of attorney is irrevocable.

§ 18

**No Protection against Competition**

The Lessor does not warrant any protection against competition on the property described in § 1.

§ 19

**Place of Jurisdiction**

Place of jurisdiction shall be . . . . . . . . . . . . . . . . if the Lessee has no place of general jurisdiction in the Federal Republic of Germany or West-Berlin or if the party against which an action is brought has, after the conclusion of the present agreement, moved its place of residence, place of business, or its usual place of abode outside the jurisdiction of the Code of Civil Procedure (ZPO), or if its place of residence, place of business, or its usual place of abode is unknown when the action is commenced. The Lessor shall be free to commence proceedings at the Lessee's place of business.

### § 20

**Restriction of Set-Off**

The Lessee may only set-off claims against the rent or ancillary charges if these claims have been either legally established in a final judgment or acknowledged by the Lessor.

### § 21

**Delay**

Should the Lessee be in arrears with the payment of rent and ancillary charges, he shall be liable to pay interest at a rate of ... % above the applicable discount rate of the Bundesbank. The Lessor shall also be entitled to claim compensation for any further damages he may suffer. The Lessee is free to prove that less damage was incurred.

### § 22

**Written Form**

All amendments and supplements to the present lease shall be made in writing. This requirement may only be waived in writing. This also applies to all declarations which are to be made in writing under the terms of the present agreement.

### § 23

**Partial Invalidity**

Should any part of the present agreement be void or voidable, the validity of the agreement as a whole shall not thereby be affected. The legally ineffective part shall then be replaced by such legally acceptable provision which approximates most closely that which the contracting parties would have made had they been aware of the ineffectiveness of the said part of the agreement. The same shall apply for the closing of contractual gaps.

### § 24

**Miscellaneous**

1.  The Lessor/Lessee shall be responsible for cleaning the real property and for removing snow and ice.

2.  The Lessor is entitled to formulate house rules and to determine the contents of these rules at his reasonable discretion.

3.  . . . . . . . . .

| | |
|---|---|
| (Place)      (Date) | (Place)      (Date) |
| (Lessor) | (Lessee) |

# 4

## MANAGING TAXES THAT AFFECT CORPORATE REAL ESTATE

The management of corporate real estate is affected by the tax policies and practices of the countries where multinational companies operate. Since corporate real estate supports the principal operating function of the company as a whole, the various national taxes affect the corporate real estate directly. Such direct effects come from ad valorem property taxes, land holding taxes, and property capital gains taxes. Allowed depreciation methods, property acquisition and stamp taxes, and tax incentives for economic development also affect corporate real estate directly. The taxes that may only indirectly affect corporate real estate include corporate income taxes on the federal, prefectural, and local levels; treatment of company operating and capital losses; presence or absence of corporate consolidation privileges; capital investment taxes; general capital gains taxes; value added or sales taxes; general stamp taxes; trade taxes; withholding taxes on international corporate distributions; employer taxes; and wealth and net worth taxes.

Multinational corporate tax strategies depend on the worldwide tax environment, the legal organizational structures permitted in the various countries, the various methods that may reduce overall corporate taxation, and currency value trends and associated taxation. The corporate real estate department is affected directly and indirectly by these multinational tax strategies that underlie corporate profitability and dividend returns to the corporate shareholders. Even though the corporate tax strategies are set by top management with the advice of the finance and corporate treasury departments, the decisions of the corporate real estate department are based partially on the company's tax strategies. For example, site selection decisions involve tax matters. The acquisition, development, and leasing decisions of corporate real estate depend partially on tax considerations.

## THE WORLDWIDE TAX ENVIRONMENT

In general, worldwide tax reform among capitalistic countries is bringing about lower corporate and personal income tax rates for economic stimulation. All countries tend to be concerned about their economic growth and their relationship within the world economy. They are individually concerned about their world trading relationships and their trade deficits and surpluses with various trading partners. Internal taxation has a significant bearing on these important economic relationships.

Tax, financial, and other economic development incentives are not now offered as freely in most countries as they have been in previous decades. Most national leaders have recognized that tax incentives for economic development only partially affect the decision making of corporations and small businesses who seek new or expanded industrial and commercial sites. At the same time, tax revenues are more and more important to the functioning of governments. Therefore, tax incentives that have been perceived as unnecessary to economic development and industrial redevelopment are culled from the former list of incentives. The federal, regional, and local incentives for industrial redevelopment and new economic development remain on a general scale in most countries, but the offerings tend to be less abundant than before and directed toward specially desired industries. Most countries offer development incentives, including tax incentives, to attract high-technology industries that employ labor at relatively high wages and salaries. Most countries want nonpolluting high-tech industries, in particular, to stimulate their economies.

## LEGAL ORGANIZATIONAL STRUCTURES AND MULTINATIONAL CORPORATE MANAGEMENT

Multinational corporations must select the legal organizational structures that fit their management, financial, and tax needs. The organizational structures must permit the company to move legally toward its management and financial goals across the world.

Usually the major corporation has a complicated management and financial structure, partially due to international tax strategies. This structure arises from matching corporate objectives to the legal organizational structures permitted by the individual countries where the company does business. The company may structure itself by regions, countries, or other management districts, divisions, and areas. In Europe, for example, in the Federal Republic of Germany legal business organizational vehicles for multinational corporations are different from those in France. Their public and private corporate vehicles have specific definitions that apply to corporate financial and tax management. Neither country is one in which a multinational company consolidates its European position; its corporate organizational structures do not attract the multinational corporations that want to reduce their overall European tax exposure. Of course, multinational companies may structure their French operations around a French-chartered corporation and their West German operations around a West German-chartered corporation. The business of the corporation in each country would be channeled through a domestic-chartered corporation, but their regional or worldwide business could be consolidated within a country that has more favorable financial and tax legislation.

When the multinational company expands its business into new areas of the world, it often establishes company branches, agents, and subsidiaries. It may acquire companies in other countries or enter into joint ventures or partnerships in order to enter markets quickly with experienced and established partners. Each of these corporate expansion arrangements has its tax implications. And the tax implications depend upon the tax legislation of the home and the foreign countries involved. So corporate tax strategy is vitally associated with corporate business and real estate organizational strategy.

Generally corporate branch profits are consolidated into home office corporate profits because the branch office is totally dependent on the home office. But the local taxing authority may have jurisdiction over the worldwide or national income of the branch office. The corporation usually pays the taxes assessed by the national government and then receives a tax credit under home office consolidated tax accounting for the taxes paid to the foreign country for the branch office's profitability. The branch office is managed entirely by the home office. In most cases, the corporate use of foreign agents for the marketing of its goods and services is treated the same way in corporation taxation. The agent is partially or totally under the management control of the home office of the multinational corporation. The branch office operates under the charter of the home office. The agent usually operates under a domestic business charter to market the goods and services of companies of various national origins.

A majority-owned corporate subsidiary is usually chartered under domestic law and is only supervised from the corporate home office. Local business management is usually left to the management of the domestic subsidiary under the overall management policies of the home office. Since it is chartered under domestic law, it is subject to the domestic laws as a national company. But its revenues and expenses may be consolidated under a regional or a worldwide corporate entity. Or its financing, leasing, and other functions might be consolidated in a similar manner. This majority-owned corporate subsidiary is subject to the taxation of the national government in which it is chartered, and to the taxation of the national government of the home office. The majority-owned subsidiary may have a national office for a group of offices within the country. For example, IBM France is a subsidiary that is responsible for the company's operations through multiple French offices, warehouses, and manufacturing plants. IBM Europe, also established in Paris in an adjacent La Defense high-rise office building, is the regional subsidiary for overall European operations covering many European real properties including the French operations and properties.

Multinational corporations also employ majority-owned subsidiaries for their worldwide or regional financing and leasing activities. In this way, their currency and financing operations can be consolidated for tax and management purposes. One well-known Fortune 500 multinational company uses a captive finance subsidiary chartered in the Netherlands for this purpose.

When a company wants to expand internationally more rapidly than is possible from development of branches or subsidiaries from scratch, the company may acquire desirable companies in key countries. The tax and operational histories of established companies should be viewed before the acquisitions are made. Plans can be made for the future tax and operational strategies as the acquired foreign company is merged into the acquiring multinational company. The tax implications of the acquired real estate of the foreign company can be merged with the tax situation already in place within the acquiring company.

If the target foreign company is not amenable to acquisition by the multinational company, the target company management may agree to a joint venture or formal partnership with the multinational company. The home country and the domestic country legislation and regulations regarding joint venture and partnership law and taxation come into play immediately. Partnership real estate is subject to different tax rulings and regulations than corporate real estate. Partnerships may be subject only to single taxation; when the individual partners receive distributions from the partnership, their partnership receipts are taxable at their ordinary domestic tax rates. Corporations, public or private, are usually subject to double taxation: one time at the corporate level and again at the corporate stockholder level when corporate distributions are made to individual stockholders. The tax rates, deductible expenses, and tax incentives usually apply differently to partnerships than to corporations. Individual tax rates and regulations often apply to partner distributions from partnerships such as joint ventures, but corporate tax rates and regulations apply to corporations.

Therefore, the expansion plans for a multinational corporation should take into account the effect of legal organizational structures on tax matters affecting multinational operations and real estate management. A complicated organizational structure may be necessary. In such a case, the taxation of corporate real estate will be affected by the multiplicity of tax regulations and rulings associated with the use of and investment in corporate real estate.

## THE TAX IMPLICATIONS FOR SITE SELECTION AND PROPERTY ACQUISITION AND DIVESTITURE

Tax regulations at home and abroad affect multinational corporate real estate directly when they are associated with:

Ad valorem property (fixed assets) taxes

Land holding taxes

Land and capital transfer taxes

Tax depreciation methods permitted

And other property taxes

Tax regulations at home and abroad affect the same corporate real estate indirectly when they are associated with:

Overall corporate income tax rates:
    federal
    prefectural
    local

Tax incentives for industrial redevelopment and economic development

Provisions for carrying losses forward and back

Group tax consolidation privileges

Capital investment and net wealth taxes

Value added taxes

Employer and payroll taxes

Withholding taxes on interest, dividends, royalties, management fees, and other intercompany payments

Other corporate taxes indirectly related to corporate real estate

Site selection and property acquisition and divestiture are affected directly and indirectly by the above-mentioned taxes that vary among countries. This book focuses on the tax variability of the most important tax regulations among the leading industrialized countries which operate under capitalistic market conditions. The rest of this chapter focuses primarily on twelve countries of Western Europe including the United Kingdom, the five industrialized nations of Asia—Japan, Taiwan, South Korea, Hong Kong, and Singapore—Australia of the South Pacific region, and the United States.

## DIRECT TAXATION OF CORPORATE REAL ESTATE

Most countries tax the appraised value or the rental value of real properties within their national borders. Malta is one exception, according to

Coopers & Lybrand. Japan has a land-holding tax. Dominica has a land value appreciation tax. Numerous countries have capital transfer or land transfer taxes; these taxes may amount to property capital gains taxes. Approved real property depreciation regulations affect corporate real estate and overall corporate taxable incomes. Stamp duties affect real estate transactions in many countries.

### Ad Valorem Property Taxes

According to a recent Organization for Economic Cooperation and Development (OECD) study, most countries use property taxes to support local governments. A few use this form of tax revenue to support the central government. For example, the central governments of Turkey and New Zealand gain financial support from property taxes. The United States and the United Kingdom governments derive over three percent of their gross domestic product from property tax revenues. But most industrialized countries gain less than 1.25 percent of their GDPs (gross domestic products) from this tax source. Here are some labels given property taxes in various advanced economies:

Australia: Land Tax, Rates

Denmark: Land Tax, Service Tax

France: Land and Building Tax, Land Tax, Property Tax

Germany: Real Property Tax

Ireland: Rates

Japan: Fixed Assets Tax, City Planning Tax, Land Holding Tax

Netherlands: Municipal Tax, Contributions to Polder Boards

New Zealand: Land Tax Rates

Spain: Rural Land Tax

Sweden: Municipal Guarantee Tax

Switzerland: Recurrent Tax

Turkey: Immovable Property Tax

United Kingdom: Rates (becoming Poll Tax)

United States: Property Tax

Examples of the various property tax bases and rates follow:

Japan: Annual taxes are imposed on land and buildings at 1.7 percent rate and on other depreciable fixed assets used in business at a rate of 1.4 percent of their taxable values.

Sweden: The assessment value of real property is based on 75 percent of the estimated sales value. The property owner usually pays a tax of 1.4 percent, 2 percent, or 2.5 percent of 33 percent or 100 percent of the assessed value, depending on the fiscal nature of the property.

Indonesia: Ad valorem property tax is imposed at the rate of 5 percent of the market value of the land and buildings. The government determines the property values.

The property tax relationships of other countries are shown in Exhibit 4.1.

**Exhibit 4.1**
**Ad Valorem Property Tax Worldwide Summary as of 1987**

---

Australia: Each state and municipality imposes an annual tax based on the value of land owned.

Austria: Real property is subject to a municipal tax on assessed value. Rates vary among the municipalities from 0.4 to 0.84 percent.

Bangladesh: Taxes are imposed at varying rates by municipalities based on the value of land and buildings. Newly constructed houses may be exempt from tax in some cases.

Barbados: Levied annually on each property owner based on the value of land and improvements thereon. The rates on unimproved land are one percent on the first $100,000 and 1.5 percent on the balance. If the property is owned by a foreign or foreign-controlled company, the rates are three percent for unimproved land and two percent for improved land.

Bermuda: Property tax is up to 7.5 percent of the assessed annual rental value of real property.

Brunei: Property assessments are levied by the local authorities and are based on the annual valuation of the property. Land rent or rates are also payable.

Canada: All municipalities levy tax on real property to finance local expenditures. The provinces levy a tax on real property outside municipal boundaries. Certain provinces and cities impose a modest tax upon the transfer of immovable property. The provinces of Quebec and Ontario levy a substantial tax upon the transfer of some types of land to nonresidents or corporations controlled by nonresidents.

Channel Islands, Guernsey: Rates are charged annually on both owners and occupiers according to the value of the property.

Channel Islands, Jersey: Rates are charged annually on both owners and occupiers according to the value of the property.

Chile: Real estate is subject to an annual tax of approximately two percent of the fiscal assessment and is payable annually in four installments.

China (People's Republic of): The Housing Property Tax is a tax on houses and buildings; the rate is 1.2 percent of the cost or 18 percent on the rental value of the houses and buildings concerned.

Colombia: An annual tax is levied on all real estate properties. The tax is based on values fixed by the municipal authorities.

**Exhibit 4.1** (continued)

Costa Rica: On a quarterly basis, land and property owners must pay a tax based on property value. The rate ranges from 3 to 12 percent.

Cyprus: Property valued over C£ 35,000 is taxed at a rate ranging from 0.15 percent to 0.35 percent.

Denmark: The assessment value of real property is based on the authorities' cash valuation. Where no valuation is published, 80 percent of the acquisition costs normally can be used. The tax on land varies from 0.6 percent up to 3.4 percent in different parts of the country (the most expensive is in Copenhagen). Furthermore, the rental value of a private dwelling is taxed by 2.5 percent or up to 7.5 percent based on the authorities' cash valuation.

Fiji: An annual tax is imposed that is based on land owned or leased within urban district boundaries.

France: Taxes are paid both on developed and undeveloped land. The tax is assessed against the owner and based on the rental value. A personal dwelling tax is levied on any individual who occupies a dwelling as of January 1, even if the individual is not the owner. The tax is based on the real value; special deductions are granted according to the number of dependent children.

Germany, Federal Republic of: A federal property tax is imposed on the owner, whether an individual or a corporation, of movable and immovable property. The tax rate is 0.5 percent for individuals and 0.6 percent for corporations, based in each case on the value of the property. In the case of land, however, the tax is not based on the market value but on a so-called unit value which is ascertained for tax purposes by a special method. This value is usually less than one half of the market value. At present, the tax is based on a sum equivalent to 140 percent of this unit value. Municipal authorities impose a land tax on the unit value of land. The tax rates vary with the location of the land.

Ghana: Municipalities levy general rates on the rateable value of properties.

Guatemala: Land and property is subject to property tax which is based on an official valuation and is paid quarterly at rates ranging from 0.3 percent to 0.8 percent.

Hong Kong: Property is charged on the net assessable value of non-owner-occupied land and buildings at the standard rate of 16.5 percent.

Iceland: Land and property tax at nominal rates is paid to the municipal authorities; the rates vary between municipalities and also in regard to use. Owners of commercial buildings must pay a tax of 1.1 percent assessed on the official value of buildings and land.

India: Taxes are levied at varying rates by municipalities on the value of land and property situated within their local limits.

Indonesia: This tax is imposed at the rate of five percent of the market value of land and buildings as determined by the government.

Ireland, Republic of: Local authorities levy taxes shown as rates of nonresidential property. The rates are normally paid by the occupier and are based on a notional rental value of the property. An annual residential property tax is payable by persons who own and occupy residential property whose market value exceeds a limit (currently IR£ 69,971) and where household income exceeds IR£ 25,307. The rate of tax is 1.5 percent on the excess of value over IR£ 69,971.

**Exhibit 4.1** (continued)

Isle of Man: An annual rates charge is made on the value of land and property owned.

Italy: Taxable income is based upon land registry data, unless actual property income can be proved to be lower or higher by certain percentages than the income calculated from land registry data.

Ivory Coast: Payable on both improved and unimproved land, property taxes are assessed against the owner and based on the rental value. The total of property taxes applicable to constructed real estate corresponds to approximately 35.5 percent of 50 percent of the property's rented value determined by the property tax authorities. All new buildings benefit from a partial exemption of property taxes over a period which may extend through 10 years.

Jamaica: Payable on all real property based on the unimproved value of the land as assessed by the government's valuation office. Rates vary with usage, that is, commercial, agricultural, or housing.

Japan: Annual taxes are generally imposed on land and buildings at 1.7 percent and on other depreciable fixed assets used in businesses at 1.4 percent of their taxable value.

Kenya: Taxes on property values are levied as rates by local authorities. The rates are normally fixed annually.

Korea, Republic of: Annual property taxes at rates between 0.3 percent and 10 percent are levied by the local authorities. Property tax rates on new factories or expansions of existing factories in the "major cities" are five times the normal rate. A 20 percent defense surtax is also levied on property tax.

Lebanon: A proportionate flat tax and a graduated tax are imposed on built property. Exemptions generally are allowed for public buildings and nonprofit organizations. The proportionate flat tax is 8 percent plus 3 percent for municipalities (total 11 percent) of gross proceeds. The graduated tax is on net proceeds in excess of LL 50,000 after deducting maintenance costs, which must not exceed 20 percent of gross proceeds. The rate ranges from 7 percent to 23 percent. A surtax of 10 percent is added to that for municipalities. Real estate profits of corporations are exempt from the graduated tax and pay the higher of either the proportionate real estate tax or the corporate tax.

Liberia: A real property tax is levied on the assessed value of real property (which is not necessarily the fair market value). Rates vary depending on the location and use of the property. The tax is payable on or before July 1 each year.

Malaysia: Property assessments are levied by the local authorities and are based on the annual valuation of the property. Land tax or quit is also payable to the state government.

Mexico: Property taxes are levied by the states and the federal district. The rates vary in each of the states and are highest on property located in the federal district.

Netherlands: A small municipal tax applies to the ownership and use of immovable property.

Netherlands Antilles: A land tax is levied on real estate at an annual rate of 0.5 percent on the value of undeveloped land and 0.6 percent on the value of built-up land.

New Caledonia: Each commune imposes an annual tax based on land owned.

**Exhibit 4.1** (continued)

New Zealand: The government imposes an annual land tax at the rate of 2 percent of the land's value less an exemption of up to NZ $175,000 for land valued at less than NZ $350,000. Certain classes of land are exempt from the land tax (e.g., land used in primary production and residential rental activities).

Nigeria: Land and property taxes are imposed by each state.

Norway: Property tax on real estate is levied by the municipality at a maximum tax rate of 0.7 percent. The local authorities are free to decide whether to levy this tax. The tax is assessed on the basis of a special evaluation of the property.

Pakistan: Taxes are levied at varying rates by municipalities on the value of land and property situated within their boundaries.

Panama: Taxes on property are levied as rates by local authorities. The rates are normally paid by the owner and are based on the value of the property. Payment is made quarterly. New properties are exempt for the first 10 years. The rates range from 1.4 percent to 2.1 percent.

Papua New Guinea: The various provinces and municipalities impose an annual tax on the value of unimproved land.

Peru: A tax is levied on vacant urban land for which a construction license is to be issued. A tax is imposed on all real estate held by persons and corporations. The tax is applied on the total value of all real estate owned by a taxpayer within each province. The property value is updated each year by local regulators on the basis of certain indicators.

Philippines: Owners of land and buildings are required to pay real estate taxes to the province or city in which the property is located. The rates (maximum is 3 percent) are based on the assessed value of the property and vary slightly with the locality.

Puerto Rico: Property tax is imposed jointly by the commonwealth and by municipalities on the assessed value of real property (generally lower than market value) and on the book value of certain personal property. The tax rates vary between municipalities and range from 3.07 percent to 4.77 percent.

Singapore: Property tax is imposed at the rate of 23 percent of the property's annual value. A 30 percent rebate is available for all industrial and commercial properties, whether leased or not, for the period July 1, 1986 to December 31, 1988. An additional 20 percent rebate is available if the owner passes the rebate down to his tenants.

Sri Lanka: There are municipal taxes on land and property.

Swaziland: Annual rates on property are payable to the town councils, based on the council valuation of the property.

Sweden: The assessment value of real property is based on 75 percent of the estimated sales value. In 1988 the last general revaluation of real estate took place. The owner of real property designed for housing or other use pays an annual property tax amounting to 1.4 percent, 2 percent, or 2.5 percent of 33 percent or 100 percent of the assessed value, depending on the fiscal nature of the property.

Switzerland: Several cantons and municipalities impose an annual tax on the officially determined values of real property.

Taiwan: A land value tax is levied on both rural and urban land on the basis of

**Exhibit 4.1** (continued)

the official assessed value of the land. A fixed yearly rate of 1.5 percent of the official assessed value is applied to urban land for industrial use. Urban land for other than industrial use is subject to tax at progressive rates from 1 percent to 5.5 percent, rising with the official assessed value of the taxpayer's holdings of urban land located in a jurisdictional area. Rural land tax is payable in kind or in cash, with the assessment expressed in terms of a tax unit equal to a number of kilograms of paddy rice.

Building tax paid by the owner of the building is 3 percent of the official assessed value if the building is used for business, 1.38 percent if used as a residence, 1.5 percent if used as a factory, and 2 percent if used as an office of professional practitioners or public organizations and institutions.

Thailand: There are two kinds of property taxes. The local development tax is imposed upon owners of land and persons in possession of land of a value ranging from 50 Stangs to Bht 400 per rai (about one-half acre). The tax is levied annually. The house and land tax is imposed upon the owner of a house, building, and land. The rate is 12.5 percent of the assessed annual lease value of the property.

Trinidad and Tobago: Taxes on property are levied by local authorities. The rates are normally paid by the occupier and are based on the assessed rental value of the property.

Turkey: Property taxes are paid on the tax values of land and buildings at rates varying from 0.3 percent to 0.6 percent.

Uganda: The local administrations levy rates on property, which vary according to valuations.

United Kingdom: Local authorities (counties, cities and towns) raise a large proportion of their revenue by taxing property. These taxes, known as rates, are normally paid by the occupier and are based on a notional rental value of the property.

United States: Taxes on real and personal property are levied by state and local governments. These taxes are generally based on the assessed value of the property (which is not necessarily the fair market value), vary widely, and are usually not significant.

Venezuela: Real property taxes, which vary from one municipality to another, are comparatively small in Venezuela.

Zaire: For purposes of the annual tax on land, Zaire is divided into three regions which each impose a different rate of tax based on the square meter.

Zambia: Local authorities levy annual rates based on property values.

Zimbabwe: Municipal and other local authorities levy annual rates on real estate—usually about one percent of the property's valuation.

*Source*: Edwin J. Reavey, ed., *International Tax Summaries 1989: A Guide for Planning and Decisions* (New York: John Wiley & Sons, 1989). Reprinted by permission.

### Land and Capital Transfer Taxes

According to Coopers & Lybrand, many countries have land transfer taxes. In their *1988 International Tax Summaries*, they report that thirty countries of Europe, Africa, the Caribbean, Southeast Asia, Asia, and Central and South America had land transfer taxes in effect. From this same authoritative tax summary, we note that three countries—Austria and West Germany of Western Europe and Nigeria of Africa—had capital transfer taxes that affect real property transfers.

### Tax Depreciation Methods Permitted

All of the 19 highly industrialized countries surveyed permitted straight-line depreciation to be used by property owners in figuring their corporate tax deductions (Appendix 4.B). There is the implication that most countries permit the use of the straight-line depreciation method. Eleven of these countries permitted the use of the declining balance method of depreciation for calculation of corporate tax deductions (Appendix 4.B). More details about the depreciation methods permitted in the eleven countries are summarized in Appendix 4.A. A sample of the approved 1989 depreciation methods for a few countries follows:

United States:

> Residential real property: straight line over 27.5 or 40 years

> Nonresidential real property: straight line over 31.5 or 40 years

United Kingdom:

> Ten percent rate for plants that are leased to most nonresident companies

> Industrial buildings in general: 4 percent on cost

> In enterprise zones, depreciation at 10 percent for all types of commercial buildings (no depreciation is normally allowed on nonindustrial commercial buildings)

> Depreciation allowances are generally recaptured on disposal

Japan:

> Straight-line or declining balance methods used on tangible fixed assets

> Law provides useful lives of various categories of fixed assets

> Special accelerated depreciation in addition to normal depreciation in year of acquisition depending on the industry and type of asset

West Germany:

> Straight-line or declining balance methods permitted

> Special depreciation available for specific building installations (i.e., research and development facilities and fixed assets located in West Berlin)

South Korea:

> Straight-line or double-declining balance methods permitted

> The double-declining balance method is automatically assumed

> Building lives range from 25 to 60 years

Hong Kong:

> Industrial building and structures: Initial allowance of 20 percent in addition to the annual allowance of 4 percent of cost of construction

> Commercial buildings and structures: An annual "rebuilding allowance" amounting to 0.75 percent of cost

Italy:

> Straight-line method based on cost of asset

> Depreciation periods set by law

> Depreciation rate cannot exceed 20 percent per annum

> In addition to normal depreciation, accelerated depreciation may be charged at a rate not exceeding 150 percent of the normal rates for the first three years

Spain:

> Straight-line method is normal on cost of asset or the written up asset

> New qualifying assets with effective lives longer than three years may be depreciated by declining balance method, constant percentage, or sum of the years digits

> Special depreciation plans for assets subject to abnormal wear and tear

## Stamp Duty

Many countries place stamp duties on real estate documents that are related to the transfer of property ownership and the placement of liens on property. According to the *1988 International Tax Summaries* of Coopers & Lybrand, thirty-nine of the countries surveyed had stamp duties in place.

## INDIRECT TAXATION AFFECTING CORPORATE REAL ESTATE DECISIONS

Various kinds of taxes that are payable by corporations indirectly affect corporate real estate decision making. The locations selected by the corporation for its business and investment properties are partially determined by the tax environment for the corporation as a whole. Most corporate managements wish to reduce their overall tax burden by selecting advantageous locations worldwide. The taxes affecting the corporate real estate decision making include:

Corporate income tax rates: federal, prefectural, and local

General tax incentives for industrial redevelopment and economic development

Provisions for carrying losses forward and back

Group tax consolidation privileges

Capital, wealth, and net wealth taxes

Value added taxes

Employer and payroll taxes

Withholding taxes on interest, dividends, royalties, management fees, and other intercompany payments

### Corporate Income Taxation Worldwide

The lowest federal corporate income tax rates among the nineteen highly industrialized countries are found in East and Southeast Asia (Taiwan, 10 to 25; Hong Kong, 17; and South Korea, 20 to 33; Appendix 4.B). In Western Europe, the federal income tax rates of Luxembourg— 22 to 36 percent—tend to be more favorable than the rates of the other industrialized Western European countries. The Luxembourg rates compare favorably with the rates for West Germany, 27.9 to 41.4 percent; Denmark, 50 percent; Belgium and Ireland, 43 percent; and France, 42 percent. In contrast, some of the Gulf States do not levy income taxes against corporations but these are not known as highly industrialized countries in the world marketplace. Their oil revenues tend to permit financing of government expenditures without resorting to federal corporate income taxation.

Prefectural and local governments tax corporations in some of the industrialized countries, including the United States, Japan, Portugal, Luxembourg, Italy, Ireland, and West Germany. Japan raises money through corporate taxes on family holding companies, prefectural enterprises, and municipal enterprises. Among the Japanese municipalities, the Tokyo metropolitan government raises money through taxation of 17.3 to 20.7 percent of the federal corporation tax. Local per capita taxes are also placed on corporate employees (Appendix 4.B).

### General Tax Incentives for Industrial Redevelopment and Economic Development

Most countries offer federal, regional, and local tax, financial, and other incentives to domestic and foreign companies for expanding their companies or locating for the first time within the country, a particular region, or a particular locality. For example, many countries have designated enterprise development areas that include special enterprise zones and foreign free-trade zones. Special tax, financial, and other incentives associated with these zones are designed to attract the desired industries and their work forces. With the special incentive packages, the public and private agencies of the country wish to promote economic growth, reduce unemployment, stimulate capital investment, raise wages and salaries, and increase tax revenues overall.[1]

## Nontax Incentives That Supplement Tax Incentives

Before surveying tax incentives in greater detail, let us look at the financial and other incentives that governments and their related public and private agencies offer companies for assistance with industrial redevelopment and economic development. Some of the financial incentives are:

Grants for various special purposes

Government assistance with favorable land purchase terms or land rental

Government offerings of government contracts or preferential government purchase arrangements

Government guarantees on loans

Government long-term loans

Loans for export market development

Government subsidies for various purposes

Availability of foreign exchange from government sources

Rail transport rebates

Two of the legal incentives for inward and capital investment by corporations are:

Elimination of property investment restrictions that may exist

Less restricted or totally unrestricted profit and capital repatriation by the foreign industrial investor

A number of nontax incentives are offered by governments and their agencies. In addition to the financial and legal incentives just mentioned, governments offer other incentives to foster exporting, manufacturing, high technology use, and research and development (Appendix 4.B). For more detail about the eleven countries' current promotion of inward and capital investment, see Appendix 4.A.

## Tax Incentives

Many countries offer tax incentives to encourage inward and capital investment. Some of the predominant tax incentives are:

Initial depreciation or investment allowance for the investment

Annual depreciation privileges

Investment allowances before first-year depreciation allowances

Business license reduction

Privileges of transferring tax losses to the parent company (consolidated tax statements for tax purposes)

Income tax credits

Reduced tax rates on a variety of national, regional, and local taxes

Tax rebates

Special tax deductibility of special industrial development related items

Permission to establish tax deferred reserves for certain purposes

These tax incentives for economic development differ by country and region (Appendix 4.C). Some of the differences and the scope of the tax incentives may be viewed in several exhibits in *Guide to International Real Estate Investment* (Westport, Conn.: Quorum Books, 1988). These exhibits cover Europe (Exhibit 12.1), Central America (Exhibit 12.2), South America (Exhibit 12.3), Asia (Exhibit 12.4), and Africa (Exhibit 12.5).

## Provisions for Carrying Losses Forward and Back

The industrialized countries permit the corporation to carry forward any tax losses that it generates. Some permit corporate losses to be carried back to prior years. In this way, the company may reduce its previous tax payments. Generally the loss carryback period runs from one to three years while the tax loss carry forward period generally ranges from three to five years. The United States, Japan, and the United Kingdom permit loss carrybacks over one to three years.

## Group Tax Consolidation Privileges

Generally the Western European countries, the United States, and Australia—among the highly industrialized countries—permit group tax consolidation privileges to their resident corporations. But exceptions in Western Europe are Belgium and Greece. According to Price Waterhouse, the highly industrialized countries of Asia, including Japan, Hong Kong, South Korea, and Taiwan, do not permit group consolidation for tax purposes.

## Capital, Wealth, and Net Wealth Taxes

According to Coopers & Lybrand, a number of countries have capital taxes. They include:

| | |
|---|---|
| Canada | Paraguay |
| Denmark | Portugal |
| Finland | Switzerland |
| Ireland | United Kingdom |
| Luxembourg | Venezuela |
| Netherlands | Zaire |
| Norway | |

Two countries have both capital and wealth taxes: Luxembourg and Switzerland.

The countries that have wealth, net worth, or net wealth taxes are:

| | |
|---|---|
| Austria | Spain |
| Bangladesh | Sri Lanka |
| Ghana | Sweden |
| India | Switzerland |
| Luxembourg | Uruguay |
| Pakistan | |

## Value-Added Taxes

While the United States and Australia have sales taxes, most of the highly industrialized countries have value-added taxes. Hong Kong and Singapore have neither value-added nor sales taxes.

If a national government imposes value-added taxes, it normally sets a standard rate, a reduced rate, and a rate for luxury goods, or at least standard and reduced rates. This is true for the majority of the Western European countries, the exceptions being Denmark and the United Kingdom. These two countries have only a flat, single value-added tax that affects corporate taxation. Taiwan and South Korea also have only a flat, single rate.

Since the value-added rates vary rather widely in Western Europe, part of the multinational adjustment preceding the formation of the new Europe is the negotiation of rates within a smaller range. Right now, for instance, Denmark has a 22 percent value-added rate while Ireland has 10 percent, 2.5 percent, and 25 percent rates. The standard rates of Luxembourg and

Spain are 12 percent. Spain has a rate of 33 percent on luxury goods but Luxembourg has no luxury goods rate.

### Other Taxes That Indirectly Affect Corporate Real Estate

Some countries, such as Japan and the United States, have employer and payroll taxes (Appendix 4.A and other sources). Withholding taxes are commonly assessed against distributions by companies of funds to entities outside the country of distribution origin. Tax treaties between the country of distribution origin and the country of distribution reception may reduce or eliminate the withholding taxes on interest, dividends, royalty payments, management fees, and other intercompany payments. Samples of current withholding taxes on each of these payment types for eleven industrialized countries may be analyzed in Appendix 4.A.

## SOME METHODS USED BY MULTINATIONAL CORPORATIONS TO REDUCE TAX INCIDENCE

Corporations can select their business locations worldwide from a tax viewpoint. Most multinational corporations consider the tax environments along with locational demand for the product, access to raw materials and semifinished goods, access to appropriate transportation facilities, labor force availability and cost, energy sources and costs, government encouragement of industrial and commercial development, and business regulations and restraints.

Corporations employ various methods to reduce their tax incidence. Before leaving tax management, we want to consider some additional aspects of tax management.

### Use of Off-Shore Tax Havens

Even though national tax authorities have eliminated some off-shore tax havens for their domestic-based multinational corporations, some still exist. Panama, the Channel Islands, Curaçao, and other locations may still offer tax advantages to the multinational corporation that channels its overseas profits through these places before remittance into the home country.

### Use of On-Shore Tax Havens

Some countries, such as Luxembourg, have unusually low federal income tax rates. Profits may be consolidated through these countries where the rates are relatively low. The finance or leasing company subsidiary may be chartered in a tax advantageous country like the Netherlands for such multinational transactions.

## Transfer Pricing

As goods and services are moved across countries from one corporate subsidiary to another, the goods and services may be priced by the corporation so that higher profits are realized in lower tax-rate countries and lower profits are realized in higher tax-rate countries. To the dismay of some national governments, transfer pricing techniques have been used by multinational corporations for overall corporate tax reduction for decades.

## Use of the DISC

Many U.S.-based multinational exporting companies utilize the DISC (Domestic International Sales Corporation) tax incentive for reduction of taxes. The tax burden on export profits of the multinational company can be reduced substantially. The company's effective tax rate on export profits may be reduced by many percentage points. The DISC must be an incorporated U.S. business that exports goods where sales is the primary activity of the company.

## SUMMARY

Tax reform, resulting in lower income tax rates, has been taking place worldwide. The organizational structures that may be used by multinational corporations in the various countries, in contrast, have remained generally unchanged. The individual organizational structures for business of the various national governments have individual tax implications as well as implications for the owner's financial and legal liability and the raising of capital for business operations and assets. Multinational corporations often charter or incorporate their subsidiaries which operate in the various countries. The multinational corporation thereby becomes a resident business and a good citizen and less susceptible to negative national sentiments about foreign companies exploiting national citizens and domestic business resources.

Corporate site selection and property acquisition and divestiture are partly determined by the tax environment of the country, region, and local community. But other considerations come into the property analysis. The tax environment may or may not be the key factor in real estate decision making.

Taxation directly and indirectly affects corporate real estate decision making. The taxation that directly affects real estate decisions involves ad valorem property and land and capital transfer taxes and stamp duties. Most countries have these taxes, as well as building depreciation methods that help the corporation reduce taxable income. Most countries permit straight-line depreciation methods using permitted property useful lives.

Many countries permit the use of declining balance and other accelerated depreciation methods. The provisions of most of these taxes and depreciation methods differ somewhat.

Some forms of taxation indirectly affect corporate real estate decision making. Most countries, excluding a few countries in the Middle East, assess corporate income taxes on the federal level. Only a few countries assess corporate income taxes on the local government level. The rates of corporate income taxation vary widely across countries as do tax and nontax incentives for industrial redevelopment and economic development. Most government tax authorities of highly industrialized countries provide corporations the right to carry forward losses, but few highly industrialized countries permit the carryback of corporate losses. Many countries—particularly in Western Europe—permit corporate consolidation of accounts for taxation purposes. Capital, wealth, and net wealth taxes are applied in quite a few countries across the world. Most nations levy value-added or sales taxes on the transfer of title of goods and services in sales transactions. Japan, for example, only recently approved the levy of a value-added tax. Other tax varieties also indirectly affect decision making in multinational corporate real estate.

## NOTE

1. The reader may wish to review the chapters on taxation of real estate and on economic development and international industrial property development and investment in this author's recent book, *Guide to International Real Estate Investment* (Westport, Conn.: Quorum Books, 1988).

## BIBLIOGRAPHY

Bischel, Jon E. and Robert Feinschrieber. *Fundamentals of International Taxation*. 2d ed. New York: Practising Law Institute, 1985.

Confederation of British Industry. *Tax: Strategic Corporate Tax Planning*. London: Mercury Books, 1989.

Coopers & Lybrand. *International Tax Summaries: Annual Guide for Planning and Decisions*. New York: Wiley, 1989.

Daniels, John D., Ernest W. Ograms, Jr., and Lee H. Radebaugh. *International Business: Environments and Operations*. Reading, Mass.: Addison-Wesley Publishing Co., 1982.

"Global Survey Reveals Widespread Relaxation of Restrictions." *Site Selection*, October 1988, pp. 1344, 1346–1349.

Hines, M. A. *Guide to International Real Estate Investment*. Westport, Conn.: Quorum Books, 1988.

———. *Investing in Japanese Real Estate*. Westport, Conn.: Quorum Books, 1987.

———. *International Income Property Investment*. Scottsdale, Ariz.: International Real Estate Institute, 1985.

Jones Lang Wootton. *The Commercial Property Investor's Guide to Germany*. Frankfurt: Jones Lang Wootton, 1989.

Organization for Economic Cooperation and Development. *International Tax Avoidance and Evasion: 4 Related Studies*. Paris: Organization for Economic Cooperation and Development, 1987.

———. *Taxes on Immovable Property*. Paris: Organization for Economic Cooperation and Development, 1983.

Practising Law Institute. *International Tax Planning for the U.S. Multinational Corporations*. New York: Practicing Law Institute, 1988.

Price Waterhouse. *Corporate Taxes: A Worldwide Summary*. New York: Price Waterhouse, 1989.

Robock, Stefan H., and Kenneth Simmonds. *International Business and Multinational Enterprises*. 3d ed. Homewood, Ill.: Richard D. Irwin, 1983.

Volhard, Rudiger, and Dolf Weber, eds. *Real Property in Germany*. Frankfurt am Main: Fritz Knapp Verlag, 1989.

# CORPORATE TAX SUMMARY FOR SELECTED COUNTRIES

## BELGIUM

### Corporate Income Tax

The basic tax rate for companies is 43 per cent. For manufacturing and trading companies, the tax rate is reduced according to a scale when the taxable income does not exceed BFr16,600,000, provided not more than 50 percent of their shares are held by another company or companies and the distributed dividend does not exceed 13 percent of the paid-up share capital. To the tax so computed, a surcharge is applicable, but it can be avoided by making quarterly advance payments equal to one quarter of the tax liability for the year.

*Branch Income.* Branch profits are usually subject to a basic tax rate of 48 percent plus the surcharge as explained above. Transfers of branch profits to the head office abroad do not give rise to further taxation in Belgium.

### Other Taxes

*Value-Added Tax.* The sale of goods and other provision of services are subject to the following rates:

| | |
|---|---|
| Standard rate | 19% |
| Reduced rate applicable to goods of basic necessity | 6% |
| Increased rate applicable to luxury goods (including special 8% tax) | 33% |

For certain goods and services, the 19 percent rate is reduced as follows:

| | |
|---|---|
| New buildings and services associated with buildings, shoes, fuel, gas, electricity, art, restaurants | 17% |
| Certain work on dwellings at least 20 years old | 6% |

*Registration Duty.* Purchases and transfers of real estate, including existing buildings (but not new buildings, which are subject to VAT), are subject to registration duty at the rate of 12.5 percent. Formation of companies and increase of capital are subject to 0.5 percent registration duty on subscribed capital or capital increase.

*Real Estate Tax*. The basis for the annual real estate tax is the assumed net annual rental income from land, buildings, and industrial equipment, assessed for the state at a rate of 1.25 percent and increased by a surcharge in favor of the provinces and the communes. These additions vary from year to year, from province to province, and from commune to commune. To some extent, real estate taxes are creditable against corporate income tax; any amount not credited is deductible as business expenses.

Corporations that benefit from exemptions of real estate taxes can deduct from their corporate income tax a deemed real estate tax (precompte immobilier ticif—fictieve onroerende voorheffing), which represents 12.5 percent of the assumed rental income. Any excess is not refundable.

*Taxes on Dividend Distributions*. Dividend distributions to resident and nonresident companies and individuals are subject to a withholding tax of 25 percent, according to the provisions of any relevant double tax treaty (15 percent on dividends to the United States and the United Kingdom).

*Withholding Taxes*. The rate of withholding tax on interest payments to the United States is 15 percent; there is no withholding on royalty payments to the United States or to the United Kingdom. The rate of withholding tax on interest payments to the United Kingdom is either 5 or 15 percent depending on specified conditions.

## Corporate Residence

Corporate residence is determined by the place of incorporation or the place where the main establishment or central management is situated. A company incorporated in a foreign country might be deemed to have its corporate residence in Belgium for tax purposes if it has its main establishment or seat of management in Belgium.

## Group Taxation

There are no provisions for companies in Belgium to file consolidated, group, or joint tax returns of any sort.

## Income Determination

*Stock Valuation*. Stocks are generally stated at whichever is lower, cost or market value. LIFO is accepted for tax purposes. Conformity is required between book and tax accounting.

*Capital Gains*. Gains on capital assets are taxed at ordinary income tax rates. Gains on capital assets held for more than five years are subject to corporate income tax at the reduced rate of 21.5 percent or exempted when reinvested within three years.

*Intercompany Dividends.* Ninety percent of the gross dividend (85 percent for holding companies) is treated as income not subject to corporate income tax, irrespective of the percentage of ownership. However, the investment must have been held during the entire tax year. The 25 percent withholding tax is refunded or deductible from the corporate income tax of the Belgian company that collects the dividends.

When a company receives a dividend on an investment not held for the entire tax year, the gross dividend, increased by a tax credit equal to approximately 50 percent of the underlying corporate income tax, is subject to corporate income tax. The tax credit and the 25 percent withholding tax are deductible from the corporate income tax. Any excess tax credit over this corporate income tax is not refundable.

*Foreign Income.* In principle, resident companies are taxed on their worldwide income. Ninety percent of net foreign dividends received by a Belgian company (85 percent for holding companies) is treated as income not subject to corporate income tax provided that the investment was held for the entire tax year. If not, the net foreign dividend (i.e., after foreign tax) is fully taxable in Belgium, but a deemed foreign tax credit of 15/85 can be offset against the corporate income tax due.

Income from foreign branches is taxable in Belgium at a reduced rate equal to one quarter of the normal tax. For countries with which Belgium has a tax treaty, the foreign branch income of a Belgian company is exempt from Belgian corporate income tax.

Foreign interest and royalties are subject to taxation in Belgium, but relief from double taxation is available by allowing a credit for foreign tax. Undistributed income of foreign or domestic subsidiaries is not subject to any Belgian income tax.

## Deductions

*Depreciation.* Rates are based on the estimated effective life of the assets and must be approved by the Belgian tax authorities. Depreciation is normally double-declining or straight-line over the useful life. For cars, a maximum annual amount for depreciation is fixed. Conformity between books and tax reporting is required. Gains on the sales of fixed assets are taxable as ordinary income except when held for more than five years (reduced basic rate of 21.5 percent or exemption if reinvested within three years). Percentage depletion is available for natural resources.

*Net Operating Losses.* Generally, losses can be carried forward for deduction from profits for five financial periods (limited to sixty months). For carry-over of losses incurred in the first five financial periods (limited to sixty months) of activity by companies formed or branches registered, between January 1, 1967 and June 30, 1970, and after January 1, 1972, and for carry-over of losses arising from depreciation, there is no time limitation. There is no provision for loss carry-back.

*Payments to Foreign Affiliates.* A Belgian corporation can claim a deduction for royalties, management services, and interest charges paid to foreign affiliates, provided such amounts are equal to what it would pay to an unrelated entity. When paid to a person or entity in a tax haven, such charges will be disallowed, except if the Belgian enterprise can furnish proof that they are real and reasonable.

## Mergers and Acquisitions

Mergers and absorptions of companies may be treated for tax purposes as neutral operations not giving rise to liquidation tax. The acquisition of the shares of a Belgian company does not result in any taxation for the buyer.

## Tax Incentives

*Regional Aid.* This aid is available for investments made in development areas that contribute directly to the setting up, development, adaptation or modernization of industrial or handicraft enterprises, public services, service-rendering enterprises dealing with commercial activities, tourism management and organization, engineering or research and development. Regional aid will be granted only for investments that contribute to the creation of new activities and employment.

*Employment Zone.* Employment zones can be established in areas defined by royal decrees where structural unemployment is severe. Qualifying enterprises (essentially those in high-tech activities) will benefit from certain exemptions from corporate income tax, and the non-Belgian executives and researchers of such enterprises will not normally be subject to social security and will not need any work permits or professional cards. Exemption from real estate tax, withholding taxes, and registration tax will also be provided.

*Coordination Center.* A qualifying coordination center is a Belgian company forming part of a group, or a Belgian establishment of a foreign company forming part of a group, and carrying out limited activities. The objective of a qualifying coordination center must be restricted, solely for the benefit of all or part of the group companies, to the development and the centralization of one or several of a number of activities. A coordination center may not hold subsidiaries.

For ten years, qualifying enterprises will be taxed on a small notional income determined on the basis of operational expenses, not including salaries, salary benefits, and interest charges. Exemption from real estate tax, withholding tax on interest and dividends, and registration tax is also provided.

*Investments Deduction.* A 5 percent tax deduction is granted on all qualifying investments and on investments used for research and development of new products and for developing new technologies (made in innovation companies) (20 percent).

*Innovation Companies.* Tax incentives, such as corporate income tax exemption on dividends up to 13 percent of the paid-up capital during ten years, increase of investment deduction, ten-year exemption from real estate tax if the investment is located in the Brussels area, and ten-year exemption from registration tax, are granted to recognized innovation companies dealing exclusively with the production and marketing of innovative high technology processes. A tax deduction of 50 percent of the capital contribution (100 percent for staff), spread over five years, is granted to shareholders.

*Depreciation.* In certain development areas, an annual depreciation equal to twice the normal straight-line depreciation may be authorized for a maximum of three consecutive tax periods. This provision relates to investment in equipment, tools, and industrial buildings that are acquired for the promoted operation. Otherwise, a double depreciation rate on declining balance may be applied.

*Registration Duty*. Capital subscribed for investments contributing to economic expansion, either for the formation or for the increase of the capital of a company operating in a development area, may be exempted from registration duty.

## Tax Administration

*Returns*. For companies with financial years ending December 31, the tax year is the following calendar year. When the financial year ends on another date, the tax year is the calendar year in which the financial year ends.

*Payment of Tax*. Corporate income tax is payable within two months after the issue of the assessment. Interest on arrears is charged if the tax is not paid by the due date.

The surcharge, which for tax year 1990 is 18 percent, can be avoided by making proper tax advance payments.

## DENMARK

### Corporate Income Tax

The state income tax rate for companies is 50 percent of taxable income.

*Branch Income*. Branch profits are subject to the basic state income tax rate of 50 percent. Transfers of branch profits to a foreign head office do not give rise to further taxation in Denmark.

### Other Taxes

*Value-Added Tax*. This is charged at 22 percent of the VAT exclusive price on the supply of goods and services.

*Stamp Taxes*. As of 1988, they are payable on many types of commercial and legal documents, normally at a rate of one percent of value, although the rate on the transfer of land is 1.2 percent.

*Share Transfer Tax*. A transfer tax of one percent on the market value of Danish or foreign shares applies if either the seller or buyer is resident in Denmark. Certain transactions are exempted.

*Capital Investment Tax*. Generally, this is one percent of an increase of share capital.

*Hydrocarbon Tax*. The rate is 70 percent on profits accruing from oil and gas extracted in Denmark and in the Danish territorial sea and continental shelf. Corporate income tax is deductible in computing hydrocarbon tax.

*Turnover Taxes*. These are a 2.5 percent levy on employers based on turnover, less export sales and purchases. Imports are not deductible. For banks and other financial institutions, payment is based on 4.75 percent of total salary costs. The employer tax is deductible for income tax purposes.

*Real Interest Rate Tax*. Insurance companies, pension funds, etc., are subject to a real interest rate tax on certain investment income earned on funds invested since 1983.

*Taxes on Distributions*. Cash dividends to resident and nonresident companies and individuals are subject to a withholding tax of 30 percent. Under the U.K.-Denmark treaty, the rate is nil if the British company has at least a 25 percent holding; otherwise it is 15 or 30 percent. Under the U.S.-Denmark treaty, the rate is five percent if the U.S. company has at least a 95 percent holding; otherwise, it is 15 percent. Stock dividends may be distributed to shareholders free of tax.

*Withholding Taxes.* Royalty payments are subject to a withholding tax rate of 30 percent which can be reduced to nil under the U.K.-Denmark and the U.S.-Denmark treaties. There is no withholding tax on interest payments.

## Corporate Residence

A company is resident in Denmark for tax purposes if it is incorporated in Denmark and registered in the Companies Register as having a Danish place of business.

## Group Taxation

A Danish company having one or more wholly owned subsidiaries, either domestic or foreign, may obtain permission to be taxed with such subsidiary or subsidiaries on a combined-income basis, provided certain conditions are fulfilled.

## Income Determination

*Stock Valuation.* Stocks are generally stated at the lower of cost or market (replacement) value and may be written down by up to 30 percent for tax purposes. A write-down should not be reflected in the official books. LIFO is not permitted for tax purposes.

*Capital Gains.* Capital gains and/or losses are included in ordinary taxable income. A gain on sale of shares kept for more than three years is tax exempt. Special rules apply to investments in tax haven companies.

A gain on the sale of a real property is the difference between the sale proceeds and the acquisition cost, adjusted for changes under a consumer price index. However, the gain is reduced by 20 percent for each year of ownership exceeding three years, so when a property is sold after more than seven years, any gain will be tax free, unless the seller is carrying on a real estate business.

*Intercompany Dividends.* Dividends received from a domestic or foreign company are tax exempt, provided the company has owned at least 25 percent of the shares during the entire year in which the dividend is received. For foreign companies, however, exemption depends on their income being taxed under rules not significantly different from Danish tax rules. Otherwise credit for underlying corporate income tax may be claimed in respect of dividends received from a foreign company in which there is 25 percent or more ownership.

If a dividend from a wholly owned subsidiary which is jointly taxed with its Danish parent is not exempt, it is excluded from joint taxable income to the extent it is covered by the taxable income (computed for Danish tax purposes) of the subsidiary concerned.

*Foreign Income.* A Danish company is taxed on the income of a foreign branch or subsidiary with which it is jointly taxed. The Danish company may claim relief for foreign trading and a tax credit or tax exemption in both cases. The relief for foreign trading is equal to 50 percent of the Danish income tax attributable to the net income (before tax) of the foreign branch or jointly taxed foreign subsidiary.

Foreign dividends received by a Danish company from a subsidiary with which it is not jointly taxed are either exempt as described above or become subject to tax when declared, but a tax credit equal to the lower of the relative tax paid by the parent and the subsidiary is available. Undistributed income of a subsidiary is not taxed in Denmark.

## Deductions

*Depreciation*. Annual depreciation allowances on all fixed assets other than buildings may be claimed under the declining-balance method at various rates up to 30 percent. The depreciation base is the cost of fixed assets, less (1) sales proceeds of disposals, and (2) depreciation allowances previously claimed. For acquisitions after January 1, 1982, the depreciation base is indexed annually in accordance with the cost-of-living index.

Depreciation allowances on buildings (but not land) other than residential property and office buildings not adjoining an industrial building may be claimed on the straight-line method. The maximum rate is six percent per annum for the first ten years and thereafter at a rate up to two percent per annum.

Advance allowances up to 30 percent may be claimed (1) on a contract amounting to at least DKr200,000 for the building of a ship and (2) on the agreed aggregate cost of buildings and/or machinery and equipment ordered in excess of DKr700,000.

An allocation to an investment fund equivalent to 25 percent of adjusted taxable income may be made for tax purposes but will be reduced by any advance depreciation allowances claimed; 50 percent of the amount allocated to an investment fund must be deposited in a blocked bank account until qualifying investments have been made.

*Net Operating Losses*. Tax losses may be carried forward for five years. Loss carry-backs are not permitted. Certain restrictions on the right to carry forward tax losses apply when more than 50 percent of the share capital or 50 percent of the voting rights at the end of the financial year is owned by shareholders different from the shareholders at the beginning of the income year in which the tax loss was incurred. Special rules apply for group companies.

*Payments to Foreign Affiliates*. A Danish company can claim a deduction for royalties and expenditures on specific services paid to foreign affiliates, provided such amounts are equal to what it would pay an unrelated entity. Interest at normal commercial rates paid to foreign affiliates will generally be allowed as a deduction.

*Other Items*. Goodwill cannot be amortized for tax purposes. Losses on the sale of real property are not deductible for tax purposes, unless the seller is carrying on a real estate business. A loss on sale of shares purchased within the last three years can be carried forward for five years, to be deducted only from taxable gains on sale of shares owned for less than three years. A loss on sale of shares owned for more than three years is nondeductible. Formation, merger, reorganization, and liquidation expenses are nondeductible.

## Mergers and Acquisitions

Provided certain conditions are fulfilled, as of 1988, mergers between companies may be carried out without any of the companies and shareholders involved having to pay tax as a result of the merger. There are no specific provisions concerning takeovers.

## Tax Incentives

*Inward Investment.* Certain concessions are granted to companies that establish industrial or other business enterprises in areas that have been designated development areas. These concessions comprise mainly long-term Danish state loans at a low rate of interest and, in certain undeveloped areas, state subventions.

*Other Incentives.* Favorable credit facilities in the form of seven-year loans at a low rate of interest on completed vessels built at Danish shipyards are available from the Danish Ship Credit Fund.

## Tax Administration

*Returns.* The financial year is April 1 to March 31. Companies must file returns for year-ends with each financial year no later than the following June 30. The tax system, in practice, is based on self-assessment. Tax assessments are made by the tax authorities on the basis of the tax return, which may subsequently be audited.

*Payment of Tax.* The total amount falls due for payment on November 1 in the financial year in question. Advance payments are generally not made, except for hydrocarbon tax.

## FRANCE

### Corporate Income Tax

The tax rate is 42 percent on profits distributed to stockholders. A 39 percent rate applies to undistributed profit. No tax is levied on income at the regional or local level.

*Branch Income.* The same tax rate applies. A distribution of branch profits is subject to a 25 percent withholding which is reduced to nil under the U.K.-France treaty and to 5 percent under the U.S.-France treaty.

### Other Taxes

*Value-Added Tax.* The standard rate is 18.6 percent. Other rates of 5.5 percent and 28 percent apply to certain sales and services. Exports and certain specific services invoiced to non-French residents are zero-rated.

*Business Tax.* This local tax is assessed at variable rates on the rental value of fixed business assets and on salaries and wages.

*Taxes on Distributions.* The total corporate tax burden on a subsidiary's profits distributed to the U.S. parent or the distributed income of a U.S. company's French branch is 44.9 percent. If the branch does not distribute some of its profits, the tax rate on these profits is reduced to 42.05 percent.

The distribution of stock dividends is exempt from income tax. The company making the distribution is subject to a three percent registration tax, which may be reduced to zero in special cases.

*Withholding Taxes.* There are no withholding taxes on interest and royalty payments to the United Kingdom. There are no withholding taxes on interest payments to the United States.

*Other Taxes.* There are numerous minor taxes including registration tax, stamp tax, and regional, departmental, and municipal taxes.

### Corporate Residence

A company is resident in France if it has been incorporated in France or if it has its registered seat in France.

### Group Taxation

French companies and domestic subsidiaries (of which they own 95 percent) may elect to file one single tax return, thus allowing offset of losses of one group company against the profits of a related company. The election for this combined reporting must be made for a five-year period. Other group consolidation systems are also available.

### Income Determination

*Stock Valuation.* Stocks must be valued at the lower of cost or market value. Cost must be determined in accordance with the FIFO or average cost methods. The LIFO method is prohibited. A form of stock relief is available in certain circumstances.

*Capital Gains.* Short-term capital gains (on assets held less than two years) are generally taxable at 42 percent, the ordinary tax rate for profit distribution. Long-term capital gains are taxable at the reduced rate of 15 percent. In the case of depreciable assets, the excess of original cost over book value (i.e. recaptured depreciation) is taxed as short-term gain. Long-term capital gains, less the 15 percent tax thereon, must be appropriated to a special reserve; the balance of corporate income tax (27 percent) becomes payable if this reserve is distributed to shareholders but not if it is offset against operating losses or later long-term capital losses, converted into share capital, or distributed on liquidation. Net long-term capital gains realized on the transfer of building sites are subject to capital gains tax at the rate of 25 percent.

*Intercompany Dividends.* French companies holding qualifying shares which represent at least 10 percent of the issued capital of other companies (French or foreign) are entitled to exclude 95 percent of the relevant gross dividends from corporate income tax. In the case of distributions, this system results in an effective tax of 3.15 percent on dividends received from French subsidiaries, which include tax credits (avoir fiscal) of 50 percent on cash dividends and 2.10 percent on dividends (including the applicable withholding tax credit) received from foreign subsidiaries. The effective tax is reduced to 2.92 percent and 1.95 percent if dividends received are not distributed.

*Foreign Income.* Resident companies are taxed on their French source income only, which excludes profits from activities carried out abroad through foreign branches. Undistributed income of foreign subsidiaries is not taxable. However, French companies are required to include in their taxable income profits made by companies established in tax haven countries if more than 25 percent of their share capital is owned.

Double taxation is avoided, as follows:

For dividends, through the 95 percent exclusion for certain inter-company dividends

For other income (interest, royalties, fees), by granting a tax credit equal to foreign withholding tax for income sourced in a tax treaty country and by granting a deduction otherwise

## Deductions

*Depreciation.* In general, the straight-line-over-useful-life method must be used; the basis of depreciation is cost. Assets qualifying include plant and machinery and office and industrial buildings (but not land).

Declining-balance depreciation is allowed for new machinery and equipment and other qualifying assets having a useful life of three years or more. The rates are equal to straight-line rates multiplied by coefficients which vary depending on the useful life of the asset.

Special accelerated rates are applicable inter alia to installations used for scientific and technological research, and industrial and commercial buildings located in certain areas. The depreciation deducted for tax purposes cannot exceed the depreciation booked. Special rules apply to companies in the oil or mining sectors.

*Net Operating Losses.* For tax purposes, net operating losses may be carried forward for five years. That portion of operating losses resulting from depreciation can be carried forward indefinitely, provided the depreciation was properly disclosed. Businesses may also elect a form of carry-back.

*Payments to Foreign Affiliates.* Payments to foreign affiliates are allowed, as long as they meet the arm's-length principle. Some limitations are imposed on the payment of interest to shareholders, as follows:

1. The interest rate paid to any shareholder, whether French or foreign, is limited to the average yield on private bonds during the same fiscal year

2. Any interest paid on the portion of a loan that exceeds 1.5 times the share capital of the paying company is disallowed when paid to a foreign corporate shareholder who has the effective management control of the debtor company

## Mergers and Acquisitions

Special rules apply to facilitate mergers.

## Tax Incentives

*Inward Incentives.* No specific incentive is available to foreign investors in France. However, the government offers a comprehensive program of tax incentives (accelerated depreciation of industrial and commercial buildings, business tax holiday) and development subsidies to encourage investment in specific areas. Tax incentives, including a ten-year corporate income tax holiday, are available in certain depressed areas.

*Investment in Research.* Qualifying research expenses may give rise to a tax credit which may be offset against corporate income tax.

## Tax Administration

*Returns.* Corporate income tax returns must be filed three months after the fiscal year-end, which may be different from the calendar year. The tax due is self-assessed.

*Payment of Tax.* Payment of tax is made in four installments during the fiscal year, totalling 40.5 percent of the taxable income of the preceding year. The balance, if any, is due not later than three and one-half months after the year-end.

## GREECE

### Corporate Income Tax

Greek companies are subject to income tax on undistributed profits at the following rates: 46 percent for commercial companies; 40 percent for manufacturing, handicraft, mining, and quarrying companies; 35 percent for certain manufacturing, mining and quarrying companies; and 40 percent for other companies.

*Branch Income.* Profits of branches of foreign companies are subject to income tax at the rate of 46 percent. No tax is withheld on profit transfers to foreign home offices.

### Other Taxes

*Value-Added Tax.* The standard rate of VAT is 16 percent. There is a reduced rate of six percent on basic necessities (three percent on books, newspapers, and periodicals) and an increased rate of 36 percent on luxury goods and services. Exports of goods and certain services are exempt.

*Contribution Tax on Capital Accumulation.* A one percent tax is assessed on capital accumulation (i.e. formation of business companies and joint ventures, capital increase, etc.) by (1) business companies and joint ventures; (2) cooperatives of all degrees, any other form of company, legal entity, or union of persons or society aiming to make profits; and (3) branches of foreign companies.

*Special Tax on Banking Activities.* A special tax is levied on banking activities at three percent for loan and credit agreements and eight percent for gross bank revenues.

*Taxes on Distributions.* Dividends paid to resident and nonresident companies and individuals are subject to a number of different rates of withholding: for quoted shares, 42 percent (registered) and 45 percent (bearer); and for nonquoted shares, 47 percent (registered) and 50 percent (bearer). Stock dividends are taxed as though they were cash dividends.

*Withholding Taxes.* There is no withholding tax on interest payments to the United Kingdom and the United States. However, royalty payments on film rentals to the United States are subject to withholding tax at a rate of 10 percent.

## Corporate Residence

Company residence is determined primarily by place of incorporation. However, regarding related tax treaty provisions, foreign companies are subject to Greek taxation if such operations as maintaining stocks from which orders are filled or leasing machinery or equipment are carried on in Greece.

## Group Taxation

There are no provisions for companies in Greece to file consolidated, group, or joint tax returns of any sort.

## Income Determination

*Stock Valuation.* Stocks are stated at whichever is lower, cost or market value. LIFO is not permitted.

*Capital Gains.* Capital gains derived from sales of any rights connected with the operations of an enterprise (trademarks, patents), excluding mining rights and realized goodwill and including gains on a business sold as a whole, are subject to income tax at a 30 percent rate. Goodwill realized through mergers of Greek companies is not taxable. Gains on sale of buildings and land are tax exempt. Gains on sale of securities are not taxable if set aside to cover losses from future sales.

*Intercompany Dividends.* Dividends from Greek companies are included in taxable income if earned from quoted or registered shares.

*Foreign Income.* Resident companies are taxed on their worldwide income. Foreign income received by a Greek company is taxed together with other income. Related income tax withheld abroad is a tax credit up to the amount of the applicable Greek income tax.

## Deductions

*Depreciation.* Depreciation at specified fixed rates for most assets and buildings (excluding land) is compulsory. Manufacturing, handicraft, hotel, and mining companies are entitled to increased rates on fixed assets directly employed in production. The increases vary from 20 percent to 150 percent on the rates, depending on the area and number of shifts worked per day, but they are not compulsory. Depreciation booked must equal tax depreciation, and any variance is not considered deductible.

Preoperating expenses, including interest, may be amortized over a maximum period of five years, but once the method is established it is binding. There are no provisions for depletion of mineral resources.

*Net Operating Losses.* These can be carried forward three years (five years for manufacturing, hotel, and mining companies). Carry-backs are not permitted.

*Payments to Foreign Affiliates.* Royalties, interest, and service fees paid to foreign affiliates are deductible expenses.

## Mergers and Acquisitions

As of 1988, there were no provisions relieving tax on the merger or acquisition of companies.

## Tax Incentives

*Inward Investment.* Foreign investments aiming at promotion of national production or otherwise contributing to the economic development of the country may obtain, with government approval, a freezing of income tax rates for a specified period not exceeding ten years.

*Capital Investment.* Manufacturing, handicraft, mining, agricultural, and hotel enterprises investing or relocated in certain areas are entitled to 40 percent, 55 percent, and 70 percent (depending on the area) tax-deferred reserve on the cost of productive fixed assets acquired between June 16, 1982 and December 31, 1992.

*Other Incentives.* Companies who export may deduct from their taxable income the equivalent of 1 percent to 3 percent of total export sales, depending on the type of products exported. Commercial enterprises acting as agents of foreign companies who export Greek products in exchange for foreign products are entitled to reduce commission income by five percent in computing taxable income. Manufacturing companies processing products for export on behalf of foreign companies may also reduce service fees by five percent in computing taxable income.

## Tax Administration

*Returns.* Income tax returns are filed via a special form within four months of the end of the company's financial year, which can be on either June 30 or December 31. Branches and subsidiaries of foreign companies may follow the fiscal year of the parent company. The income tax return constitutes the basis for assessment.

*Payment of Tax.* Income tax based on the tax return is paid in seven equal monthly installments, the first of which should be paid upon filing. If total tax assessed is paid when the first installment is due, a 10 percent discount is granted.

# REPUBLIC OF IRELAND

## Corporation Tax

The rate applicable to all profits is 43 percent. A rate of 10 percent applies on certain manufacturing activities. Closely held companies are liable to a 20 percent surcharge on after-tax nontrading and professional service income not distributed within eighteen months of the end of an accounting period. Branches of foreign companies are liable to corporation tax at the normal rates. No tax is withheld on repatriation of branch profits.

## Other Taxes

*Value-Added Tax.* The standard rate on the supply of goods and services is 25 percent. Certain items, such as exports, are exempted while others, including real property and building services, are subject to a lower rate of 10 percent.

*Local Taxes.* Rates based on notional rental values are imposed on the owner-occupiers of certain land and buildings. They are an allowable deduction for corporation tax purposes.

*Stamp Tax.* As of 1988, this tax is payable on the issue and transfer of shares in a limited company at one percent of value.

*Taxes on Distributions.* An Irish resident company paying a dividend or interest on certain loans must pay advance corporation tax (ACT) equal to 28/72nd of the payment after April 5, 1989. The company's corporation tax liability will be reduced by the amount of ACT paid.

Advance corporation tax is not payable on dividends to 75 percent foreign parent companies located in countries such as the United Kingdom and the United States with which the Republic of Ireland has a tax treaty. Interest paid to a 50 percent foreign parent company is treated as a distribution to which a rate of 35 percent is applied. There are no withholding taxes on dividend payments. Irish companies may, in general, issue stock dividends, but if there is a cash option, the stock dividend is taxed as income.

*Withholding Taxes.* There are no withholding taxes on interest and royalty payments to the United Kingdom. There are no withholding taxes on dividends, patents, or royalties to the United States.

## Corporate Residence

Corporate residence is determined by reference to the location of the central management and control of the company.

## Group Taxation

A company and all its Irish-resident 75 percent subsidiaries may group operating losses with profits of corresponding accounting periods. Assets other than development land may be transferred between members of a group without liability to corporation tax on capital gains.

## Income Determination

*Stock Valuation.* Each item of stock is valued for tax purposes at the lower of either cost or market value. Ascertainment of cost or market value must be consistent and not in conflict with tax law. The base stock and LIFO methods are inappropriate for tax purposes but FIFO is acceptable.

*Capital Gains.* Short-term gains (within one year) are taxed at 60 percent, gains on assets held between one and three years at 50 percent, and gains on assets held between three and six years at 35 percent. In all other cases, gains are taxed at 30 percent. The base cost in computing capital gains is indexed for inflation. There are special provisions dealing with gains from development land.

*Intercompany Dividends.* Dividends from Irish companies are not liable to further tax, other than a surcharge on closely held companies if the dividend is not redistributed. Companies within a 51 percent group can elect not to account for ACT on intercompany dividends.

*Foreign Income.* Where income, whether dividends or branch income, is derived from a foreign country with which the Republic of Ireland has a tax treaty, a credit is usually given for the foreign tax paid against Irish taxes on that income. If there is no tax treaty, the foreign tax is normally deducted from the foreign income. Although no special rules exist to tax the undistributed income of foreign subsidiaries, there are special rules to tax the undistributed capital gains of certain closely controlled nonresident companies.

## Deductions

*Depreciation and Depletion.* Qualifying industrial buildings and new machinery and equipment other than road vehicles are eligible for 100 percent depreciation. Twenty percent of the written-down value of vehicles is allowed annually.

*Net Operating Losses.* Trading losses may be set against any income of a current or immediately preceding accounting period or carried forward indefinitely against profits of the same trade.

*Payments to Foreign Affiliates.* In general, there are no prohibitive rules on payments, other than interest, to foreign affiliates, provided the amounts are reasonable and computed on an arm's length basis.

## Mergers, Amalgamations, and Reorganizations

There are a number of provisions designed to facilitate mergers, amalgamations, and reorganizations. These include a provision that on a transfer of a trade between 75 percent associated companies, losses can be passed to the transferee, and assets can be transferred, without balancing adjustments. Where shares in one company are exchanged for shares in another, it generally does not constitute a disposal for capital gains tax purposes.

## Tax Incentives

*Inward Investment.* The following incentives are available:

1. Profits on the export of goods manufactured in the Republic of Ireland can, subject to certain restrictions, qualify for total relief from corporation tax up

until April 5, 1990 if the trading operations commenced prior to January 1, 1981.

2. Companies that commenced operations within the Shannon Free Airport Zone before January 1, 1981 or commenced after that date with a commitment that the relief would be available can obtain full exemption from corporation tax until 1990 if the income is derived from certain activities, including exporting goods and a wide range of services.

3. Companies carrying on manufacturing operations in the Republic of Ireland are liable to a reduced rate of corporation tax of 10 percent on profits from manufacturing operations arising between January 1, 1981 and December 31, 2000, regardless of whether the goods are exported or not. The reduced rate of corporation tax will apply to certain service operations establishing in Shannon.

4. Companies engaged in the provision of international financial services for nonresidents in the Custom House Dock Site in Dublin can qualify for the 10 percent corporate tax rate up until December 31, 2000.

*Capital Investment.* Nontaxable and nonrepayable capital grants are available for capital expenditure on machinery and equipment and industrial premises. Rates depend on location of new industry.

*Other Incentives.* The incentives below are also available:

1. When certain trade assets liable to capital gains tax are sold and the proceeds reinvested in other specified assets, the tax liability on any gain is deferred.

2. Government and semi-state agencies operate a comprehensive system of cash grants, including assistance for research and development, obtaining export markets, and creation of employment in the service industry sector.

## Tax Administration

*Returns.* A company may make up its accounts to any date it chooses within the calendar year. However, an accounting period for corporation tax may not extend longer than one year. The system is one of information filing, with assessment by the tax authorities.

*Payment of Tax.* An assessment is made for the payment of corporation tax, which is payable in a single installment six months after the end of the accounting period. A company must make an ACT return within six months of the end of the accounting period in which a distribution is made, at which time the ACT due has to be paid.

## ITALY

### Corporate Income Tax

The basic tax rate for companies is 36 percent.

*Branch Income.* Branches of foreign companies are taxed at the same rates as resident companies. There is no withholding tax payable on the transfer of profits to a foreign head office.

## Other Taxes

*Local Income Tax.* This is levied at 16.2 percent on income arising in Italy but not on dividends or income subject to a final withholding tax. Income earned abroad by resident companies is also subject to local income tax, when such income results from business activities that are carried out abroad with a permanent establishment. The tax is deductible in computing corporate income tax.

*Value-Added Tax.* VAT is levied on most goods and services at the standard rate of 19 percent, with other rates applying as follows:

| | |
|---|---|
| Export sales | Exempt |
| Food | 4% or 9% |
| Mass consumption goods, utilities | 9% |
| Luxury goods | 38% |

*Tax on Property Appreciation.* This tax is imposed on the transferor whenever land or real estate is transferred. A property company must pay tax on the capital appreciation on its land and buildings. For nonproperty companies, this applies only to land and buildings not used directly for their own commercial or industrial activity. The tax rate is determined by the local authorities, but cannot exceed 30 percent of the appreciation. The tax is deductible from profits for corporate income tax purposes.

*Registration Duties.* On contributions in cash to a company in exchange for stock or shares, a registration tax of one percent is due.

*Taxes on Distributions.* If a company distributes to its shareholders more than 64 percent of the income declared for the purposes of corporate income tax, an additional corporate income tax equal to 56.25 percent of the excess is imposed. This additional tax also applies to distributions from other reserves created tax free after November 30, 1983 which are not otherwise subject to corporate income tax on distribution. (For example, a monetary revaluation reserve is normally created tax free, but on distribution, corporate income tax is imposed.) If sums are distributed from other reserves that were already in existence on December 1, 1983, an additional tax of 15 percent of the reserves distributed is due even if the reserves were created out of taxed profits.

Dividends to nontreaty nonresidents are subject to a withholding tax of 32.4 percent. Under the U.K.-Italy treaty this is reduced to 15 percent (or 5 percent if the U.K. company holds at least 51 percent of the voting rights). Under the U.S.-Italy treaty, if the recipient of a dividend is a U.S. corporation that controls more than 50 percent of the voting power of the Italian company declaring the dividend and subject to certain other conditions, the rate of withholding is reduced to 5 percent. If the U.S. corporation controls more than 10 percent, the withholding is reduced to 10 percent. In all other cases, the withholding tax is 15 percent.

In the case of a bonus issue, the new shares do not constitute taxable income and do not give rise to the application of withholding tax on dividends. However, if in the following five years a reimbursement of capital is made to the shareholders, this will be considered as a distribution of profits up to the amount of the reserves capitalized.

*Withholding Taxes.* Interest payments to the United Kingdom are subject to a withholding tax of 12.5 percent and 15 percent. Withholding cannot exceed 5 percent if the British company holds at least 51 percent of the entire voting rights. There is no withholding tax on royalty payments to the United Kingdom. The withholding is 5 percent when the royalty derives from artistic, scientific or literary work; 8 percent when the royalty derives from movies or films; and 10 percent in all other cases.

## Corporate Residence

Companies having their legal or administrative headquarters or their principal business purpose in Italy are taxable on their worldwide income. Other companies are subject to Italian income tax only on income arising in Italy.

## Group Taxation

Consolidated business taxation is not permitted for income tax purposes.

## Income Determination

*Stock Valuation.* Basically a LIFO method is used. Companies may elect to use another acceptable method as long as the resulting cost is higher than the cost arrived at by using the LIFO method.

*Capital Gains.* Capital gains are taxed as part of corporate income and are normally taxable when realized or reported in the books of the company. Tax on the gain realized on the sale of fixed assets may be declared as taxable income in equal instalments over a period not exceeding five years.

*Local Dividend Credit.* Italian companies and permanent establishments in Italy of foreign companies receiving dividends from companies having their legal or administrative seat or main business purpose within Italy are entitled to a tax credit equal to 56.25 percent of the amount of the dividend. This credit should be included in the taxable income and credited against the ultimate tax due.

*Intercompany Dividends (Foreign Affiliates).* Dividends received by Italian companies from foreign-associated companies (those owned over 10 percent or 5 percent if quoted on a stock exchange) form a part of the taxable income only to the extent of 40 percent of the income. Such dividends as reduced are not eligible for the local dividend credit and are subject to corporate but not local income tax.

*Intercompany Dividends (Italian Affiliates).* No special provisions exist for dividends received by an Italian company from Italian-associated companies. Such dividends are subject to corporate income tax but not to local income tax, and they benefit from the local dividend credit.

*Foreign Income.* An Italian resident company is taxable on all income whether produced in Italy or abroad. There are no special rules for the taxation of the unremitted income of a subsidiary. Foreign tax credits are granted in the year in which the foreign tax on such income is paid.

## Deductions

*Depreciation and Depletion.* Depreciation is deductible on a straight-line basis starting from the first tax period in which the asset concerned was used. In the first period the assets must be depreciated at a rate that does not exceed one half of normal rates.

Depreciation rates are determined in accordance with a ministerial decree. No depreciation allowance is granted on land. The rates for intangible assets should conform to the period of utilization as laid down by the relevant contract; in their absence, the rate used cannot exceed 20 percent per annum. Goodwill (if it is recorded in the books) can be depreciated at a maximum rate of 20 percent per annum.

*Net Operating Losses.* Loss carry-over for five years is applicable for corporate income tax but not for local income tax. Loss carry back is not permitted.

*Payments to Foreign Affiliates.* Transactions with foreign affiliated companies are closely scrutinized in order to determine whether or not the arm's length concept has been adhered to and whether the transfer price may be considered normal.

## Mergers and Acquisitions

In the case of a merger between two or more companies, no profit realization or profit distribution is deemed to arise. However, there is no special tax treatment for takeovers.

## Tax Incentives

Certain nontax incentives apply to enterprises in southern Italy and certain depressed mountain regions in central and northern Italy. The benefits are available for all qualifying investors, foreign or Italian. In the Trieste area there is an exemption from the local income tax of 16.2 percent for a period of ten years which may not be granted later than December 31, 1995 and also a reduction from basic corporate income tax from 36 percent to 18 percent for ten years.

Tax incentives in southern Italy include (1) for manufacturing companies established between March 29, 1986 and December 31, 1993, an exemption from corporate income tax (usually 36 percent) for ten years from the year or incorporation and (2) for other manufacturing companies, an exemption from local income tax (usually 16.2 percent) for ten years from the first year in which the company makes a profit. This incentive applies to factories built prior to December 31, 1993.

## Tax Administration

*Returns.* Tax returns, which in all cases are self-assessments, must be accompanied by financial statements which have been prepared as of the close of the financial year and which have been approved by shareholders. Corporate tax returns must be submitted within one month of the date of approval of the financial statements, while a branch's tax return must be submitted within four months of the close of its financial year.

*Payment of Tax.* A payment of 98 percent of the taxes paid in the prior year must be made in the 11th month of the company's financial year. The balance is due when the annual tax return is submitted.

## LUXEMBOURG

### Corporate Income Tax

Tax is payable at a rate of 34 percent on profits in excess of Luxfr1,312,000. A lower average rate is charged on profits below this amount, the average rate being a combination of a low basis rate and a high marginal rate. Profits below Luxfr400,0001 are taxed at a flat rate of 20 percent. Profits between Luxfr600,001 and Luxfr1,000,000 are taxed at a flat rate of 30 percent with a marginal rate of 46.8 percent applying between Luxfr1,000,001 and Luxfr1,312,000, at which point the average rate is 36 percent.

Against the tax so determined, the following are credited: the tax withheld from income from Luxembourg capital, tax withheld from income from capital arising abroad, and temporary tax assistance for certain investments. In addition to the above tax, there is an unemployment fund contribution of 2 percent of the tax.

*Branch Income.* Branches are taxed at the rate of 34 percent. If the Luxembourg and the foreign income of the company as a whole is lower than Luxfr1,312,000, the taxpayer can request that the tax due be determined at the rate applicable under the above scale to the whole of the taxpayer's income. The two percent unemployment supplement also applies.

### Other Taxes

*Value-Added Tax.* VAT is levied on sales of goods and services rendered in Luxembourg at the standard rate of 12 percent or at 6 percent or 3 percent on certain transactions. Banking operations are generally exempted.

An exemption from corporate income tax and municipal trade tax on income is granted on 25 percent of the profit arising from new businesses and new business-related service companies or from the introduction of new manufacturers and new high technology services, up to a variable limit during a period of eight years. Holding companies and investment funds are subject only to the annual tax on share capital and to the capital investment tax.

Several other incentives are available, which are not given in the form of tax incentives but rather as financial incentives, such as:

Loans at reduced interest rates

Cash grants for capital and high technology investments, reorganizations of economically justified sectors, research and development of new products or services or new fabrication or commercialization procedures, organization or management or promotion studies that have had a positive impact, and technical transfers related to the use of patents, licenses, and know-how. The lessee benefits from the cash grant if the investments are financed by leasing

Government guarantees on loans

Government and communal intervention in the acquisition or renting on favorable conditions of industrial sites and buildings

Regional incentives with ceilings varying between 17.5 percent and 25 percent

The Societe Nationale de Credit et d'Investiessement promotes the creation, expansion, reorientation, and rationalization of industrial and service organizations

The Comite pour la Promotion des Exportations Luxembourgeoises grants interest rebates on loans financing the export of goods

The Ducroire Office gives guarantees against export risks, especially those relating to credit

## Tax Administration

*Returns.* Companies must file their returns for all taxes at the latest by May 31 of each year following the calendar year during which the income was earned. Assessments are issued after the end of the tax year and can normally be finalized within five years.

*Payment of Tax.* Quarterly tax advances have to be paid which are fixed by the tax authorities on the basis of the tax assessed for the last preceding year or the estimated current year tax if the information provided justifies this.

*Tax on Net Worth.* Resident companies and branches of foreign companies are subject to a 0.5 percent tax on the "unitary value" (see below) of the working capital invested in commercial or industrial enterprises.

*Annual Tax on Share Capital.* Most resident companies and branches of foreign companies are subject to a tax on the value of share capital at the rate of 0.36 percent (0.18 percent for an Sarl) with a minimum of Luxfr500. For a holding company, the rate is 0.2 percent with a minimum of Luxfr2 million.

*Communes.* Two taxes are levied by communes. Municipal business tax is levied at 0.2 percent per annum of the net worth of the business. It is applicable to all business establishments situated in Luxembourg. The taxes are multiplied by a coefficient that ranges from 180 percent to 300 percent according to the commune where the business is located. The taxes thus determined are deductible as an expense for computing income subject to corporate income tax.

The second tax is ground tax, the basis of which is the "unitary value" of real estate, which represents 5 percent to 10 percent of market value. The rate varies between communes and different types of property. The basic rate changes from 0.7 percent to 1 percent of the unitary value according to the category of property and is multiplied by a coefficient. The tax is deductible for income tax purposes.

*Capital Investment Tax.* This tax is 1 percent on capital introduced into a business by its shareholders. The tax is deductible for income tax purposes.

*General Registration Taxes.* These are generally 6 percent on the market value of real estate purchased or transferred (9 percent in the commune of Luxembourg City); 1 percent on mortgages on real estate; and 0.6 percent on the total lease payments for registered lease contracts. The taxes are deductible for income tax purposes.

*Taxes on Distributions.* Dividends are subject to a 15 percent withholding tax subject to the provisions of a double tax treaty. Under the U.K.-Luxembourg treaty the rate is reduced to 5 percent where the British company has a 25 percent holding. Under the U.S.-Luxembourg treaty, the rate for portfolio dividends is 7.5 percent if the beneficiary has no permanent establishment in Luxembourg. The rate is reduced to 5 percent where the recipient U.S. company has held during the entire year 50 percent of the Luxembourg shares and where a maximum of 25 percent of the gross income of the Luxembourg company originates from interest and dividends from nongroup companies.

*Withholding Taxes.* There is no withholding tax on interest payments; royalty payments are subject to a 5 percent withholding tax when paid to United Kingdom recipients. There is no withholding tax on royalties to U.S. entities. The withholding rate on portfolio dividends to U.S. recipients is 7.5 percent; on dividends to U.S. companies with substantial holdings, 5 percent.

## Corporate Residence

A company is considered resident in Luxembourg if either its registered office or its principal establishment is located in Luxembourg. The registered office of a company is the place so designated in the company's statutes, and the principal establishment is the place from which a company's activities are directed. A foreign company is only subject to Luxembourg taxation if it has a permanent establishment in Luxembourg.

## Group Taxation

Consolidated tax returns may be submitted for a minimum period of five years by resident companies, together with their resident corporate subsidiaries, as long as at least 99 percent of the subsidiary's capital is directly or indirectly held by the parent corporation, an economic and organizational integration exists, and the fiscal year-ends are coterminous.

Tax losses that occurred before the consolidation period have to be set off against profits of the company that incurred the loss. Losses arising during the consolidation period are attributed to the parent company.

## Income Determination

*Stock Valuation.* Stocks are generally valued at the lower of actual cost or market value. In general, both the FIFO and LIFO methods of valuation are unacceptable for income tax purposes, unless it is shown that the method accords with the facts.

*Capital Gains.* Capital gains are generally taxed as ordinary income. It is possible to postpone the taxation on gains on certain fixed assets where the gain is offset against the cost of certain replacement items.

*Intercompany Dividends.* Income from a holding of at least 10 percent in the capital of another company (or a minimum investment of Luxfr50 million) is exempt from tax if the other company is resident or nonresident, but subject to a tax corresponding to Luxembourg corporate income tax. The holding must have been held for at least twelve months.

*Foreign Income.* A Luxembourg company is liable to corporate income tax on its worldwide income whether derived from Luxembourg or foreign sources. Dividends from foreign subsidiaries are taxed when received, except where relief is given as mentioned above.

## Deductions

*Depreciation.* Rates must be approved by the tax authorities. The depreciation must be calculated on the total acquisition cost, bearing in mind the normal life of the asset and the estimated residual value.

Depreciation is normally calculated on the straight-line method. However, the declining-balance method is permitted for fixed assets other than buildings and intangible assets. The depreciation rate may not, however, exceed three times the rate applicable according to the straight-line method, or 30 percent (in the case of assets used exclusively for scientific and technical research, four times and 40 percent). Fixed assets of a value not in excess of Luxfr25,000 or a life not in excess of one year can be totally depreciated in the year of acquisition. Special depreciation of 50 percent of the cost of movable assets and 30 percent of the cost of immovable assets that protect the national environment or save energy in Luxembourg is granted under certain conditions.

*Net Operating Losses.* Losses for tax purposes may be carried forward and offset against taxable income of the following five years. No carry-back of losses is permitted.

*Payments to Foreign Affiliates.* Royalties, management services, and interest charges paid to foreign affiliates are deductible items, provided such amounts are equal to what the company would pay an unrelated entity for comparable services.

## Mergers, Amalgamations, and Reorganizations

Mergers of Luxembourg companies effected by share exchange do not give rise to taxation of the profits realized. The transaction is considered neutral, the taxation being postponed to a future date. Similar arrangements can be applied to the splitting of companies.

A taxable profit is deemed to arise if the registered office or the principal establishment of a resident company is transferred abroad. The same applies if the Luxembourg branch of a nonresident ceases or is transferred abroad or to a third party.

## Tax Incentives

*Inward Investment and Capital Investment.* A variety of incentives are available.

An investment tax credit of 12 percent is allowed in respect of additional investments in fixed assets, other than land and buildings. The additional investment represents the difference between the balance sheet value of the assets set out in the application and their reference value. The reference value, which must be at least Luxfr75,000, represents the arithmetic average of the respective book values at the end of the preceding five financial years. The book value of the new investments forms the ceiling.

Another credit is allowed in respect of new investment in tangible depreciable assets (other than land, buildings, and motor vehicles) with a depreciable life in excess of four years, as follows:

| | |
|---|---|
| First Luxfr6 million | 6% |
| On excess | 2% |

These credits are deducted from corporate income tax payable and can be carried forward to the four following tax years.

## THE NETHERLANDS

### Corporate Income Tax

As of 1989, corporate tax is assessed at 40 percent on income up to Fl.250,000 and 35 percent of any excess. (Previously a flat rate of 42 percent applied.)

*Branch Income.* Rates on branch profits are the same. No tax is withheld on transfers of profits to the head office.

### Other Taxes

*Value Added Tax.* VAT is payable on the supplies of goods and services rendered in the Netherlands and on the importation of goods at the rate of 18.5 percent, 6 percent on certain prime necessities, and zero percent on exports, imports stored in bonded warehouses, and certain other services. Rents, banking, and insurance transactions are exempt.

*Transfer Tax on Immovable Property.* Acquisition of immovable property in the Netherlands is subject to 6 percent transfer tax on market value; some exemptions are available.

*Capital Tax.* This tax is payable on issued share capital at one percent of the par value of shares or the value of the consideration paid for shares, whichever is the higher.

*Taxes on Distributions.* Dividends are subject to a 25 percent withholding tax, but under the U.S.-Netherlands treaty the rate is reduced to 15 percent, or 5 percent if a U.S. company owns at least 25 percent of the share capital.

*Oil Taxes.* As of 1988, for the Dutch sector of the continental shelf, production profit tax (PPT) is levied on profits from the exploration and production of oil and natural gas. The rate is 70 percent or 50 percent depending on the form of license. Corporate income tax paid is credited against PPT, and the PPT is a deductible item in calculating the corporate tax liability.

*Withholding Taxes.* There are no withholding taxes on interest or royalty payments.

## Corporate Residence

Corporate residence is determined by the circumstances. Management and control are important factors in this respect, but companies incorporated in the Netherlands are always deemed to be tax resident.

*Group Taxation.* A resident company and its wholly owned resident subsidiaries may under certain conditions file a tax return as one entity.

## Income Determination

*Stock Valuation.* In general, stocks are stated at the lower of cost or market value. Cost may be determined on the basis of FIFO, LIFO, base stock, or average cost. The LIFO system can be used for book and tax purposes, but there is no requirement to have conformity between book and tax reporting.

*Capital Gains.* Capital gains are taxed as ordinary income. However, gains realized on disposal of a shareholding qualifying for the "participation exemption" (a holding of 5 percent or more) are tax exempt. Tax may be deferred by transferring the profit on disposal of tangible fixed assets to a special reserve which must then be applied against the cost of replacement assets. Except in special circumstances, the reserve cannot be maintained for more than four subsequent years. Capital losses are deductible unless they relate to shares qualifying for the participation exemption.

*Intercompany Dividends.* Subject to fulfillment of the conditions of the "participation exemption," a Dutch company or branch of a foreign enterprise is exempt from Dutch tax on all "benefits" connected with a qualifying shareholding (5 percent or more), including cash dividends, dividends in kind, bonus shares, and hidden profit distributions. To qualify for the participation exemption, the holding must be held for the whole of the tax year. In addition, if the participation is in a foreign company, the holding must not be a portfolio investment and the foreign company must be subject to a national profits tax.

*Foreign Income.* A Dutch resident company is subject to corporate tax on its total foreign and domestic income. Double taxation of certain foreign source income, including foreign branch income, is relieved by proportionally reducing Dutch tax by the ratio of foreign income (subject to a foreign income tax) to total income.

Double taxation of foreign dividends, interest, and royalties is relieved by tax credit under Dutch tax treaties or, if no treaty applies, by deduction in computing net taxable income. However, dividends from foreign investments qualifying for the participation exemption are exempt from tax.

## Deductions

*Depreciation and Depletion.* Depreciation may be computed on a straight-line or declining-balance method, or in accordance with any other sound commercial basis. Depreciation is applied from the date the asset comes into use. Specific depreciation rates are not prescribed by law.

The sale of depreciated property triggers tax on the difference between the sale price and the depreciated book value unless a replacement reserve is set up. A depletion allowance for natural resources may be granted for tax purposes where it is in accordance with sound commercial practice and appropriate for accounting purposes.

*Net Operating Losses.* Losses can be carried forward for eight years. Losses incurred during the first six years of the existence of a company or branch may be carried forward indefinitely. There is also a three-year carry-back facility.

*Payments to Foreign Affiliates.* A Dutch company can claim a deduction for royalties, management services, and interest charges paid to foreign affiliates, provided such amounts are equal to what it would pay an unrelated entity.

*Other Significant Items.* The cash value of future pension premiums related to employees' past service may be actuarially computed and deducted from taxable profits. Interest on borrowings to acquire participations in foreign companies qualifying for the participation exemption is not deductible.

### Mergers and Acquisitions

As of 1988, companies involved in mergers and reorganizations may qualify for privileged tax treatment. In particular, gains that arise may be exempt from tax.

### Tax Incentives

*Inward Investment and Capital Investment.* The principal investment incentive (the WIR) has largely been withdrawn but there remains a wide range of financial incentives for investment projects in certain growth areas.

### Tax Administration

*Returns.* Tax returns are filed on either a calendar-year or a financial-year basis. On the basis of the return, the authorities generally make a provisional assessment prior to issuing final assessment after an audit of the return.

*Payment of Tax.* The corporate tax assessed must be paid within one month of the date of the final assessment. In addition, installments are paid based on the prior year's taxable income.

## PORTUGAL

### Corporate Income Tax

Corporate tax is charged at the rate of 36.5 percent on taxable business income. The rate is increased by a municipal surcharge which varies from 10 percent to 40.15 percent depending on the municipality. The surcharge is deductible in the year of payment when calculating industrial tax.

*Agricultural Tax.* This tax is applicable to profits derived from agricultural production (crops and livestock) and afforestations at the rate of 10 percent.

*Real Estate Tax.* The tax is assessed at 1.1 to 1.3 percent (urban real estate) or at 0.8 percent (rural real estate) on notional income (as determined by local district land authorities) or actual income less allowable percentages for maintenance and administration. The urban tax does not apply to property directly used for business activities by its owner.

*Branch Income.* Branch profits are taxed on the same basis as corporate profits. No tax is withheld on transfers of profits to head office.

## Other Taxes

*Value-Added Tax.* This is charged at a normal rate of 17 percent, a reduced rate of 8 percent, and higher rate of 30 percent. Food, books, and pharmaceutical products are generally exempt, and exports of goods and certain services are not subject to the tax.

*Taxes on Distributions.* Dividends are subject to a withholding tax of 15 percent, but under the U.K.-Portugal treaty the rate is reduced to 10 percent where the U.K. company has a 25 percent shareholding. There is no treaty with the United States.

*Withholding Taxes.* Dividends, interest, and royalties from a Portuguese source (and from some foreign sources) are subject to the tax on income from moveable capital, which is normally withheld at source. Interest payments to the United Kingdom are subject to a 10 percent withholding and royalty payments to a 5 percent withholding. Withholding taxes affecting U.S. entities are: dividend withholding rates, 16 to 25 percent; interest withholding rates, 16 to 25 percent; royalties withholding rates, 15 and 16 percent; and withholding rate on income on real estate paid by a business entity required to have proper books of account, 16 percent.

## Corporate Residence

Corporate residence is defined as the place of head office (i.e., central management), but a company with its head office abroad is considered resident if effective management is exercised in Portugal.

## Group Taxation

Consolidation of accounts and taxation on a group basis may be authorized for local companies with a head office and effective management in Portugal provided one of them (directly or indirectly) holds 90 percent of the capital of the others. Previous tax losses can only be carried forward against the particular company's taxable income. Dividends, interest, royalties, and capital gains within the group are tax exempt.

## Income Determination

*Stock Valuation.* Stocks are stated at cost. A provision of up to 10 percent of year-end stocks is allowed to reduce cost to estimated net realization. The FIFO and average cost methods of valuation are accepted.

*Capital Gains.* Capital gains less losses are taxed as part of normal income with exemption to the extent that the taxpayer undertakes to reinvest the sale proceeds in tangible fixed assets within the second tax year following that of the sale. Net book values are adjusted by a special price index for the purpose of defining the taxable gain or loss if the assets have been held for more than two years.

*Intercompany Dividends.* In the case of residents of the country, ninety-five percent of the gross dividend is deducted. Tax withheld constitutes a tax credit if the shares represent more than 25 percent of total capital and if they have been held for more than two years or with an undertaking to hold them for this period if the company was formed later. This also applies to regional development corporations and private development corporations regardless of the proportion of capital or the period held.

*Foreign Income.* A Portuguese company is taxed on foreign income as earned and when earned in the case of a branch operation. In other cases, tax is assessed on the basis of income received. Double taxation is avoided by means of giving credit for foreign taxes.

*Other Significant Items.* Provisions other than up to 10 percent of cost of year-end stock and up to 5 percent (8 percent for retail installment and motor vehicle sales) of total receivables are not deductible.

## Deductions

*Depreciation and Depletion.* Depreciation which is available for most tangible fixed assets (but not land) must be computed by using the straight-line or the declining-balance method. Acceptable rates are normally those used for accounting purposes by business and industry but can be reduced by 50 percent in any one year on election. Sixty percent of additional depreciation resulting from a revaluation of fixed assets, as permitted from time to time, is allowed for tax. Some intangible assets (e.g. patents but not goodwill) are also depreciable. Depreciation of yachts and motor vehicles that are not essential for business activity and depreciation on the excess over Escl.4 million on all other passenger vehicles are not allowed for tax purposes.

*Net Operating Losses.* Losses can be carried forward for five years. There are no provisions for loss carry-back.

*Payments to Foreign Affiliates.* A Portuguese company is allowed to deduct royalties and interest paid to foreign affiliates, provided the amounts do not exceed normal rates. Service fees paid are allowed if there is adequate proof that the service was received.

## Mergers and Acquisitions

There is no general regime of reliefs available on reorganizations. However in certain circumstances where it can be shown that a reorganization will benefit the economy as a whole without impeding free competition, there may be exemptions from tax for gains resulting from the merger.

## Tax Incentives

*Inward Investments and Capital Investment.* As part of the tax reform of 1989, these incentives were expected to be revised. As of 1988, profits appropriated to reserves for the purchase of fixed assets are allowed as a charge against future income, provided they are used within three years to acquire plant or machinery. This deduction may be doubled if the investment meets certain criteria for the creation of jobs and for the improvement of the foreign currency balance of payments. Additionally, a new investment tax credit has been established that allows a deduction from corporation tax payable for investment in new plant and machinery of 6 percent of investments concluded in 1988, and 4 percent of any concluded in 1989 and subsequent years.

These two tax credits are cumulative and are restricted to tangible assets effectively employed in the business, excluding land, buildings (other than factories), light vehicles, furniture, equipment used for social purposes, and other assets not directly and necessarily associated with the company's productive capacity. Hotels and the tourist industry are generally allowed income tax exemption for a period of seven years with a 50 percent reduction for a further equal period.

*Other Incentives.* A regional tax incentive scheme is available, relating to (1) the establishment of new production units, the expansion of existing units and the relocation of productive units, provided they fall within the strategy for regional development; (2) research, development, and demonstration; and (3) the modernization of and innovation in production.

## Tax Administration

*Returns.* The tax year is the calendar year. For industrial tax purposes, the annual declaration is submitted in April.

*Payment of Tax.* Tax is paid in four installments. The first three each correspond to 25 percent of the previous year's corporate tax assessment and are paid in June, September, and December of the year in which taxable income arises. The fourth installment is paid or received through self-assessment upon filing the annual tax return in April of the following year.

If the tax year ends on a date other than December 31, interim payments take place on the sixth, ninth, and twelfth month of the tax year. Filing of the annual tax return together with the final payment is in the fourth month following the close of the tax year.

## SPAIN

### Corporate Income Tax

The standard rate of tax on corporate income is 35 percent. Some companies are not directly subject to corporate tax but may elect to be assessed through their shareholders. This imputation system is obligatory in certain cases; the most important examples are unquoted portfolio investment companies, portfolio investment companies where more than half of the assets are invested in securities, and companies that merely possess assets (i.e. more than half of such assets are not used for business activities). However, the imputation system only applies when more than 50 percent of the capital belongs to the same family unit or to ten shareholders or less.

*Branch Income.* Branch income is taxed at the standard corporate income tax rate of 35 percent. Management and general administrative expenses incurred by the foreign head office are deductible to the extent that they are allocable to the branch but are subject to withholding tax of 14 percent.

## Other Taxes

*Value-Added Tax.* VAT is payable on supplies of goods and services in Spain and on the import of goods. There are three rates: (1) an "ordinary" rate of 12 percent; (2) a "reduced" rate of 6 percent, applied to basic necessities (food, agricultural products, books, medicine, etc.); and (3) an "increased" rate of 33 percent, applied to luxury goods and services (vehicles, with certain exceptions, recreational boats and airplanes, jewelry, luxury furs, etc.).

*Transfer Taxes.* Transfer tax is levied normally at a rate of 1 percent of value on issues of shares, capital reductions, and such.

*Other Taxes.* There are many other taxes such as excise, stamp, Chamber of Commerce, license to open premises, and production taxes.

*Taxes on Distributions.* Dividends are subject to a withholding tax of 20 percent subject to the provisions of a double tax treaty. Under the U.K.-Spain treaty, the rate is 15 percent reduced to 10 percent if the recipient is a company holding at least 10 percent of the paying company's capital. No treaty exists with the United States.

*Withholding Taxes.* Interest payments to the United Kingdom are subject to a 12 percent withholding, and royalty payments to the United Kingdom are subject to a 10 percent withholding. Interest and royalty payments to the United States and other nontreaty countries are subject to a rate of 20 percent.

## Corporate Residence

Companies incorporated in Spain or having their domicile or place of management in Spanish territory are resident and therefore subject to corporate income tax on their worldwide income.

## Group Taxation

Approval must be obtained to consolidate for tax purposes; authorization is at the discretion of tax authorities. The main requirement is that the consolidating company must own directly or indirectly more than 90 percent of dependent companies. Losses prior to consolidation can only be offset against profits earned by the same company, and consolidated losses cannot be carried forward into the subsidiary when it is no longer consolidated.

## Income Determination

*Stock Valuation.* Stock is valued at the lower of cost or market value. The average and FIFO methods are accepted, but replacement, LIFO, or base stock are not.

*Capital Gains.* Capital gains are taxable when realized and are treated as normal income subject to the standard corporate income tax rate of 35 percent.

*Intercompany Dividends.* All dividends must be included gross in the recipient company's taxable income. The withholding rate of 20 percent is available as a tax credit. A further tax credit is available equal to 50 percent of the amount that results from applying the effective rate of corporate tax paid on net taxable income to such dividends. The credit may be increased to 100 percent of this amount if the direct or indirect holding exceeds 25 percent and in certain other circumstances.

*Foreign Income.* When specific tax treaties do not give credit, the taxpayer may claim a credit up to the amount of Spanish tax on any item of income.

*Other Significant Items.* The following other items are excluded from taxable income: (1) capital contributions, share premiums, and contributions by shareholders or participants within the financial year, for the purpose of reinstating losses; (2) capital gains arising on the sale of certain fixed assets when the proceeds are reinvested in similar assets and used for the same purpose; and (3) the writing up of assets according to revaluation laws.

## Deductions

*Depreciation and Depletion.* All fixed assets, except land, are depreciable for tax purposes. There are guideline rates by both industry sector and asset type, expressing a maximum per annum rate and a maximum number of years. The straight-line method over the useful life is normally used and applied on the cost of the asset or the written-up value.

New qualifying assets that have an effective life of longer than three years may be depreciated according to the declining-balance method. Mining and hydrocarbon entities have a special tax depreciation regime. Also special depreciation plans can be approved when assets are subject to wear and tear at a higher rate than normal.

Recapture of depreciation on disposal of assets is not applicable in Spain; capital gains are regarded as ordinary income and taxed at the standard corporate income tax rate.

*Net Operating Losses.* Tax losses may be carried forward to the following five financial periods, but they cannot be carried back.

*Payments to Foreign Affiliates.* To be deductible for tax purposes, charges for royalties, interest, service fees, and management back-up services must be supported by a contract. If remittable overseas, the contracts require prior verification. Management back-up services paid to a parent company are subject to withholding tax of 14 percent.

## Mergers and Acquisitions

Tax benefits are available to encourage companies to form mergers that, without jeopardizing free competition, improve their productive or organizational structure in the interests of the national economy.

## Tax Incentives

*Inward Investment.* There are no tax incentives specifically for the foreign investor. Incentives may be granted to Spanish- or foreign-owned corporations alike.

*Capital Investment.* There is a credit of 5 percent on new fixed assets (excluding land). If new products or industrial processes are being formulated through research and development, the tax credit is 15 percent on intangible expenditures and 30 percent on new fixed assets.

*Employment.* Incentives involving employment include a tax credit of up to Pta500,000 for each man-year of increase in the annual average of personnel; incentives to stimulate the employment of young persons; a reduction of 50 percent in the employer's social security contribution for personnel who are over 45 when hired; a subsidy of up to Pta400,000 to the employer for each officially registered unemployed person hired.

## Tax Administration

*Returns.* The system is one of "self-assessment," with audit by the tax authority. The tax year is the calendar year; however, businesses file their tax returns on the basis of their accounting year.

*Payment of Tax.* A payment on account of the current year's tax is required to be made by October 31 of each year; the amount of the payment is the equivalent of 30 percent of the previous year's tax charge. The balance of the tax due is payable at the time of filing the annual tax return.

# WEST GERMANY

## Corporate Income Tax

Corporation profits tax rates are 36 percent for profits distributed to shareholders and 50 percent for undistributed profits. Higher West Berlin rates apply to dividends received from a company resident in Germany. For the purposes of allocating income after tax to the various categories of retained earnings, income taxed at 38.7 percent is deemed to have been taxed at 50 percent, permitting a higher return to be paid to shareholders entitled to the imputation tax credit. The tax rate of 27.9 percent applies if all of the income is distributed. However, the lowest tax rate that can be achieved is 24.75 percent, and this is possible if 11.3 percent of the taxable income is retained by the company.

*Municipal Trade Income Tax.* The effective rate varies from 11.1 percent to 20 percent according to the municipality (9.1 percent in West Berlin, for example). This is deductible as an expense for corporation profits tax.

*Branch Income.* Both corporation profits tax and municipal trade income tax are imposed on the taxable income of a foreign entity's German branch. While the municipal trade tax rates are the same as for resident Germany companies, corporation profits tax is levied at 50 percent with no reduction for distributions. Transfers of branch profits to its foreign head office do not give rise to further taxation in West Germany.

## Other Taxes

*Net Assets Tax.* This tax is six-tenths of one percent of 75 percent of taxable business assets over DM125,000 and is not deductible as an expense for corporation profits tax purposes.

*Capital Element of the Municipal Trade Tax.* Approximately 0.5 percent to 1.0 percent on capital is computed for this tax, which is deductible as an expense for corporation profits tax.

*Capital Transactions Tax.* This tax is 1 percent on capital introduced into a business by its shareholders and is deductible as an expense for corporation profits tax purposes.

*Value-Added Tax.* This is levied at the standard rate of 14 percent or at 7 percent on certain transactions, on proceeds of sales and services effected in West Germany. The taxpayer is entitled to offset against his VAT payable, the amount of such tax charged to him by his suppliers or the amount assessed on imports. There is a significant number of exemptions from VAT including exports, insurance, and banking services.

*Taxes on Distributions.* Dividend payments nontreaty are subject to a withholding tax of 25 percent, whether paid to resident or nonresident nontreaty companies or individuals. When the recipient is a U.K. resident, the rate is reduced to 15 percent. When the recipient is a U.S. resident, the rate is reduced to 10 percent (5 percent in 1992). In the case of dividends paid to German residents, the corporation tax borne by the company (36 percent) and the dividend withholding are both creditable in full against the shareholder's final tax liability. For trade tax purposes, dividends are tax exempt if the shareholder holds at least 10 percent of the company's shares.

*Withholding Taxes.* There is presently no withholding tax on interest, rentals from movable assets, or royalty payments to the United Kingdom or the United States.

## Corporate Residence

A company is resident in West Germany for tax purposes if either its place of incorporation or its place of central management is there. If the company is resident by reference to its German central management only, but is incorporated abroad under legislation less stringent than the German rules, the German tax authorities may ignore the corporate form and tax the profits of the entity as though they had been earned by the shareholders directly.

## Group Taxation

Resident companies that have their seat and place of management in West Germany may be taxed as a unit, thus permitting losses of one company to be offset against profits of another company.

## Income Determination

*Stock Valuation.* Stocks are normally valued at the lower of actual cost, replacement cost, or net realizable value. From 1990 LIFO will be acceptable. If specific identification is not possible, valuation at standard cost, or use of an averaging method is acceptable. Conformity is required between book and tax accounting.

*Capital Gains.* Capital gains and losses are generally taxed as ordinary business income or losses. It is possible to postpone the taxation of gains on certain fixed assets where the gain is offset against the cost of certain replacement items.

*Intercompany Dividends.* These are taxed as normal income for corporation profits tax purposes, with a tax credit being granted for the full underlying (36 percent) imputation tax and 25 percent withholding tax. For municipal trade tax purposes, dividends are tax exempt if the shareholder holds at least 10 percent of the company's shares.

*Foreign Income.* Income received by a German company from foreign sources is included in taxable income unless a tax treaty provides for exemption. Irrespective of a tax treaty, for municipal trade tax purposes, income or dividends from a foreign branch, partnership, or a direct or indirect shareholding may be reduced if the shareholder has at least a 10 percent interest. Double taxation is also avoided by means of foreign tax credits or, at the taxpayer's option, by a deduction of the foreign taxes as an expense.

Generally, undistributed income of foreign subsidiaries is not taxed in West Germany. However, antiavoidance rules are in force with respect to subsidiaries in low tax countries in certain lines of business.

## Deductions

*Depreciation and Depletion.* Depreciation is normally calculated on either the straight-line or declining-balance method over the anticipated useful life. Depreciation is available at a wide range of rates and on most assets (including goodwill) and buildings, but not on land. Apart from buildings, under certain conditions, the declining-balance method may be used at present only for movable fixed assets, and the annual rate may not exceed three times the rate that would have applied under the straight-line method or 30 percent. The residual value of the asset needs to be taken into account only where this is material—gains on a sale being treated as normal business income. Tax depreciation must be reflected in the accounts prepared for commercial purposes.

*Net Operating Losses.* Losses for tax purposes must first be carried back and offset up to the amount of DM10 million against taxable income of the preceding two years to the extent that such income has not been used for distribution. Any excess amount may be carried forward for five years. The loss carry-back is not permitted for municipal trade tax purposes.

*Payments to Foreign Affiliates.* A German company can claim a deduction for royalties, management services, and interest charges paid to foreign affiliates, provided such amounts are equal to what it would pay an unrelated entity for comparable services.

## Exchange Gains and Losses

Exchange gains and losses are part of the normal trading income and expenses, even if incurred in connection with purely speculative activities.

## Mergers and Acquisitions

Reorganization and restructuring of companies can be carried out tax free so that it is possible to merge two or more entities under common ownership without triggering a tax charge. If there is no common ownership, a tax charge may arise.

## Tax Incentives

*Inward Investment and Capital Investment.* The German Tax Reform Act has repealed or cut most of the incentives for investment. However, a limited range of incentives is available.

Incentives available for capital investments range from 12 percent or 20 percent grants (in the form of a tax reduction) for loans made to specified Berlin banks for capital investment in Berlin and cash premiums of 7.5 percent to 15 percent for new assets used in a Berlin business, and additional grants up to a total of 25 percent under the regional program which have to be treated either as income or as a reduction in the cost of the investment.

## Tax Administration

*Returns.* Returns are filed for each calendar year and reflect the financial statements for the business year ending in that calendar year. Assessments are issued once the tax office has reviewed the return.

*Payment of Tax.* Taxes are payable in quarterly installments during the year, with a final settlement when the assessment is issued. The quarterly installments are based on the estimated ultimate liability. Usually this is the total tax due as shown by the last assessment issued.

Source: Price Waterhouse, *Corporate Taxes—A Worldwide Summary.* Information Guide Series, New York: Price Waterhouse, 1989. (Any errors of omission or commission are the reponsibility of the author.) Based on the book prepared by Price Waterhouse for the Confederation of British Industry, *Tax: Strategic Corporate Tax Planning.* London: Mercury Books, 1989.

# SURVEY OF DIRECT CORPORATE TAXES AND INCENTIVES

|  | Belgium | Denmark | France | Germany | Greece |
|---|---|---|---|---|---|
| **INCOME TAX RATES %** | | | | | |
| Federal | 43 | 50 | 42 | 27.9-41.4 | 35/40/46 |
| Local | - | - | - | 11.1-20 | - |
| **TAX DEPRECIATION** | | | | | |
| Basis | useful life | st.-line, reducing balance acceptable rates | straight line useful life | st. line or declining balance over useful life | straight line fixed rates |
| Accelerated allowances/ investment reserves or incentives | x | x | x | x | x |
| **INCENTIVES** | | | | | |
| Regional/ employment | x | x | x | x | x |
| Export (other than guarantees) | - | - | - | - | x |
| Manufacturing | - | - | - | - | x |
| High tech/R&D | x | - | x | - | x |
| Tax holidays | x | - | x | - | x |
| **LOSSES** | | | | | |
| Carry-forward (yrs.) | 5 | 5 | 5 | indefinite | 3-5 |
| Carry-back | - | - | Specific conditions | Limited amount 2 years | - |
| Group | - | 100% subs | 95% subs | x | - |
| **CAPITAL GAINS TAX** | x | x | Lg term cap gains to 15% | x | Reduce. rate of 30% |
| Transfer of real property | - | x | 25% | - | - |
| **VALUE ADDED TAX %** | | | | | |
| Standard | 19 | 22 | 18.6 | 14 | 16 |
| Reduced rate | 6 | - | 5.5 | 7 | 6 |
| Luxury goods | 25 | - | 28.0 | - | 36 |

|  | Ireland | Italy | Luxembourg | Netherlands | Portugal |
|---|---|---|---|---|---|
| **INCOME TAX RATES %** | | | | | |
| Federal | 43 | 36[1] | 22-36 | 35-40 | 36.5 |
| Local | x | 16.2 | 4-12 | - | 10 |
| **TAX DEPRECIATION** | | | | | |
| Basis | x | straight line | straight line | straight line or declining balance | straight line or decl. bal. approved rates |
| Accelerated allowances/ investment reserves or incentives | x | acceptable rates | approved rates | | |
| | | x | x | x | x |
| **INCENTIVES** | | | | | |
| Regional/ employment | x | x | x | x | being revised |
| Export (other than guarantees) | x | - | x | - | being revised |
| Manufacturing | x | x | x | - | being rev. |
| High tech/R&D | x | - | x | - | being rev. |
| Tax holidays | - | x | x | - | being rev. |
| **LOSSES** | | | | | |
| Carry-forward (yrs.) | indefinite | 5 (fed. only) | 5 | 8 | 5 |
| Carry-back | 3 | - | - | 3 | - |
| Group | 75% subs | - | 99% subs | 100% subs | 90% subs |
| **CAPITAL GAINS TAX** | x | x up to 30# | x | x | x |
| Transfer of real property | x | x | | | indexed |
| **VALUE ADDED TAX %** | | | | | |
| Standard | 10 | 19 | 12 | 18.5 | 17 |
| Reduced | 2,5 | 4,9 | 3,6 | 6 | 8 |
| Luxury goods | 25 | 38 | - | - | 30 |

| | Spain | United Kingdom | United States | Japan | Australia |
|---|---|---|---|---|---|
| **INCOME TAX RATES %** | | | | | |
| Federal | 35 | 35 | $15-34^2$ | 28-37.5 | 39 |
| Local | - | - | 1-12 | $x^3$ | - |
| **TAX DEPRECIATION** | | | | | |
| Basis | st. line approved rates on cost or written-up values | declining balance fixed rates | st. line or declining bal. methods, specified by useful lives | st.line or declining balance over useful life | st.line or decl. balance method on expected life |
| Accelerated allowances/ investment reserves or incentives | x | x | x | x | x |
| **INCENTIVES** | | | | | |
| Regional/employment | x | x | x | - | x |
| Export (other than guarantees) | - | - | x | x | x |
| Manufacturing | - | x | | - | x |
| High tech/R&D | x | x | x | x | x |
| Tax holidays | - | - | - | - | - |
| **LOSSES** | | | | | |
| Carry-forward (yrs.) | 5 | indefinite | 15 | 5 | 7 |
| Carry-back | - | 1 | 3 | 1 | - |
| Group | 90% subs | x | x | - | x |
| **CAPITAL GAINS TAX** | x | x | Taxed as ord. income | Taxed as ord. income | Taxed as ord. income |
| Transfer of real property | x | | | Plus 20-30 | Same as above |
| **VALUE ADDED TAX %** | | | | | |
| Standard | 12 | 15 | Sales, franchise | 3 | Sales |
| Reduced | 6 | - | | 0 | |
| Luxury goods | 33 | - | | 6 | |

|  | Taiwan | South Korea | Hong Kong | Singapore |
|---|---|---|---|---|
| **INCOME TAX RATES %** | | | | |
| Federal | 10-25 | 20-33[4] | 17 | 33 |
| Local (deductible for federal) | - | - | - | - |
| **TAX DEPRECIATION** | | | | |
| Basis | st. line declining balance & machine-hour methods acceptable | st. line or declining balance on specified useful lives | initial allowances and annual allowance on cost at 3 rates (10, 20, 30%) st. line & decl. balance | st. line at specified rates |
| Accelerated allowances/ investment reserves or incentives | x | x | x | x |
| **INCENTIVES** | | | | |
| Regional/employment | - | x | - | x |
| Export (other than guarantees) | - | x | - | x |
| Manufacturing | x | x | - | x |
| High tech/R&D | x | x | - | x |
| Tax holidays | x | x | - | x |
| **LOSSES** | | | | |
| Carry-forward (yrs.) | 3 | 5 | indefinitely | unlimited |
| Carry-back | one | | - | - |
| Group | - | - | - | no, except for invts. in new technology and venture capital cos. |
| **CAPITAL GAINS TAX** | Taxed as ordinary income | Taxed as ord. income | - | - |
| Transfer of real property | - | add'l 32-53% | - | Taxed as ord. income |
| **VALUE ADDED TAX %** | 5 | 10 | - | - |

[1]Italy: Equalization tax up to 56.75 percent (of excess distribution to corporate shareholders)
[2]United States: Plus 20 percent of alternative minimum taxable income. Personal holding
    co., 28 percent
[3]Japan: Family holding company surtax: 10-20 percent
Prefectural enterprise: 6-13.2 percent
Prefecture: 5-6 percent (percentage of corporation tax)
Municipality: 12.3-14.7 percent (percentage of corporation tax)
Tokyo metropolitan: 17.3-20.7 percent (percentage of corporation tax)
Local per capita: 50,000 yen-3,750,000 yen
[4]South Korea: Defense: 20-37.5 percent (percentage of corporation tax)
Resident: 7.5 percent (percentage of corporation tax)

*Source:* Price Waterhouse, *Corporate Taxes: A Worldwide Summary.* Information Guide
    Series, New York: Price Waterhouse, 1989. (Any errors of omission or commission are
    the responsibility of the author.)
*Note:* x means yes or available; — means no or not available; blank space means no
    information available

# INTERNATIONAL INVESTMENT INCENTIVES

| Investment Incentives | Percentage of Foreign Participation Allowed for Most Common Type of Investment | Percentage of Foreign Participation Allowed for Least Common Type of Investment | Minimum Annual Percentage Capital Repatriation per Year | Minimum Annual Percentage Capital Repatriation per Year | Minimum Percentage Permitted Capital Repatriation per Year | Minimum Percentage Permitted Capital Repatriation per Year | Customs Guarantee Treaties with the United States | Customs Guarantee Treaties with Other Nations | Specific Incentives to Attract Outside Investment | Special Incentives to Certain Industries |
|---|---|---|---|---|---|---|---|---|---|---|
| Antigua & Barbuda | 100 | 50 | 100 | 100 | 100 | 100 | | | * | |
| Australia | 100 | 15 | 100 | | 100 | | | | | R |
| Austria | 100 | | 100 | 100 | 100 | 100 | | | * | * |
| Barbados | 100 | | 100 | | 100 | | | | * | |
| Belgium | 100 | 100 | 100 | 100 | 100 | 100 | | | * | * |
| Belize | 51-100 | 49 | 100 | 100 | 100 | 100 | | | * | * |
| Botswana | 50 | 100 | 75 | 0 | | | | | * | * |
| Brazil | 100 | | 100 | | 100 | | | | * | * |
| Brunei | 100 | | | | | | | | * | * |
| Bulgaria | 100 | | 100 | 0 | 100 | 0 | | | * | * |
| Canada | 100 | 100 | 100 | | 100 | 100 | | | * | * |
| Chile | 100 | 100 | 100 | | | | * | | * | * |
| Colombia | 65 | 49 | 20-30 | | 100 | | * | | * | * |
| Denmark | 100 | 100 | 100 | 100 | 100 | 100 | | | * | * |
| Dominican Republic | 100 | | 100 | 25 | 100 | 100 | | | * | * |
| Ecuador | 100 | 20 | 100 | 30 | 100 | 100 | * | | * | * |
| Egypt | 100 | 49 | 100 | 100 | 100 | | * | | * | * |
| France | 100 | 20 | 100 | | 100 | | | | * | * |
| Greece | 100 | | 100 | | 100 | | | | * | * |
| Guam | 100 | | 100 | | 100 | | | | | |
| Guatemala | 100 | 100 | N/A | N/A | N/A | N/A | * | | * | * |
| Haiti | 100 | 49 | 100 | | 100 | | * | | * | * |
| Hong Kong | 100 | 100 | 100 | 100 | 100 | 100 | | | * | * |
| Ireland | 100 | 100 | 100 | 100 | 100 | 100 | N/A | N/A | * | * |
| Jamaica | 100 | 100 | 100 | 100 | ? | | * | | * | * |
| Japan | 100 | | 100 | | 100 | | | | * | * |
| Luxembourg | 100 | 100 | 100 | | 100 | | | | * | * |
| Malaysia | 100 | 30 | 100 | | 100 | | * | | * | * |
| Morocco | 100 | 100 | 100 | 100 | 100 | 100 | * | | * | * |
| Netherlands | 100 | | 100 | | 100 | | | | * | * |
| Netherlands Antilles | 100 | 49 | 100 | | 100 | | * | | * | * |
| New Zealand | 100 | 100 | 100 | | 100 | | | | * | * |
| N. Mariana Islands | 100 | 100 | 100 | 100 | 100 | 100 | * | | * | * |
| Norway | 100 | 3 | 100 | | 100 | | | | * | * |
| Pakistan | * | * | 100 | | 100 | | * | | * | * |
| Philippines | 100 | 30-40 | 100 | | 100 | | * | | * | * |
| Puerto Rico | 100 | 100 | 100 | 100 | 100 | 100 | | | * | * |
| Senegal | 49 | | 100 | | 100 | | * | | * | * |
| Singapore | 100 | 100 | 100 | | 100 | | * | | * | * |
| South Africa | 100 | | 100 | | 100 | | | | * | * |
| South Korea | 100 | 100 | 100 | | 100 | | * | | * | * |
| Spain | 100 | 0 | 100 | 0 | | | * | * | * | * |
| St. Lucia | 100 | 100 | 100 | | 100 | | | | * | * |
| St. Vincent/Grenadines | 100 | 49 | 100 | | 100 | | | | * | * |
| Swaziland | 100 | 100 | 100 | 100 | 100 | 100 | | | * | * |
| Switzerland | R-100 | R-33 | R-100 | R-100 | R-100 | R-100 | | | R | R |
| Taiwan | 100 | 100 | 100 | 100 | 100 | 100 | | | * | * |
| Tunisia | | | | | | | | | | |
| Thailand | 100 | 49 | 100 | | 100 | | | | * | * |
| United Kingdom | 100 | 100 | 100 | 100 | 100 | 100 | | | * | * |
| Uruguay | 100 | | 100 | | 100 | | | | * | * |
| Venezuela | 100 | 19.9 | 20 | | | | | | * | * |
| West Germany | R-100 | R-100 | R-100 | R-100 | R-100 | R-100 | | | R | R |

R  Indicates regional information.
1  Most manufacturing concerns. Mining and non-residential commercial real estate development is require some local country participation.
2  Radio and TV/media communication.
3  After taxes.
4  Special tax deductions offered to foreign investors.
5  Although the director's VAT is 33%, it ranges from 10% to 37%.
6  Manufacturing only, 10 years.
7  Maximum 5 brands.
8  Variable tax incentives.
9  Less than 15.
10  Local value added.
11  15 years.
12  Above 12%, taxes increase substantially.
13  With the obligation of becoming a closed enterprise (49%) within 15 years. In some cases, this requirement may be suspended.
14  Negotiable.
15  No restrictions provided payment takes place not later than 30 days after shareholders' general meeting.
16  10 years.
17  Telecommunications, radio and television, broadcasting and natural gas distribution are effectively closed to private enterprise.
18  For free zone industries.
19  Up to 25% from a registered foreign investment outside a free zone may be repatriated.
20  For reinvestment benefits, but only in certain industries.
21  Depending on type of industry.
22  Must be approved.
23  Depending on type of good and/or designation.
24  Tax holiday can range from 10-15.

| Investment Incentives | Special Incentives According to Status of Investment (pioneer, etc.) | Special Incentives Offered for Certain Areas | Other Types of Special Incentives | Percentage Corporate Income Tax Exemption (for limited number of years) | Percentage Property Tax Exemption (for limited number of years) | Percentage Customs Duty Exemption on Goods in Transit | Percentage Value-Added Tax on Finished Products and Services | Industrial Sites Free or for Less Than Market Price | Industrial Buildings Free or for Less Than Market Price | Subsidized Training for New Workers | Wage Subsidies for New Workers |
|---|---|---|---|---|---|---|---|---|---|---|---|
| Antigua & Barbuda | | | | 100[24] | 0 | 100 | | | | | |
| Australia | R | R | R | | | | | | | * | * |
| Austria | * | * | * | | | | 20[5] | * | * | * | |
| Barbados | | | * | 100[9] | | 100 | N/A | * | * | * | [7] |
| Belgium | * | * | | 6 | 6 | 6 | 6 | * | * | * | * |
| Belize | * | * | *[10] | 100[11] | | 100 | N/A | * | * | | |
| Botswana | * | * | | 100 | 100 | 0 | 0 | | | * | * |
| Brazil | | * | | | | | | * | | * | |
| Brunei | * | * | * | | 0 | 0 | 0 | * | * | * | |
| Bulgaria | | | | | | | 0 | | | | |
| Canada | R | R | R | 100 | | | | | | R | R |
| Chile | | | | | | | | | | | |
| Colombia | | * | | 50 | | 100 | 10 | | | | |
| Denmark | | *[48] | *[48] | 0 | 0 | 100 | 22 | | | * | |
| Dominican Republic | | | * | 100[20] | 100[21] | 100[18] | 6 | | | | *[21] |
| Ecuador | | * | * | 100 | 100 | 100 | | | | * | |
| Egypt | * | * | * | 100 | 100 | 100[22] | 0[22] | * | | * | * |
| France | | * | * | | R-100 | 100[21] | 5-33[23] | R | R | R | |
| Greece | * | * | * | | | | | * | * | * | * |
| Guam | | * | | 75 | | | | * | | | |
| Guatemala | * | * | *[27] | N/A | N/A | N/A | N/A | * | * | | |
| Haiti | * | * | | 100 | N/A | N/A | | | | | |
| Hong Kong | | | | | | | | | | | |
| Ireland | | * | *[29] | 90[28] | | 100 | 100[31] | * | * | * | * |
| Jamaica | | *[18] | | 100 | | 100 | 0 | * | * | * | * |
| Japan | * | * | * | | | | 0 | * | * | * | * |
| Luxembourg | * | * | | 25 | | 100 | 5-12.5[33] | * | | * | |
| Malaysia | * | *[34] | | 100 | | 50 | 5-10 | * | | | |
| Morocco | | * | * | 100 | 100 | 100 | N/A | * | | * | * |
| Netherlands | * | * | *[35] | | | 100 | | R | R | * | * |
| Netherlands Antilles | * | * | | 98[16] | 100 | 100 | 0 | * | * | * | * |
| New Zealand | | * | | | | | | | | | |
| N. Mariana Islands | | * | * | 95 | 4[?] | 0 | 3 | | | | |
| Norway | | * | | | | 100[23] | | | | | |
| Pakistan | * | * | * | | | N/A | | * | | * | |
| Philippines | * | * | * | 30[?] | 39[?] | | | * | * | | |
| Puerto Rico | * | * | * | | | | | * | * | * | * |
| Senegal | * | * | * | 100 | | 100 | | | | | |
| Singapore | * | | | 100 | | 100 | | | | | |
| South Africa | | * | | R-100[40] | | 41 | | | | *[42] | *[42] | *[42] |
| South Korea | | | | 100 | 100 | 100 | 100 | | | | |
| Spain | | * | | 25 | | | 6-12 | | | * | * |
| St. Lucia | | | | 100[43] | 100 | 100 | N/A | * | * | * | |
| St. Vincent/Grenadines | | * | * | 100 | 100 | 100 | 0 | | | * | |
| Swaziland | * | * | | 100 | N/A | 100[23] | R-0[23] | * | * | * | |
| Switzerland | R | * | R | R-50 | R-50 | 100[43] | | | | | |
| Taiwan | | | | | | | 100 | | | | |
| Thailand | | * | * | 100[44] | N/A | 100 | N/A | * | * | | |
| Tunisia | | * | | 0 | 0 | 0 | | | | | |
| United Kingdom | * | * | * | | | 45 | 46 | * | * | * | * |
| Uruguay | | * | | | | 100 | 21 | | | | |
| Venezuela | | * | | 20 | 20 | 20 | | | | | |
| West Germany | R | R | * | | N/A | N/A | 14 | R | R | R | R |

25 Customs duty may be waived on importation of any capital item, packaging material or raw material.
26 Emphasizing drawback operations, particularly in the textiles and electronics industries.
27 Export-oriented businesses.
28 Special training grants for ASIC design engineers.
29 Value added to local economy.
30 To year 2000.
31 Rebate on exports.
32 After two years, capital can be repatriated in three annual installments.

33 Manufactured goods: 10-12.5%.
34 5% investment tax allowance for less developed areas.
35 Other factors include amount of fixed assets, building and equipment. Special emphasis is given to high tech: biotech, laser and medical research.
36 For postal, telephone and broadcasting services and the production and sales of spirits, wine and drugs.
37 Flexible.
38 For capital equipment only: 50% for non-pioneer, 100% for pioneer.
39 50% for non-pioneer, 100% for pioneer.

40 100% exemption available only in the Republic of Ciskei. Not available in larger cities, such as Johannesburg.
41 Available on case-by-case basis.
42 Only in developing areas.
43 No real property tax.
44 3-8 years.
45 100% for 10 years in Northern Ireland enterprise zones.
46 100% in freeports only.
47 U.S. Commonwealth: All U.S. treaties apply.
48 Must be approved Jan. '90.
Source: Conway Data, Inc., 1988 Survey of Governments.

Reproduced from *Site Selection*, September/October 1988, by permission of the publisher, Conway Data, Inc., Atlanta. No further reproduction is permitted.

# 5

# *RISK MANAGEMENT*

The global corporation assumes many risks. Producing products for the marketplace at home and abroad has its risks, as does marketing those products. It can be risky to manage personnel working in various corporate capacities who are drawn from different work ethic environments, cultures, languages, and educational backgrounds. The corporation also assumes many risks including those associated with its leased and purchased real estate. Since the company's real estate serves the principal functions of the global business, these assets are affected in general by any risks encountered by the company. However, some risks are more specifically associated with the real estate itself.

## WHAT ARE THE RISKS ASSOCIATED WITH GLOBAL REAL ESTATE MANAGEMENT?

One might classify the global corporate real estate risks as (1) financial, (2) political, (3) environmental, (4) corporate takeover, and (5) other types. The financial risks involve currency value change, changes in funds repatriation policies, expectations of under-the-counter payments, real estate investment risks in general, price controls, and the geographical locations of prospective real estate buyer capital. Political risks include (1) the time, personnel, and cost of government approvals of requested land use changes; (2) possible government nationalization of foreign companies and their properties; and (3) contract enforcement systems.

Environmental risks tend to come from:

Environmental protection controls including
> waste disposal controls such as water and air pollution controls
> noise pollution controls

Adequate water supply for company operations, employee homes, and related community facilities

Adequate transportation facilities for company operations and employee transportation between workplace, home, and other locations ·

Appropriate and adequate labor supply

Only hostile corporate takeovers present substantial risk to the director of corporate real estate. Friendly takeovers, as well as hostile takeovers, could cause the director of real estate to lose employment, but the "friendly acquirer" might leave the global real estate holdings of the company in place.

Other risks might involve security for the property and the personnel, construction management, atmospheric and geological conditions, and antinational sentiments that are expressed in numerous ways. Even though the real estate manager faces extensive risks along with the plant, administrative office, personnel, and distribution managers, these risks are perceived as manageable in light of the prospective profitability from international manufacturing and distribution of products.

## SHARING THE RISK MANAGEMENT WITH OTHER CORPORATE DEPARTMENTS AND DIVISIONS

Unlike the real estate portfolio manager, the corporate real estate manager shares responsibilities for risk management affecting corporate real estate with colleagues and other departments within the company. Currency management affecting real estate usually is the primary responsibility of the headquarters foreign exchange or treasury department. The foreign exchange specialists hedge the current and expected net cash flows from the total corporate operation including the real estate financial activities in numerous currencies. In this specialized headquarters position, the treasury department may merely conduct hedging operations to reduce financial risk or they may go a step further and take some currency risk in hopes of earning currency profits. The insurance department of corporate headquarters generally provides self insurance for perceived company risks. This self insurance may extend to property hazard insurance. The foreign investment and finance department may have the job of reducing losses from capital, profits, royalties, and management fees repatriation policies of the local government. The company may have a barter department for transactions which may involve no negotiable currency, only real assets and various products. The legal department might examine the legality of special types of payments such as key money deposits for leased space.

Political risk assessment may be the principal responsibility of top company executives. Plant and distribution center locations are finalized by the executive committee and the board of directors. Often political risks must be considered as part of the deliberations. Top management may gain the assistance of specialized political risk analysts who offer their services to global industrial, transportation, and financial service companies.

The legal department can enter into the acquisition of land use approvals from the local government. The corporate legal department or the real estate attorneys of the real estate department enter into real estate contract negotiations and title transfer and recording. The legal staff also is associated with local and national environmental protection regulations that may affect the acquisition and leasing of properties in individual countries. When friendly or unfriendly offers for corporate acquisition come from various sources, the legal department usually analyzes the offers in conjunction with the finance officers, top management, and board members.

A logistics and materials department analyzes the availability of the right forms of transportation, warehousing systems, and materials and natural resources that may or may not adequately serve the foreign company operation. This group of specialists could be closely associated with the international and domestic real estate specialists. At the DuPont corporation, the real estate function falls within their Logistics and Materials Department.

The engineering and architecture departments normally take care of the project planning, design, building permit acquisition, contract negotiations for construction, on-site construction management and supervision, and occupancy permit acquisition after construction is finished. These departments often are closely affiliated in a major corporation with the real estate department. At Abbott Laboratories the Real Estate Department is a part of the Engineering Administration Department. The same relationship is true of AT&T. Therefore, in such companies, the reduction of risks from construction management is shared by real estate and engineering.

The public relations and marketing departments may help in countering any community resistance for foreign company ownership and operation. Employee relocation and other personnel matters are handled at least partially by the personnel department on site and at the corporate headquarters.

## THE PRESENCE OF UNCONTROLLABLE RISKS

Many risks encountered in global corporate real estate are uncontrollable, but they need satisfactory responses. Such risks include atmospheric and geological conditions that could threaten the corporate activity and real property. For example, seismic faults that predict possible earthquakes exist in many parts of the world. Recently, for example, an earthquake registering 6.4 on the Richter Scale took the lives of a dozen people in northeast Africa. There are well recognized earthquake prone areas in Japan, northern Taiwan, the Midwest and West Coast areas of the United

States, and Greece. Monsoons and drought are uncontrollable environmental hazards of serious proportions.

The corporation cannot control a government's management of inflation, the economy, employment, and financial payments and reserves. It cannot control a government's use of price and rent controls, of the power of eminent domain, or of the power to nationalize foreign business and assets or to privatize its state-owned businesses. Since these factors affect the use of a corporation's property, it must monitor the government's plans and changes in policies so that it can take counter steps if necessary. Some legislative and executive branch lobbying might be beneficial to counteract unfavorable government tendencies.

## THE MANAGEMENT OF FINANCIAL RISKS AFFECTING GLOBAL REAL ESTATE

First, the financial risks must be recognized by top management and by the director of corporate real estate. Second, personnel must be assigned to the management of the strategic and the less important risks. Most of the financial risks affecting global real estate are usually assigned to the treasury, finance, and legal departments rather than the real estate department. If the financial risk management is not assigned to the treasury, finance, and legal departments, it remains a management responsibility of the real estate department.

### Inflation and Its Management

While the highly industrialized nations continue to experience low levels of inflation, some of the developing nations experience very high levels of inflation. Inflation risk, therefore, is evident primarily in the less developed countries even though advanced economies must expect inflation and take precautions. For example, the inflation of the United States approximates 5.5 percent; Japan, 1.5 percent; West Germany, 4.5 percent; and the United Kingdom, 8 percent.

High levels of inflation should prompt the corporation to buy or build its real properties. The value of the property will probably rise with inflation. Rents in such high inflation countries as Brazil and Argentina are indexed to current inflation. Therefore, rents for leased premises will increase steadily unless the government takes strong measures to reduce the inflation. Most governments cannot take such strong economic measures because employment would immediately be reduced, and personal and corporate incomes would suffer as the government bureaucracy was reduced, employees were laid off, and taxes were raised.

The company that leases space under indexed contracts often finds that the government establishes price controls on the corporation's products at the same time. Rents steadily increase while revenues are stabilized at a low level. If the company is financially able to buy or build its own premises, it faces these fixed costs at the same time it faces price controls. It is a more manageable situation than leasing space on an indexed basis while prices are controlled.

If the corporation financed its new premises with interest-bearing debt, the inflation may reduce the effective cost of the debt over time, particularly if the rate of inflation is high. Of course, the interest on debt in high-inflation countries is usually indexed to inflation. Even so, interest payments are normally tax deductible expenses under most income tax administrations. So the cost of the financing—after-tax debt financing—may be less than the cost of all-equity financing of the real estate.

Properties in one country may be financed in another country. Fixed interest-rate debt financing for the real estate in a high-inflation country is preferable and may possibly be acquired through debt financing in a low-inflation country. Many U.S.-based corporations acquire fixed-rate debt financing for foreign operations in the United States or in the Euromarkets, perhaps through interest rate swaps.

### Repatriation of Funds

When a multinational corporation sells a property, it normally wishes to take the funds from the buyer and add them to the home office's other cash resources. If it is a U.S.-based company, it usually wishes to receive U.S. dollars at the home office as a result of the infrequent sales transaction. Sometimes the payment cannot leave the country in which it is received due to government control of capital and profit repatriation. And the government controls over the foreign capital and profit repatriation may change over time with the state of the nation's economic affairs.

Most multinational firms build or buy their properties and hold them indefinitely. The properties merely facilitate their manufacturing, processing, and distributing of their products. But occasionally properties are sold for various reasons.

When properties are sold, the company has several options. The property can be leased back for the investor. The monies can be sent back to the company headquarters to raise the cash balance on the next set of corporate financial statements. If the buyer pays in cash, notes, and other assets, these assets are all added to the corporation's balance sheet in the proper accounts. Or the sale proceeds can be used for reinvestment in property or other assets within the original country. When the particular national government restricts or forbids capital repatriation, the company thinks twice about selling a property and, when it does sell a property, it tends to reinvest the proceeds within the same country. The proceeds can be used to purchase equity in another company, the equity in another property or applied to the construction or purchase of another well-designed and well-located property that fits the company's needs.

If the government restricts repatriation of capital previously invested in the country, perhaps the government will still permit repatriation of profits in the form of dividends. Sometimes interest payments to the home office can be repatriated.

If the government restricts repatriation privileges associated with one currency, the government may permit repatriation of the country's currency or another currency. The foreign exchange or treasury department of the company may accept the currency that may be repatriated and then swap or trade this currency for a desired currency at a reasonable exchange rate. Eventually the home office can receive the proceeds of the property sale in the desired currency. Companies doing business in Hungary are negotiating on this basis when they enter into transactions originally. Multinational companies signing agreements in Russia are also negotiating future capital and profit repatriation on this basis. If capital and profits cannot be repatriated, the company might have to negotiate a barter agreement.

### The Risks of Barter Agreements and Their Management

Barter agreements are used when a company cannot repatriate its earnings or capital from a country such as the Iron Curtain, Latin American, and African countries. Barter agreements amount to the taking of goods and perhaps services instead of the currency of the local country in payment for goods and services sold to its government or businesses. Computers for nonmilitary use may be sold to Yugoslavia, for example, and, in lieu of currency payment, the seller may receive blue jeans, ceramic goods, or agricultural products. After the vendor agrees to the barter arrangement, the vendor must turn around and sell the offered goods or services to another buyer who will pay currency. Actually, many companies will not agree to a barter arrangement until they have already sold or have an advance commitment for the sale of the offered goods or services. The company that is to receive goods in exchange for goods wants to be reasonably certain that the offered goods can be sold at a fair price. At the end of the total transaction the vendor wants to receive a market price for the goods sold, taking into account the demand for the offered goods and the exchange rates of the foreign currencies eventually received. Of course, the customer for the goods from the original customer may pay in the currency of the headquarters country of the multinational firm.

Global companies are often permitted to buy or build properties that are used for their businesses in countries that permit limited or no repatriation of capital and earnings. When the properties are no longer needed because of obsolete production processes, discontinued products, or closed subsidiaries, a repatriation problem may develop. The receipts from the property sale—which may amount to a capital gain—may be taken out of the country only by way of a barter agreement.

Most major U.S.-based multinational companies have established barter departments which operate in order to make possible some foreign sales of goods. The major aircraft companies have often bartered in order to sell planes to countries that can only exchange goods. Global fast food chains have had to engage in barter arrangements where foreign agricultural products have been received in payment for capital and profit repatriation. Specially built machinery and equipment has been sold to the less developed countries of Latin America through barter agreements arranged by the International Finance and Investment Department of FMC Corporation. This major machinery manufacturer would lose many large sales if it could not engage in barter. Major chemical companies also maintain barter departments to enhance their overseas sales.

When it is necessary to sell the goods and services received in lieu of currency in a major sales transaction, there is always risk. The purchasing country may offer a range of goods and services for the barter agreement. The seller, the receiving company, must sort out the goods and services that it thinks it can sell to eventually gain the market price for the original goods or services.

## Management of Special Payment Provisions

The United States government, since the latter 1970s or early 1980s, barred U.S.-businesses and government agencies and personnel working abroad from taking or giving bribes and under-the-counter payments. Bribes are payments for services rendered made to gain unfair advantages over competitors. Under-the-counter payments amount to expenditures that are not recorded for income tax purposes. They are requested as partial payment for a transaction in order to avoid taxation.

Key money payments for the acquisition of leased space may be construed by the U.S. government in the same light as the taking or giving of bribes and the payment or receipt of under-the-counter amounts. Key money payments may be requested by landlords because the demand for the particular type of property is extremely strong. The space demand is so strong that the landlord asks for key money, security deposits, and high rents payable in advance. The key money, which may not be an interest-bearing deposit, may be accumulated by the landlord in order to construct the building at the specified location. The prospective tenant is so anxious to acquire the existing or proposed space that the key money would be paid readily except for the intervention of the tenant's government. Most governments do not intervene in this process, particularly in the prime office building central business sectors of many countries. Corporations need space in these foreign markets and encounter the requests for key money. Otherwise, the landlord will turn around and take key money from the next prospective tenant for the same space to the chagrin of the major corporation.

Key money payments are requested in the United Kingdom in the retail sector. They are requested by landlords of prospective office buildings in Bombay, India. These payments are expected by Japanese landlords in the middle of Tokyo. The merchants of France who wish to buy or lease scarce shopping center storeroom space are required to pay key money. A heavy demand for any type of building space may create a situation which prompts key money requests from the landlord or developer.

When a major chemical conglomerate from the United States sought new office space near the heart of Tokyo, they encountered a request for key money from the Japanese developer of the twin tower location. Since the U.S. government frowns on such payments in addition to the payment of a security deposit and rent in advance, they negotiated an agreement which amounted to the payment of interest equal to the interest the developer would have received from the key money deposit. The U.S. corporation could deduct the interest for U.S. federal income tax and the key money deposit was avoided, but the company did acquire prime new office building space that fits its needs in downtown Tokyo.

In South Korea, officially the Republic of Korea, a major pharmaceutical company sought manufacturing space in this market of expanding pharmaceutical demand. The corporation scouted South Korea and found eleven possible manufacturing facilities that could be purchased for their company's use. As they spent time examining what each of the eleven plants had to offer, they discovered that most of the plant owners required a substantial payment that would not be reported to the government tax authorities. In each case the remaining portion of the purchase price would be reported to the government. The amount of the requested "under-the-counter" payments was substantial. A U.S. company is allowed to pay small consulting fees for services but not immense amounts for no services rendered, according to the U.S. government's regulations for U.S. companies operating abroad. One of the plants that suited the needs of the pharmaceutical company was owned by an American pharmaceutical company which was leaving the market. A purchase agreement that did not entail possibly illegal payments was worked out. The American property seller was not a part of the local culture that expected the special payment arrangement.

Corporate bribery of government and business officials is a recognized way of doing business in many countries in the world. Since the U.S. government does not consider bribe payments from U.S. companies to be legal, U.S. companies must find other ways to accomplish the same results. Recent examples of rampant bribery of government and business officials have been associated with Italy and the financial capital of Milan, in particular. Even the Italian government has not been able to tolerate some of the bribery among real estate developers and government officials in the land use approval area. Government reports have appeared in European newspapers about this and other excesses. Taking bribes is tempting for government officials dealing with land use approval anywhere because of the relatively low salaries these public servants earn compared to their real estate and business colleagues.

How does one get around payment of the expected bribes? One major U.S. corporation which is determined to establish a series of delivery depots in Italy and other foreign countries responds that the normal domestic procedure will be used to find good locations and acquire land use approvals. The company will wait out the normal time required for planning approvals for site use and will employ local specialists who are acquainted with the planning approval process and the persons involved. Use of local joint venture partners' assistance and the employment of a domestic expert will help to get the numerous required depot locations. The global company is "in that market to stay." The company has patience.

### Currency Management

Currency value fluctuations affect the net proceeds from foreign property sales, the net cash flows from investment real estate or land development projects, and the payment of rent to landlords. Properties are occasionally disposed of when no longer useful to the company or when properties which are better located and designed are available. Some companies, like Philip Morris, have land development projects that are intended to add profits to the companies from eventual project sales. These investment properties are usually designed and built to be sold. Many multinational corporations pay rent to landlords for leased industrial plants, warehouses, and office and retail buildings. The industrial plants are sometimes sold, after construction to multinational company specification, to financial institutions or partnerships and then leased back by the company.

When a property is sold, the selling price may exceed the depreciated purchase price. Thus, a capital gain is created. The government's income tax service must define "long-term capital gain" before the company can declare whether it has realized a capital loss, a short- or long-term capital gain, or broken even on the sale. On the other hand, there may be a difference between the price paid and the price received in terms of the company's headquarters currency. Let's look at a situation involving a U.S.-based multinational company. An auto plant in West Germany may have cost U.S. $10 million dollars or 25 million Deutsche marks (U.S. $10,000,000 × 2.5 Deutsche marks equals 25 million Deutsche marks) in 1975 when the U.S. dollar equalled 2.5 Deutsche marks. When a purchaser is found for the property in 1990, the sale price is 30 million Deutsche marks with the U.S. dollar equal to 1.9 DM (Deutsche marks). The U.S. dollar has weakened in comparison to the Deutsche mark. Thirty million Deutsche marks equals U.S. $15,789,473.68. There is a capital gain of U.S. $5,789,473.68 (U.S. $15,789,473.68 sale price less U.S. $10,000,000 purchase price). If the U.S. dollar had strengthened instead, the sale price of 30 million DM would have equalled U.S. $9,375,000 if the U.S. dollar equalled 3.2 DM. There would have been a loss on the sale of U.S. $625,000. (U.S. $10,000,000 purchase price less U.S. $9,375,000 sale price equals U.S. $625,000.) The exchange rate change made the difference between a capital gain or a capital loss to the parent company in the United States. The parent company knows that it is better to invest in a country where the currency is expected to strengthen in comparison with the currency of the parent company. When Japan's yen was strengthening against the U.S. dollar for a long stretch of months in the mid-1980s, an American corporate investor could have gleaned profits merely from the purchase of an asset at the beginning of the yen's uptrend and sale of the asset when the yen had risen measurably against the U.S. dollar. When a country deliberately devalues its currency, as the United States did in the mid-1980s, its leadership knows that foreign exchange capital gains can be realized when the foreign currency goes up in value while the domestic currency declines in value.

Most multinational companies lease space overseas. This rent is usually paid in the currency of the country where the property is domiciled. If the currency of the headquarters country is strong in comparison with the foreign currency, the effective rent is lower. If the headquarters country's currency is weak, the effective rent is high. For example, the Alpha Company has negotiated monthly rent of 70,000 French francs for the space it needs. When the U.S. dollar equals 7.5 French francs, the effective rent is only U.S. $9,333.33 a month. When the U.S. dollar slips to 6.5 French francs in value, the effective rent climbs to U.S. $10,769.23. When the U.S. government devalued its currency in the 1980s, the U.S. corporation's effective prices for foreign buyers declined, but the established overseas corporate expenses increased in U.S. dollar terms.

*Management of Risk through Company Operations in the Local Overseas Currency.* The corporation avoids some foreign exchange risks by buying, selling, leasing, paying operating expenses, and receiving local payments in the local currency. It may also finance its acquisitions and sell properties and other assets in the currency of the country. Therefore, the corporation might receive only the net amount from the foreign country's total operations as converted one time into the headquarters country's currency. Actually net amounts may be repatriated to the home office more than once a year, but only one or a few currency translations are necessary rather than numerous translations from numerous transactions. The foreign division may have only infrequent financial reporting responsibilities.

*Treasury or Foreign Exchange Department Countermoves at the Head-
quarters Office.* Real estate operations overseas involve two cash conversion or foreign exchange situations: infrequent sales of properties and
continual net cash flows from property financing and operations. They may
be handled differently by the headquarters foreign exchange or treasury
department—if they are singled out from the other corporate foreign exchange transactions related to main line business operations.

The isolated cash flows from property sales exhibit foreign exchange risk
that might be handled through forward contracts once the timing of the
net cash receipts is known. Once the tax payments, selling costs, and other
expenses at sale time are deducted from the local currency sale price, the
foreign exchange department may know the cash amount at risk. The profit
or loss at the time the net cash receipts are known may be locked in by
the sale of forward contracts in the foreign currency. If the headquarters
currency increases in value or the foreign currency declines in value between that time and the actual receipt of the net cash flows from the
property sale, the company will receive the value set on the forward sale
of foreign currency. If the forward contract must be covered at the time
of the actual receipt of foreign currency—since the currency sold had to
be borrowed—the foreign currency equal to the forward contract sale
amount will be purchased. If the foreign currency has weakened and the
headquarters company currency has strengthened in the interim period, a
smaller amount will be paid to close out the forward contract. The gain
on the forward contract will be counteracted by a loss on the decline in
the spot market value of the net property price. If the foreign currency
has strengthened, a greater amount will be paid for the foreign currency
than was received from the forward contract sale. The foreign exchange
transaction will result in a gain while the spot market value of the net cash
receipts from the property will have declined.

The continual net cash flows from property operations abroad usually
amount to net negative currency flows. The properties used in manufacturing and distribution are absorbing currency for operating expenses. Generally corporate properties overseas are not leased to outside tenants; they
usually do not generate income to counterbalance the properties' operating
costs. But the net negative currency flows from the overseas properties
within a country may be counterbalanced by the net positive currency flows
from the country's marketing activities. Therefore, if the national division
reports only net cash flows and profits from the country's total operations,
the treasury or foreign exchange department will handle the exchange risk
of the total country currency flow.

## The Contracts Available for Hedging Currency Risks

Forward and future contracts are available for the hedging of currency
risk. Since forward contracts are arranged through banks with international

or foreign exchange departments, the banks may tailor the forward buy or sell contracts to any time length and to any recognized currency to fit the multinational corporation's needs. Few forward contracts offered by a bank extend beyond a year or two. The risk to the financial institution increases with the length of the contract. The risk depends on the frequency of fluctuation of the particular currency and the nature of any defined trend in the currency. The more risks the bank itself takes in hedging its own position against the offering of the forward contracts, the higher the fees to the corporation. But the forward contract fees are relatively reasonable.

Futures contracts are bought and sold on major securities exchanges around the world. Most future contracts extend 30, 60, 90 or 180 days and have fixed dimensions for each contract. The fluctuation in the value of the futures contract may be restricted to only one-half to two percent a day. The particular securities exchange wants to maintain stability in the values of the contracts to some degree.

Only the major currencies, such as the Japanese yen, the British pound sterling, the French franc, the Swiss franc, and the West German Deutsche mark are traded by futures contracts. Therefore, if currency flows from a country without representative futures contracts, the futures contracts of another currency, which is closely correlated in value trends with the needed currency, may be used by the foreign exchange department for hedging purposes.

### The Importance of Forecasting Foreign Exchange Rates

A company's staff and its consultants may constantly attempt to forecast the exchange rates of the leading currencies. Hedging of the total amount of the expected corporate net cash flows may or may not be necessary. If the currency is moving in a direction that enhances corporate profits, the corporate transaction may be left unhedged or only partially hedged. In other words, if the amount of net cash flows from the particular country's transactions is 10 million French francs, the hedge may be set for only a part of this amount.

One of the responsibilities of the multinational corporation's finance operations is to forecast exchange rates. Part of the responsibility for this duty may be delegated to outside consultants, such as a commercial or investment bank's foreign exchange departments.

If a country's currency is forecasted to weaken or the headquarter's currency is forecasted to strengthen, the periodic net negative real estate obligations will decline in value. The periodic net positive corporate cash flows will decline in value also. Continuous hedging with forward or futures contracts might stabilize the value of the net positive currency receipts.

## The Costs of Hedging versus the Benefits Derived

Top management will have to decide whether the costs of hedging will be offset by the benefits from the hedging process. If short-term forward and futures contracts must be constantly "rolled over" to keep the necessary hedge in place to cover the forecasted cash flows, the cost of "rolling over" the contracts may become significant. Hedging "one-time" capital gains from infrequent property sales in advance of expected property payments might be more cost effective for the company.

## The Responsibility for and the Results from Corporate Currency Management

Seldom does the real estate department have responsibility for currency management in a large multinational firm. This management process is normally assigned by top management to a specialized treasury, foreign exchange, finance, or international finance and investment department. The real estate department does not usually have any financing responsibilities other than leasing of space. Even the financial analysis of the lease versus the buy or build decision usually rests with the finance department, and rarely with the real estate department.

The recent annual financial statements, publicly distributed, indicate how successful the currency management operations of selected U.S.-based multinational firms have been. In 1988, 10 of the 14 selected companies took net currency management losses (Exhibit 5.1). In 1986, in contrast, 13 of the same 14 companies generated net currency gains. The year between, 1987, was a transition year; nine of the companies netted currency gains while only five generated currency losses. Since recent years have been turbulent in the foreign exchange markets, these results show evidence of good currency management. Most of the selected multinational firms have well-established foreign exchange traders and hedgers with substantial experience in the field of finance. Most of the companies are well entrenched in international trade with manufacturing and distribution positions in many countries of the globe. The currency risks from these major operations have given the currency management specialists much work over the years.

Hedging permits cost cutting. Instead of taking losses from doing nothing, hedging of appropriate currencies may reduce losses to amounts far less than they might have been. The FMC Corporation has repeatedly experienced this benefit from currency hedging in their international sales of specialized machinery and equipment.

Cost cutting from currency management can also be obtained from other areas of management. The multinational company may negotiate a home currency price as the company enters the transactions. If it is a U.S.-based

**Exhibit 5.1**
**Currency Management Results, Selected U.S.-Based Multinational Corporations,**
**1988 (Millions of Dollars)**

| Selected Multinational Companies | 1988 | 1987 | 1986 |
|---|---|---|---|
| **Abbott Laboratories** | | | |
| Effect of exchange rate changes on cash and cash equivalents | ( 0.6) | 7.6 | 0.6 |
| **Amoco** | | | |
| Foreign currency gain (loss) reflected in income | 14.0 | ( 71.0) | 41.0 |
| Net translation adjustment reflected in shareholders equity | 13.0 | 110.0 | 40.0 |
| **AT&T** | | | |
| Translation adjustments | ( 3.0) | 148.0 | 94.0 |
| **Campbell Soup** | | | |
| Foreign exchange gains (losses) net | ( 16.6) | ( 4.8) | ( 0.7) |
| **DuPont** | | | |
| Effect of exchange rate changes on cash | ( 13.0) | 70.0 | 11.0 |
| **FMC Corporation** | | | |
| Balance sheet: For currency translation adjustment | ( 5.7) | 45.1 | 31.0 |
| Effect of exchange rate changes on cash | ( 18.3) | ( 4.1) | 6.6 |
| **McDonald's** | | | |
| Translation adjustments excluding tax benefits | 19.9 | 35.8 | - 0 - |
| **Morton Thiokol** | | | |
| Translation adjustment | 15.7 | 11.9 | 11.7 |
| **Motorola** | | | |
| Foreign currency gains (losses) | 1.0 | 8.0 | 4.0 |
| **Philip Morris** | | | |
| Effect of exchange rate changes on cash | ( 44.0) | 113.0 | 54.0 |
| **United Parcel Service** | | | |
| Effect of exchange rate changes on cash | ( 8.4) | 4.9 | 9.1 |
| Shareholders equity: Foreign currency adjustments | ( 19.7) | 22.0 | 17.1 |

**Exhibit 5.1** (continued)

| Selected Multinational Companies | 1988 | 1987 | 1986 |
|---|---|---|---|
| Union Carbide | | | |
| Foreign currency adjustments | 23.0 | 10.0 | 5.0 |
| Equity adjustment from foreign currency translation | (106.0) | ( 75.0) | N/A |
| Warner Lambert | · | | |
| Stockholders' equity cumulative translation adjustments | ( 75.5) | ( 64.8) | N/A |
| Effect of exchange rate changes on cash | ( 6.6) | ( 0.6) | 6.2 |
| Xerox | | | |
| Shareholders equity: Translation adjustments | 79.0 | 113.0 | 95.0 |
| Effect of exchange rate changes on cash | ( 25.0) | 55.0 | 14.0 |

N/A = Not available

*Source*: 1988 corporate annual reports.

corporation, the company can negotiate for receipt of U.S. dollars only. Otherwise, expenditures in the country will be paid in the domestic currency. This currency management has been employed in Mexico by astute corporations.

Currency value management can also be accomplished through corporate borrowing in the local currencies as a form of currency hedging and through corporate finance in *ecu's* (European Currency Units) or *acu's* (Asian Currency Units). Since European Currency Units represent a weighted basket of European currencies combined to comprise an artificial currency for trade use and the Asian Currency Units represent a weighted basket of Asian currencies for the same use, the corporation can reduce its risk from currency fluctuation by dealing in one of these more stabilized artificial currencies.

Royalty payments for the transfer of technology to a lesser developed nation are important to many multinational corporations. Often they will only transfer technology to the foreign country through the establishment of a subsidiary if they are promised rights of royalty repatriation by the local government. Otherwise, the corporation will not consider a site and a plant in locations in those countries.

If the government will not permit royalty repatriation, as is true in

Mexico, for example, the company may negotiate for other valuable concessions. McDonald's and IBM have negotiated for 100 percent foreign ownership for their subsidiaries even though Mexico generally bars 100 percent foreign ownership of companies operating within its national boundaries. But it wants the transfer of technology so it has been willing to negotiate terms.

### Interest Rate Management and Interest Rate Hedging

The financing of overseas real estate may entail loans from overseas sources. This type of financing can be a currency hedge that benefits the real estate area of the company. Local currencies are acquired for local real estate purchase or construction and operation. Then the loan can be repaid in local currency if such terms go into the original loan agreement.

In the case of local overseas financing, the real estate department or the finance department, whichever makes the financing decision, needs to be aware of the interest rate forecasts for the particular foreign country. The decision maker in real estate finance also needs to understand the basis for the interest rate. Once the basis for the loan interest rate and the national interest rate forecasts are known, the decision maker can manage the interest rate exposure.

If interest rates are expected to rise in the foreign financial market, the local foreign lender will probably negotiate a floating rate loan. If rates are expected to remain relatively stable, the foreign lender may negotiate a fixed rate for the loan that will finance the real estate acquisition, construction, and operation. (Since real estate is being financed, the local lender may suggest real estate collateral for more favorable loan terms.) If higher and fluctuating interest rates create undue risk in the profitability of the real estate transaction, the real estate or financial manager will possibly consider an interest rate swap to move from a floating rate position to a fixed rate position. Third parties exist in many financial markets for the creation of an appropriate interest rate swap.

If interest rates in the foreign financial market where the real estate is located are expected to decline soon, the lender will prefer a fixed rate loan. The company will probably prefer a floating rate loan for the same expected interest rate scenario. If so, the overall cost of the foreign fixed rate loan can be accepted and an interest rate swap for a floating rate loan negotiated at the same time with a third party in the financial community at home or abroad. Costs can be reduced by interest rate swaps when the cost of the less desirable loan plus the swap fee is less than the cost of the desired type loan.

The loan for real estate purposes may have a rate that is determined by several factors. Most of the U.S. loan interest rates are based on the lender's cost of funds. The cost of the lender's funds may be the federal funds cost or the cost of a short-term Euromarket loan. It may be the rediscount loan cost when the lender borrows from a federal regulatory authority such as the U.S. Federal Reserve or the U.S. Federal Home Loan Bank. Since the lender wants an adequate spread over his or her cost of funds, the interest rate on the loan is usually based on one of the lender's cost of funds, the "prime" local city or New York bank rate, or LIBOR (the London Inter Bank Offered Rate). Overseas, the loan rate may be set in the same manner, but the funds sources may be quite different. Many lenders do acquire funds from the Euromarket where LIBOR sets the rate on the high-credit financial institution and multinational corporation loans. If LIBOR's spread does not determine the multinational business lending of the financing source, then a local basis may be established for the important multinational corporate loan. In Latin America, the loan rate is often established on a spread over the government Treasury bill rate. As the government T-bill rate moves, the rate on the floating rate multinational corporation real estate loan moves. Since many corporations hedge interest rates affecting their international transactions, the basis for the foreign loan needs to be understood before a hedging program that will cover the loans in the particular foreign market is established. The international forward and futures markets contain interest-rate hedging contracts negotiable at a commercial bank (in the case of forward contracts) and in the securities markets (in the case of futures contracts).

### Price Controls

Another financial risk for the multinational corporation is the setting of price controls. The government may impose controls on prices paid for properties as well as set controls on the selling prices of the corporation products. While the product price controls threaten the operating profitability of the company, the property price controls threaten the eventual capital gains from the properties sold. Of course, the purchase price of needed property may be less than free market conditions would dictate. The costs of labor might be controlled through the government programs, but the cost of materials and equipment to the company might not be controlled. Some operating costs may be permitted to rise with demand and supply conditions while the prices to the ultimate consumers of the consumer and industrial goods may be controlled on a lower level than demand and supply conditions would warrant. A profit squeeze would result. But between the acquisition of property at controlled government price levels and the eventual sale of the property, the company has time for the government to possibly raise these price controls.

### Circumstances Prompting Government Consideration of Property Price Controls

When does a government consider and possibly implement a policy of property price controls? An environment of steeply rising property prices usually creates a situation demanding government attention. The government may see that property price rises are increasingly more rapidly than personal and corporate incomes. The housing sector may need attention as house and apartment condominium price rises substantially exceed personal income increases. The government also considers the affordability of standard housing for the nation's citizens. When housing prices are rising more rapidly than personal incomes, the government must give even more attention to this important economic and political sector. If commercial and industrial property prices are rising far more rapidly than corporate incomes, the government pays little attention.

### Use of Government Property Price Controls

Corporations who wish to sell their properties in Japan encounter property purchase price controls. The government has noted a high degree of property speculation and demand and supply conditions that prompt large and continuous increases in property prices. It has stepped in with property purchase price controls to try to control the land speculation and to restore satisfactory affordable housing.

When foreign or domestic corporations seek to buy property in Japan, they negotiate a purchase price which is then submitted to the appropriate government agency for approval before the property sale can be finalized. The same thing is true when the corporation's expatriate and domestic personnel seek to buy houses and apartments. The government must approve the purchase price. If the landlord realizes a heavy demand for the particular property, he may be tempted to take additional payments which may be offered to persuade him to deal with a particular buyer in preference over the other potential buyers. Key money payments are common to the Japanese commercial rental property sector.

When the corporation or corporate personnel seek to sell their properties, they encounter the government property price approval system. The seller might have to take a price lower than demand-supply conditions would dictate. The purchase/sale price is registered by the government. Additional payments to the seller beyond the government approved sale price are not sanctioned and registered by the government.

### Results of the Property Price Controls

The corporation and its employees may receive lower than market-determined selling prices for their properties. The capital gain may be lower than normally expected when demand and supply conditions determine the sale price. But in Japan large capital gains are still realized between the government approved purchase price and the government approved sale prices. The increases in property prices, particularly in the Tokyo and Osaka metropolitan areas, are unusually high compared to prices in other major cities of the world. Japan has little space for new development; therefore, land prices are constantly pushed higher as the domestic economy expands and multinational companies desire more production, distribution, and administrative office space in that expanding market.

## THE MANAGEMENT OF POLITICAL RISK

There is political turmoil in a number of countries where multinational businesses operate. The companies manage to the best of their abilities to protect their assets against loss in such political environments. The property of multinational corporations is subject to nationalization, vandalism, and partial or complete destruction caused by local unrest and civil insurrection.

### Iranian Nationalization of Property

In the 1970s, the United States government learned, for example, that a country like Iran can take over foreign corporate and government property when political conflicts occur. When Iran nationalized U.S. properties, it also took many American citizens as hostages for an extended period. To counteract this hostage taking, the United States froze Iran's bank accounts which were held in financial institutions.

In the Iranian incident, many types of foreign properties were nationalized by Iran. Hotels were used as military headquarters during the conflict. Foreign corporate offices and oil production, refining, and distribution facilities were claimed by Iran. Whatever business and government properties were located in Iran at the time were subject to nationalization. The U.S. government repeatedly, over the succeeding years, has requested appropriate compensation for its government and corporate properties. The corporations and local assets were at the mercy of a hostile government which had no intention of compensating the owners for the values of their confiscated properties. In this instance, the companies had no recourse against Iran except what the U.S. government could do. It was a political and military matter with no corporate defense.

### Argentine Nationalization of Foreign-Owned Properties

Argentina nationalized foreign corporations and their assets in the 1970s. As the Argentine government took over the multinational production plants and office buildings, they sought training for the Argentine persons who were entrusted with the operation of the companies and their properties but they did not promise compensation for the confiscated properties. Some of the U.S.-based companies received some compensation for their nationalized assets and operations from both the U.S. and Argentine governments, according to brief, undetailed public reports.

### The 1989 Chinese Student Revolt and the Political Clampdown

In May and June of 1989, the student uprising in the People's Republic of China (PRC) threatened the existing properties of foreign companies wherever they were located in the PRC. Several foreign corporations have offices and commercial properties in the vicinity of Tiananmen Square in Beijing. During the student riots that involved hundreds of thousands of Chinese citizens, these nearby properties were subject to vandalism and partial or total destruction. The Chinese Army was posted in the area mainly to protect Chinese property and the citizens who were not involved in the political conflict. They were also posted on the outskirts of the central Beijing square to control the demonstrators themselves.

In reaction, many of the multinational companies withdrew their employees, who were threatened in any way, from the country at least temporarily until stability was regained within the Chinese government. Top management of multinational corporate headquarters tried to stay abreast of the political developments in the summer of 1989. Most of the companies wished to retain their manufacturing and distribution facilities within China. The companies that had Chinese operations and properties on their planning boards wanted to proceed with only necessary changes to their proposed operating schedules in China. Chinese production and marketing are important to many multinational corporations who wish to operate and sell their products in such an immense marketplace. The labor supply of China is known to be trainable, manageable, and economical regarding wage scales. China particularly encourages multinational company operations because it gains foreign exchange, tax payments, and employment opportunities from the exporting activities of these companies. China also benefits from the transfer of technology that results. The nation's leaders want this transfer of technology ranging from military defense to industrial and consumer product manufacturing. In return, the PRC permits relatively long-term leases of land, but generally no capital or profit repatriation rights. The PRC leadership wishes to retain the scarce foreign reserves.

### Glasnost and Perestroika Policies of the USSR and Its Satellite Countries

As the Russian policies of glasnost and perestroika continue, foreign company entry to the communist marketplace is encouraged. The transfer of technology from the other advanced economies into the communist bloc will develop its civilian or domestic economy. The military establishment is well developed in the USSR and its satellites. The injection of elements of capitalism into the Soviet economic system will aid the domestic economies of the various communist countries.

There is risk that the new "capitalistic" economic policies will be rejected by the succeeding administrations of the governments of Russia and its satellites. As corporations from capitalistic countries enter the Soviet marketplace, they establish offices, manufacturing plants, and distribution centers. At present, the communist governments of USSR, Hungary, Poland, and the other Eastern countries are permitting only the lease of land for new corporate properties. Most of the properties are jointly owned by government entities. Therefore, capital commitment by foreign corporations for wholly owned properties is not permitted. But foreign joint-venture partners are putting in cash to build the commercial structures that will house foreign company operations.

How does the foreign corporation protect itself from nationalization of the property interests in communist countries? There is no direct protection of the foreign property interests. Indirectly the corporation must stay informed about the actions taken by the local and national governments in supporting or opposing foreign corporation operations and their property ownership. If there tends to be a rejection of the "capitalistic" methods of economic development, the foreign company top managements will probably request that the joint venture partner that is a local government entity buy out the interests of the foreign joint venture partners. In the meantime, the multinational corporation can withdraw its personnel and operations from the hostile government environment.

### Beirut, Lebanon, and the Ongoing Military Conflict in the Middle East

While the shelling and other fighting goes on in Beirut, Lebanon, multinational corporations continue to do business there. As long as it's possible to operate their businesses in this environment of military conflicts, most of the foreign countries will continue to manufacture and distribute. Management strives to stay abreast of current economic and military policy changes while it maintains the necessary security for its personnel, properties, and other assets.

Military conflicts in Central America also affect the operations of U.S.-based multinational companies. As long as materials and supplies can be procured and a demand exists for products generated in the various Central American markets, the multinational companies can continue to operate, perhaps profitably, until better economic times arrive. U.S. fast food companies, for example, have tried to retain their businesses in Nicaragua and Honduras even though consumer spending continues on a low level and military action persists. If the governments can attain stability in the coming years, these companies can regain normal profitability.

## Government Approval of Land Use Changes

Corporations need property in urban areas. Office space is usually acquired in a central business district, in the business districts surrounding it, or in the outlying suburban business districts. Industrial space is usually needed in the suburbs of a major city. If housing for expatriate employees is needed, this needs to be located in good residential areas devoted to the safety and convenience of expatriate corporate families. If a corporation needs retail property, it usually will be located in the central or secondary business districts near offices and housing.

If existing property is acquired, it may need conversion to new land use. It can be refurbished to accommodate the technological equipment, business operation, and staff of the new occupant. A corporation which does not find satisfactory existing premises at a reasonable price or rent may wish to construct buildings for its occupancy. Any excess space in the new building, which represents company accommodations for expected business expansion, may be leased temporarily to outside companies. If property is rented, leasehold improvements may be necessary to allow the new corporate tenant to operate profitably. Any contemplated building and land use changes must be approved by the local government.

*The Government Land Use Approval Process.* If a corporation wants to make any change in the use of land within the local government's jurisdiction, a government agency must approve the land use change whether it constitutes building construction, reconstruction, or renovation or change in leasehold improvements. The corporation must submit to the local authority the proposed architectural plans and specifications for the land use change. The corporation's architect and builder must prepare the necessary sketches and plans for the government authority at the request of the corporate real estate department. If the plans are approved, the government entity will grant construction approval in the form of a building permit, license to build, or other such authorization.

Building plans and specifications are usually submitted to the property government agency. They will be turned over to a department or committee who is charged with reviewing plans for land use change. Once the department or committee has approved the projected changes, a board of overseers, planning commissioners, or building supervisors will take the recommendations and proceed with public hearings on the planned land changes. In advance of the public hearing or the board's final decision, newspaper announcements usually inform the public of the impending actions. At the public hearing, any citizen may be heard. The hearing can produce positive and negative remarks from interested parties about the proposed land use change. The decision-making body of the government agency will hear comments during the hearing and also before and after the hearing. They must deliberate about the land use change precedents, the need for corporate land use change, the views of the public and closely associated private and public real estate interest groups, and their agency's plans for the future of the particular urban area before making a decision to approve or disapprove the land use change. The current zoning and building codes and the master plans for the urban area must be compared to the corporation's building plans.

The time necessary for this decision-making process may be short or it may be quite lengthy and costly. The change posed by the corporation may cause little interest or some mild interest. In the extreme, the public may immediately express a strong opinion about the impending corporate building change. Newspapers might report strong political sentiments about the corporation's application. A political controversy might occur with a lengthy public airing and numerous public hearings over a period of time. Eventually the governing board will either approve or disapprove the government extension of the necessary permit or license for the proposed property change.

*The Corporation's Position in the Government Land Use Approval Process.* The corporation is concerned about the time necessary for property acquisition and changes in the property. The price of the government approval may be a major factor in building acquisition and improvement costs or building development and construction costs. The employment of local specialists in land use approval may be another consideration. The company might employ corporate legal, real estate, construction engineering, and urban planning specialists. The corporation—particularly one making an initial entry into a country's market—may or may not appreciate being in the public eye if its actions promote a political controversy. There can be a public relations impact as a result of the application for government approval of the land use change. Some corporations actively guard their corporate images against all possible negative intrusions.

In countries with strong urban planning legislation and regulations, corporations find that even the most amiable land use planning situations take considerable time. When political controversy arises in such environments, the land changes may never be approved. If approval is received—perhaps in the form of a building permit—it may result from extensive petitioning and consultation with various members of the decision-making group. An expensive corporate public relations effort might be necessary to sway public opinion. Paid civil servants and the decision-making board members may expect some personal compensation for their time and effort in a particular case.

*Management of the Corporate Risks from Government Approval of Land Use Changes.* The chances of disapproval of the proposed land use changes are reduced if the corporation is seen as a "good national citizen." Local people are more willing to grant the land use change if the corporation is seen as a "member of the community" and works to benefit the community with its employment practices and other contributions. Therefore, the corporation must cultivate a good image before it can expect rapid approval of requested land use changes. If the company does not want to stir up the animosity and jealousy of its competitors and of the real estate society in which it must operate, it must publicly display its congeniality and acceptance of the local social and economic institutions. It does not want to appear to challenge its associates in the political arena or the marketplace.

To avoid conflict with local traditions, a corporation can employ local public relations, land use planning, and real estate personnel. It might ask local political and business leaders to serve on the board of its subsidiary, as does IBM Italy.

Through long-range real estate and corporate operations planning, company moves into new foreign locations can be anticipated long in advance of the expansion. This longer lead time permits normal negotiation for land use planning consents without generating corporate emergencies in the new market setting. Mature growth companies have the luxury of long-range planning. Companies that are growing rapidly do not have this luxury to enter into time-consuming negotiations with local government officials over property needed immediately.

The real estate director must inform top management of the normal process for land use change approval. Otherwise, top management may be frustrated with the lengthy negotiations and the costs of the process. Alternatives to immediate occupancy of premises in the new market may have to be presented to the corporate decision makers.

Two alternatives to an immediate move into desirable owner-occupied premises may be to either (1) lease temporary space that generally meets corporate space requirements, or (2) enter the new foreign market through extension of the personnel, production, and distribution facilities of a nearby country until government approvals are acquired for appropriate sites for the necessary production plants, office buildings, and retail and wholesale distribution facilities. When the company must lease temporary space without the most advantageous leasehold improvements, it may find that space in several buildings in several urban locations is required to accommodate the growing corporate management, staff, and production personnel. For example, International Business Machines is said to have a dozen or more property locations in the Milan, Italy metropolitan area. A location for a large property complex has not been acquired to accommodate the entire Milan company operation. Land use approvals for adequate sites for major multinational firms come slowly from the government.

The land use approval systems of many non-U.S. locations are routinely handled with payoffs and bribes of political and urban planning officials. Federal laws in the United States make such payments illegal so U.S.-based multinational companies cannot enter into the normal business practices in many countries. Only justifiable consulting or other reasonable fees can be offered local people who are knowledgeable in land use planning systems and who can assist the corporation in preparing the necessary applications and in presenting them effectively to the local decision makers.

## Contract Enforcement Systems

Private property rights and their enforcement are the rule in the United States, Canada, Western Europe, the Scandinavian countries, parts of Asia, and Japan. Where the government is controlled by a communist party or by tribal and religious leaders, the property rights of private citizens and companies may not be enforced.

Even where private property rights are honored and protected, some countries, such as South Africa, make a difference between the property rights of one group of citizens and another group of citizens. Generally the property rights of white South Africans are different and are enforced differently than the property rights of black South Africans. Therefore, the corporate properties of primarily black South African shareholders may be treated differently by statute and regulation than the corporate properties of white South African stockholders.

In communist countries, such as Russia and China, corporations from other countries may enter into agreements with the government entities and businesses controlled by the communist legal system. The communist partner to the agreement is not subject to the terms of the contract in the same manner as the other partner. Contract law under the common law and the civil codes is entirely different from law under the communist legal systems. Property in communist countries is owned by the state and is merely allocated on a leasehold basis through the individual communes to the commune members. There are no private property rights except for certain leasehold rights attributable to the commune-allocated properties and properties built by commune members for their personal and business use.

Even in the countries that preserve private property rights for their citizens and private companies, the legal enforcement systems differ measurably. For example, in Japan there are few attorneys for its 125 million population. The Japanese prefer negotiation and compromise to litigation. They continue to believe in the power of group consensus. Only rarely does a corporation in Japan enter into lengthy and costly litigation to solve a property dispute. In contrast, the United States is a litigious society. Suits involving property disputes are constantly filed in the courts for legal resolution. The number of attorneys per capita in the United States is relatively high. There are many attorneys available and capable of handling real estate disputes. Through international law, the international real estate disputes can be resolved.

Contract law regarding real estate contract enforcement varies among the non-communist countries. After a property buyer in the United Kingdom has signed a purchase agreement with a seller and deposited earnest money with the estate manager (called a licensed real estate salesperson, broker, or agent in the United States), the seller may without legal consequences contract and sell the same property to another buyer offering a higher price. It is reportedly the same in South Korea. In the United States, the seller in such a situation would be liable for prosecution in the courts. Even within the United Kingdom, such property purchase situations are subject to varying legal enforcement. Scottish purchase agreement systems are different from English ones.

It has already been mentioned that under-the-counter property payments and bribery of government officials and business people may be condoned in some societies but that they are illegal in other societies such as in the United States. In addition, lease provisions are different under a European civil code than under the common law of England, the United States, and Hong Kong. In the early 1980s, mortgage law was enacted in Hong Kong which took on the general legal dimensions of the mortgage law under the English common law. The British rule of Hong Kong for so many decades has made the colonial government leadership receptive to the adoption of the British common law. When Hong Kong becomes a special administrative district of the People's Republic of China in 1997, the leases on the majority of Hong Kong will be honored. Perhaps other portions of the English common law will also be honored by the parent communist government.[1]

## The Implications of Corporate Takeovers

To the multinational corporation director of real estate, corporate takeovers imply:

Possible sale of key properties of the acquired company

Possible replacement of the real estate director and/or staff with the real estate director and/or staff of the acquiring company or demotion of acquired company personnel in favor of higher level staff from the acquiring company

Broader responsibilities of the existing real estate director due to wider global property coverage with the assumption of the properties of the acquiring company

New responsibilities and duties from different policies of the acquiring company or a diminution of responsibilities and duties for the same reason

Consolidation and restructuring of the resulting company which may mean disposal of unnecessary properties and acquisition or development of new properties for joint company operation

Expansion into new markets with new properties from the infusion of new corporate capital

Corporate takeovers are fraught with risk and with opportunities for the officers of the acquired company. Even the officers of the acquiring company may feel threatened if the acquired company is seen to have an experienced, competent, and well-qualified international real estate department.

## ENVIRONMENTAL RISKS AND THEIR MANAGEMENT

Corporations may be subject to environmental protection controls of many kinds in each country in which the company is located. Some of the environmentally sensitive areas are:

Asbestos insulation

Nuclear waste disposal

Chlorofluorocarbon (CFC) waste disposal

Waste water disposal

Water pollution

Air pollution

Noise pollution

Many countries have environmental protection legislation in effect, but not all countries enforce their legislation; just as many countries have comprehensive building codes in place but not all those countries have the financial capacity and personnel to enforce the observance of the building codes. In like manner, environmental protection regulations require substantial financial capacity and personnel to investigate and enforce the legislated requirements.

### Corporate Environmental Investigation and Management Policies

A multinational corporation normally wants to comply with the environmental protection standards of the community and country in which it wants to do business. Therefore, the company can take an aggressive stance toward environmental protection and investigate thoroughly the environmental impact of a proposed industrial plant, office building, or distribution facility and then voluntarily take steps to minimize the expected impact.

Otherwise, the company can passively investigate the environmental impact and wait until national and local environmental protection authorities specify actions to alleviate the recognized pollution elements from the proposed or existing plant, office, or distribution facility.

The industrial plant is the property most likely to pollute the local environment with its waste water, air, and noise emissions. An office building may promote dangerous water runoff due to the extensive paved parking lots that lead to residential and commercial neighborhoods. An incinerator operation at a retail or wholesale facility may pollute the air. The delivery truck entry and exit and the loading and unloading of cargo may cause noise pollution and lighting problems from nighttime work when residential neighborhoods abut the commercial or industrial location.

When corporation buildings are constructed or renovated, the environment is affected by debris falling into trash containers below. Trash collection conduits may be used to connect the higher floors with the ground-level containers. The operation of construction machinery may disturb walking passersby. Covered walkways may be installed to protect people walking on the bordering sidewalks. Workers are subject to falls from high places on the building iron work if unusually high winds arise. They need protection in the form of temporary building sheathing and safety nets below to reduce injury from possible falls.

When buildings are constructed or renovated in densely populated central cities, traffic congestion often occurs on the surrounding streets. Construction trailers must be parked at the site. They tend to require a lane or so of the normal street so that traffic is restricted to less space for two-way passage. The corporate owner of the property and its general contractor can work with the city government authorities to place the construction trailers most advantageously and to alleviate the traffic congestion as much as possible. The city may have detailed ordinances about environmental precautions for inner city construction and reconstruction work. The city and the company will want the construction work concluded as quickly as possible. Thus, the city government preserves its livable and workable environment, and the company reduces costs through shorter financing periods for the construction and less man-hours and payroll obligations.

### Adequate Water Supply and Adequate Waste Water Treatment

Most industrial plants need ample water supplies at adequate water pressures. A company might seek to buy the needed water supplies from neighboring municipalities and their public utilities. If this course of action does not work, the company may have to seek other sources of water.

Perhaps a location on a major water source is one answer. Most chemical companies find that this is the best solution to their major water need. If the pressure of the water must be increased for manufacturing processes, a water tower can be erected to gain pressure from the height of the water reserve tank.

If an industrial plant site in a rural area is being contemplated, the company may need to consider waste water treatment. For example, often in rural India a neighboring community will drink and otherwise use water expelled from an industrial plant. If the company wishes to avoid health and safety problems for its employees and others living in the vicinity, it must consider waste water treatment. Perhaps secured sedimentation ponds can be used for water treatment before it is permitted to flow back into the community water supply. Many countries permit industrial waste to be dispersed into the rivers and streams from which water for residential communities is drawn. Multinational corporations may plan to treat their industrial waste water before it is permitted to flow into the neighboring rivers and streams. This would exhibit an aggressive environmental policy. Otherwise, the company could wait until local authorities specified the minimal steps the corporation must take to satisfy environmental protection regulations. The company's attorneys should keep abreast of the changes in the local environmental protection rules.

## Adequate Energy Supply and Its Management

Industrial plants need continuous sources of energy for their operations. Office buildings require continuous sources of power for their elevators; heating, ventilation, and air conditioning systems; lighting; and office equipment operation. Warehousing and other distribution facilities need power for lighting, air conditioning and heating, and automated inventory control and conveyor systems. Power sources may be so strategic to industrial plants that site selection specification may be headed by a demand for immediate access to power plants including nuclear plants.

Even though an adequate energy supply may be assured the company by the purchase of energy from nearby utility companies, the company may wish to conserve its fuel usage and reduce utility expense. Therefore, the company may install computerized energy conservation systems in its office buildings, warehouses, and industrial plants. Automatic, computerized temperature controls in corporate buildings are becoming the general rule in leading industrialized countries in the world. Like an adequate water supply, the corporation needs an adequate power supply for its corporate property operation, its employee homes, and the community facilities that serve corporate management, staff, and industrial workers.

### Adequate Transportation System and Managerial Policies

The employees must get to and from the workplace. The materials and supplies must get to and from the industrial plant and the distribution center. Clients, suppliers, and employees of office buildings must get to and from those locations. The most basic transportation need is adequate travel accommodations between the home and the workplace. Then travel accommodations must adequately connect the office with the industrial plant and the warehouse. The delivery trucks of the company must travel from their permanent storage locations to the necessary delivery sites and the docks of the company warehouses and plants and back to the storage locations. These transportation needs fit most corporations no matter what the national locations.

*Airport and Roadway Adequacy.* A specialized delivery corporation, such as United Parcel Service, which operates in many countries must consider transportation facilities strategic to their service and operating costs. All companies, including U.P.S., primarily consider sites that are close to the forecasted delivery points and the airport serving the particular delivery station. Much of the multinational delivery company's business is overnight delivery of documents and packages. Therefore, airport delivery at night from distant pickup points links with the early morning delivery facility to meet the customer requirements. Airport property leasing, facilities for efficient plant loading and unloading and truck loading and unloading at night, and take-off and landing fee agreements are important to such delivery companies.

Roadway adequacy is also important to companies. Their materials and supplies must reach their production plants, and their finished materials must reach customers as soon as possible. Employees must be able to reach work from their homes within reasonable times and then reach their homes within reasonable time after work. The materials moved by truck must be safe and secure on the roadway. Therefore, the roadways need to be reasonably level, paved, and safe. Problems arise in the area of highway transportation when manufacturing plants are sited in rural areas of less developed countries. The local government may be asked to improve the highway system if it seeks to entice major multinational employers. This element may be only part of the infrastructure normally provided by local government that the corporation may need for reasonable operation of its plants and other buildings. The roadway systems of suburban and rural areas of Latin America, Africa, and parts of Asia are a problem for the truck and personnel transportation needs of major companies.

*Employee Payment for Unusual Commuting Time.* On occasion, multinational employers face extra payment to employees, including real estate department employees, who must travel an unusual distance to reach the workplace. These payments are made in special commuting situations in the headquarters country as well as in foreign countries. While companies have paid workers with unusual commuting times in Houston, Texas, they have paid extra amounts to employees in their London locations for unusually long commuting times there.

## Appropriate and Adequate Labor Supply and Its Training

Corporate operation of plants, office buildings, and warehouses depends on appropriate and adequate labor supplies. As part of the site selection process, the company team must analyze the availability of trained and skilled labor required by company operations or of labor that is amenable to training and skill development. Then the company must explore the possibility of the local government training and educating the available labor. Local government incentive packages for prospective corporate employers often contain this attractive provision. Local governments might even pay for local employees to be trained and educated in the home country of the multinational corporations. Recently foreign employees were brought in for four- to six-week stays in Virginia and Florida to be trained by a major multinational telecommunications company for their job assignments in the foreign country. The training expenses for these prospective employees were subsidized by the foreign government while the training was conducted by the multinational company employees in the United States.

*Management Policies of Hiring Local Managers and Nonmanagerial Employees.* Local people are hired by multinational corporations to fill most of the middle- and lower-management and nonmanagerial positions of the company subsidiary. Hiring local people allows the foreign company to become a part of the community immediately in the eyes of its citizens. Any criticism of the intrusion of foreign people and companies is immediately squelched by this employment tactic. Besides, the company may require only one or two foreign managers at the location to get the operation going and operating continuously. The costs of supporting a manager from the home office at the particular foreign site are prohibitive for most multinational companies.

*Employment of Local Property Managers.* The company seeks local people who have the qualifications and experience that will enable them to manage or assist in the management of the plant, office buildings, and distribution facilities. Most home office real estate departments are short-staffed. Home office people may not be able to even set up the property management operation at the new foreign site. But the corporate project manager may select one or more property managers from the qualified and experienced people in the community. The home office real estate department may assist with this selection. In some instances, a property management contract is drawn up between the corporation and a local estate management firm for the services required. International real estate firms, such as London-based Cluttons, Knight Frank & Rutley or Jones Lang Wootton, may be located in the marketplace and offer property management services on a contract basis.

### Adequacy of Local Raw Materials Sources

Companies cannot operate without a ready and continuous source of raw materials that fit their production needs. Oil companies such as Amoco and Royal Dutch Shell require continuous and plentiful sources of oil and gas. Therefore, most of the major oil company exploration locations are in the North Sea; off the South China Sea coast; in the Bering Straits north of Alaska; in Saudi Arabia, Kuwait, and other Middle Eastern locations; and in other similar oil producing locations of the world. Morton's, a worldwide salt company, must be located near adequate sources of salt. They take the basic salt product and refine it into table and industrial salt products for worldwide marketing. McDonald's must supply itself with quality food products in every location. Since potatoes of the right texture and quality are difficult to buy from local suppliers in many markets, varieties of Russet potatoes must be provided for local producers who often have to be taught how to grow such quality products. After local suppliers have learned how to produce the right potatoes and McDonald's source of quality potatoes is assured, McDonald's usually enters into long-term production contracts with these local sources. Importing potatoes or potato products to McDonald's retail outlets at great distance from the sources is prohibitively expensive. Finding appropriate beef product sources is also a problem for McDonald's Corporation in some parts of the world, such as the Middle East.

## OTHER RISKS OF MULTINATIONAL CORPORATIONS IN FOREIGN LOCATIONS THAT AFFECT PROPERTY MANAGEMENT

In addition to financial, political, and environmental risks, multinational corporations face other risks. Security, anti-national sentiment, construction management, and atmospheric and geologic risks affect most global firms.

### Security Risks and Their Management

Security of plants, office complexes, and distribution facilities is strategic both at home and abroad. The security systems at home may be adapted to overseas property needs. For example, the Warner Lambert production plant in Beirut, Lebanon needs strong security for defense against the military unrest in the city. They maintain a plant in an area that needs the employment and the products they create. In Lima, Peru, security is so important to a major multinational corporation that it has a security lookout tower on the premises of the plant. Since most Peruvians have relatively low incomes and the many problems associated with low incomes, there continues to be civil unrest within the country. In addition, illegal drugs are produced and distributed in the mountainous regions, according to recent international newspaper reports. Many companies have production plants in Pakistan and India where continuous political unrest is the rule, not the exception. Company security systems in place and operating are vital to company success in such locations.

Other Latin American locations experience civil unrest due to poor economic conditions and weak political leadership. One major U.S.-based company experienced hand-thrown and hand-made explosives even though its premises were set back many yards from the security fences surrounding the facility. Since the company was wise enough to set its premises back from the exterior boundaries where the security fences were maintained, the premises did not suffer major damages.

Inner city corporate buildings are subject to vandalism and other destruction due to the unrest caused by high unemployment levels or drug trafficking. The relatively new office building of IBM France in the area of La Defense office complex has built into its premises an elaborate magnetic card computerized walk-through entrance for IBM employees and visitors. The world headquarters of FIABCI, the International Real Estate Federation, located on the Left Bank of Paris, has a security system to keep out passersby. These Paris office building locations are subject to the constant strikes of civil servants and private company employees and disruptive demonstrations for one reason or another. Of course, high levels of thievery are common in all cities.

## Antinational Sentiments That Affect Company Operations

The West Germans and British have continually demonstrated and picketed at European and U.S.-based military establishments and plants which produce military products and nuclear power. Citizens of many nations express anti-American sentiments. Perhaps these sentiments express their frustration at America's continual military presence in their countries. Even McDonald's has experienced the expression of anti-American sentiments by local people. Since McDonald's is located in 70 or more countries, they are one of the leading American corporate ambassadors. If local people are dissatisfied with a recent American government action or purported action, a few people may demonstrate or boycott the local McDonald's or another American corporate subsidiary. Most multinational corporations feel antinational sentiments occasionally and must be prepared to counteract such negative expressions that may have little to do with the operation of their particular company.

In some African countries, including Nigeria, company security must extend to protection of the home and family of plant managers. Political and military unrest continues in most African nations.

The local public relations and advertising efforts of a company may focus on the dissipation of the antinational sentiment which affects the company subsidiary's operations. News releases and advertising may express the positive community relationships that the company represents. Generally the company efforts focus on:

Company employment of local managers and workers

Company support of community facilities that benefit the general community as well as their managers and employees

Company acquisition of local raw materials, equipment, and machinery

Company payment of local property, sales, and income taxes

Company provision of services to the local community such as rapid and overnight document and parcel service from distant places

Company housing for employees in well-designed communities with quality environmental features

### Atmospheric and Geological Conditions Pose Risks for the Multinational Corporation

Many atmospheric and geological conditions pose risks for corporations locating around the world. Earthquakes have recently occurred in Greece, eastern Sudan, Taiwan, Japan, southern California in the United States, Eastern Europe, Ecuador, and Mexico. Once an earthquake has occurred in one place, there is a likelihood that another will occur there. Where seismic faults exist, earthquakes may repeatedly cause damage to the area and its properties.

Monsoons occur periodically in East, South, and Southeast Asia. In recent years, safe harbors have been built for monsoon protection. Properties have been built back from the waterfronts that are usually subject to huge waves and driving winds. Countries are planning similar protections in hurricane-prone areas of the world. The Caribbean islands and the coastal regions along the Caribbean are affected repeatedly by hurricanes. The swirling wind conditions of the Caribbean gulf create tornadoes which move to locations on land and do tremendous destruction to properties.

Fires often damage the many wooden structures in Latin America. This was true of Hong Kong and Japan before extensive rebuilding occurred after the Second World War. Steel and concrete buildings dispel the threat of structural fires, but the threat of fire which destroys interior furnishings remains.

The heat of the sun near the equator may interfere with building activity. Corporate structures should be positioned so the sun's heat will not directly penetrate the working premises. The cold of the polar regions requires adequate insulation to permit corporate work to continue within the structures.

*Precautions against Atmospheric and Geological Risk Conditions.* In addition to well-insulated structures positioned to repel hot sun, fire repellant furnishings should decorate office spaces, and steel and concrete be preferred to lumber for construction. The company gains protection locating adequate fire extinguishers on the premises and by building structures that can be reached by the ladder trucks of the local fire departments.

Engineers have discovered methods of building structures to prevent massive damage from earthquakes. The newer buildings in earthquake-prone areas have generally been built to such engineering specifications. For example, the newer residential and office buildings of Mexico City withstood damage in the recent earthquakes better than the older buildings not built according to the new building codes. Japan's newer buildings— particularly the high-rise office buildings of the central business district of Tokyo—are built by new codes that give earthquake protection. Also the older wooden residential and commercial buildings are fast disappearing, replaced by steel and concrete structures that are less prone to fire and earthquake damage.

Damage from monsoons, hurricanes, and tornadoes can be minimized with buildings constructed to withstand high winds and some standing water. Some sway in high-rise buildings may be needed in order for the building to withstand winds, so the engineers must estimate how much flexibility is necessary in the structural components. Window covers reduce hurricane and tornado damage. Underground levels for strategic building and computer operating systems are often needed in tornado-prone areas. Some owners employ architects to design totally or partially earth-covered buildings for family living and commercial enterprises. The low level of the roof line does not impede the low-level tornadoes passing through the area.

## The Risks of Construction Management

The architect can design protection against earthquakes, monsoons, hurricanes, and tornadoes, but the construction manager must build the structure to actual specifications and must be well qualified to adapt to changes caused by local supply conditions as well as to manage the job to prevent cost overruns from delayed completion. Strikes, unexpected foul weather, delays in importation of building materials, and other emergencies can occur and those need the attention of good construction management.

Most corporations with large real estate and construction engineering departments design and orchestrate the construction process from the home office, but require local subcontractors and perhaps a local general contractor for the on-site work. Well-qualified construction labor and management may be scarce in the country where the structural project is underway. For example, for the last ten years the major building programs of Singapore have required the importation of large amounts of construction labor and management. People from Japan and other southeast Asian countries have been temporarily housed in Singapore to accomplish the work associated with the construction of high-quality hotels, industrial buildings, apartment complexes, and shopping centers. A case that illustrates some of the risks and their management may be found in Appendix 5.A.

## SUMMARY AND CONCLUSIONS

There are many controllable and uncontrollable risks associated with global corporations and their properties. These risks may be categorized as financial, political, environmental, and other types. The risk management associated with the corporate properties may be shared by the corporate real estate, finance, foreign exchange, international finance and investment, and other departments within the company.

The company must manage financial risks such as inflation, repatriation of funds, barter agreements, special payment provisions, currency, and interest rates. Also some companies must manage the risks associated with governmental nationalization of foreign property, political unrest and government repercussions, daily military conflicts in the immediate vicinity of corporate operations, government approval of land use changes, various procedures for contract enforcement, and corporate takeovers.

Environmental risks that must be managed by the multinational company include the environmental protection policies of the various countries and the adequacy and appropriateness of the water supply, water treatment plants, energy supply, transportation system, and the labor supply. The available labor must have the necessary job skills or be trainable and willing to work at new jobs requiring new skills and abilities.

Corporate management must provide security when foreign and domestic conditions call for it. Public relations and advertising efforts may be employed to combat antinational sentiments which affect the use of company property and the operation of the business. Precautions must be taken against atmospheric and geological risks which may interfere with property use. These risks involve earthquakes, monsoons, tornadoes, and hurricanes. Fire protection is also needed. Experienced construction management reduces the risks of poor construction from using inexperienced construction labor.

## NOTE

1. The reader may learn more about the differences in international law and the risks to the corporation by reading Chapter 4, "Development Trends and Differences in International Law" in this author's book, *Guide to International Real Estate Investment* (Westport, Conn.: Quorum Books, 1988).

## BIBLIOGRAPHY

Beatley, Paul Cullen. "The Benefits of a Global Environmental Compliance Strategy." *Site Selection*, June 1989, pp. 15+.

——. "Environmental Considerations for Foreign Direct Investment in the United States." *Site Selection*, April 1988, pp. 4+.

Dobie, Maureen. "E. I. (Everett I.) Brown Firm Hoping to Profit from Perestroika." *Indianapolis Business Journal* 10, no. 17, August 7–13, 1989, pp. 1, 50.

Hines, Mary Alice. *Guide to International Real Estate Investment*. Westport, Conn.: Quorum Books, 1988.

——. *International Income Property Investment*. Scottsdale, Ariz.: International Real Estate Institute, 1985.

Huntley, Judith. "More Ways to Limit Financial Risks." *Financial Times*, July 12, 1989, p. III.

Price Waterhouse. *Foreign Exchange Information: A Worldwide Survey*. New York: Price Waterhouse, 1989.

# APPENDIX 5.A

# SITE SELECTION IN INDIA: A CASE STUDY

## Harry S. Thomes and Robert G. Fulton

This paper will focus on the selection of a large industrial site overseas. We will begin with a brief review of how Du Pont conducts overseas site selection and then present a case study.

Although Du Pont's site-selection procedures are quite formalized domestically, on the international scene the process tends to be less structured. This is because within the U.S., where everything is under the control of the parent organization, Du Pont is more rigid with the requirement that the search for a new site begin and end with the corporate real estate section. We are the only corporate section that has the authority to execute agreements pertaining to real estate.

Internationally, with the myriad of separate, independent subsidiaries, the real estate section's official role is not to approve or execute but to exercise a veto if a project seems to be contrary to Du Pont's business interests. In any case, as Du Pont expands overseas, we in real estate and the other necessary disciplines of site selection are being called into a project earlier than was the case in the past. And we believe that the result has been that the time and cost of acquiring a foreign site are being cut significantly.

The impetus for an overseas site originates with a business need to be in a particular place with a particular product. The need could be to serve the local market for regional or worldwide export or a combination of reasons. In most countries, Du Pont already has a staffed representative office primarily for marketing purposes and has a country manager in place. The industrial department or business unit will work initially through the real estate office to determine what government approvals are necessary and what are the acceptable areas in which to locate.

In many cases, particularly in the Far East, but also in Europe and Latin America, there are only certain areas of

countries where certain products can be produced. For chemical businesses, locational constraints are a factor especially with respect to environmental concerns. Sometimes, only certain types of products can be manufactured in what the real estate section would consider a desirable location. For example, Du Pont recently acquired a small site in China in a special economic zone, a very promising location just outside of Hong Kong. Here the authorities will only accept industries that produce high-tech goods and that will export a high percentage of their product.

Also, there is a great desire in many countries to locate industry far away from major cities and out into the less-developed countryside. Such locations can be difficult for expatriates who Du Pont must move there, for recruitment of professionals such as engineers and for locating maintenance and other local support services to serve the operation.

The Indian government only granted four licenses for plants located in four different locations to make the product lycra spandex for swimsuits. The siting of one of those facilities is discussed below. The Indian officials' desire was to get industry out into less-developed areas and away from the major cities. Du Pont's site is near where most of the knitting mills are located in northeast India. Three other companies got in ahead of Du Pont and got the three other good areas designated for lycra spandex production, better areas quite possibly than Du Pont's site. So Du Pont was pretty much locked into this area.

Many times, the only way to enter a foreign market is through a joint-venture partner. Again, the business unit will seek out such a partner. The site-selection team often then gives the partner responsibility for obtaining the necessary government approvals and for coming up with the candidate sites. In some countries, it is nearly impossible for a non-domestic company to even attempt to acquire property

**Harry Thomes** *is manager of international real estate for E. I. Du Pont. He has been with Du Pont for 15 years in the corporate real estate group, where he has handled commercial, industrial, residential and planning assignments.*

**Robert Fulton** *is responsible for logistics planning at Du Pont. His work has taken him to 49 countries, including India, for site-selection work. This article is taken from Thomes and Fulton's joint presentation to a workshop of IDRC's Hilton Head World Congress.*

Reproduced from *Site Selection*, July/August 1989, by permission of the publisher, Conway Data, Inc., Atlanta. No further reproduction is permitted.

in its own name. In any case, Du Pont's corporate site-selection team formulates criteria that it feels are essential to a successful site and forwards this information to the potential partner.

### International Site-Selection Team

When the list of candidate sites has been narrowed to a few choices, a select group from Du Pont, the site-selection team, visits the sites to evaluate them and make a recommendation regarding which one should be chosen. The team usually consists of a real estate person, civil engineer, manufacturing representative, logistics expert and other specialized personnel if needed. If there is no joint-venture partner, the real estate representative works with the local Du Pont office to develop candidate sites before the site team goes to work. And if it is a large enough project, one of Du Pont's regional planning people may also assist. To aid in this search, the site-selection team frequently seeks out government industrial development people, university professors, transportation companies, etc. Real estate brokers are seldom of any value in selecting a large industrial site, and there may not even be any brokerage firms in the area.

Now, we will expand on the roles of each site-selection team member. The real estate representative is interested in making sure that all of the necessary bases are covered by the other members of the team and in evaluating the costs and methods for site procurement. He will also investigate the possibilities for expatriate housing and any off-site support requirements, such as warehousing and office space. The real estate representative will summarize his findings for the business unit for inclusion in that unit's project report, which they submit to the appropriate corporate level for authorization to proceed with the project.

The civil engineer is interested in soil stability, utilities (water and electricity, etc.), wind direction, environmental concerns, methods of construction, etc.

The logistics expert evaluates the feasibility of getting raw material into the site and finished product out. This was a particular concern in the case study that we will come to later in this article.

The manufacturing or operations representative concentrates on the workforce, work rules, quality of labor and the overall suitability of the location for the product.

The whole team or subgroups visit existing plants operating in the area to gather information on the work force, local government, reliability of the electrical service, etc. The site-selection team also visits the utility companies and examines their facilities and the local communities and schools, which are of great interest to expatriates and their families. Utility service will be provided to the site by the local government, which will arrange for hookups from the state-owned electrical water companies.

Back home in the office, the site-selection team presents its findings to a steering committee made up of management, legal, public affairs and finance representatives. This committee gives the site-selection team guidance on corporate concerns and regarding who will have input into the final recommendation and start-up of the facility.

### Site Selection in India — A Brief Case Study

Within the last several years, Du Pont has begun to look at India and to consider serving this market. With over 700 million people, India can no longer be ignored as a market for Du Pont's products. In this country, at least for the products Du Pont is interested in manufacturing, it is mandatory to have an Indian joint-venture partner. The typical company ownership breakdown is 40 percent to the Indian partner, 40 percent to the non-Indian partner and 20 percent to the Indian government. Also, to manufacture a product in the country, the company must obtain a license from the government for a particular area, which limits the number of alternative sites.

Du Pont gave its joint-venture partner the tasks of evaluating general areas according to the following criteria:

- proximity to market,
- proximity to port,
- raw material transport,
- state government stability,
- cooperation to be expected of state government,
- ease of obtaining license clearance,
- industrial relations,
- labor costs,
- site costs,
- the power situation,
- pollution clearance,
- financial incentives,
- proximity to infrastructure and
- proximity to Delhi, the capitol of India and the location of headquarters offices of both Du Pont and its Indian partner.

Those locations that the site-selection team identified as having insurmountable obstacles, such as a general lack of acceptance of the chemical plant and state government instability, were excluded from further consideration. The Indian state of Uttar Pradesh in the northeast portion of the country at the foothills of the Himalayas was chosen as a potential location. Even so, this site is located 1,700 kilometers (900 miles) from the nearest ocean port, with road access and driving conditions treacherous at many points along the way accessing the site.

> ❛
> *The logistics expert evaluates the feasibility of getting raw material into the site and finished product out.*
> ❜

Du Pont's joint-venture partner obtained the license for a manufacturing facility and located the 570-hectare (230-acre) site in Bhang Wan, population 200. This is near Pontseib, which happens to be the sixth most important Seikh shrine in India. Obtaining the license was a very long and arduous process. Our job as the site-selection team was to evaluate this site to determine if there were any fatal flaws that would preclude its use for the intended purpose.

The critical issues that we highlighted before we physically visited this site were:

- We were dealing with a potentially hazardous raw material, isocyanate (also referred to as NDI in this article);
- We would have to transport this raw material 1,700 kilometers (900 miles) inland;

- We suspected poor quality or even lack of expatriate facilities;
- We did not know the quality of the local work force; and
- We needed to address local environmental concerns.

With respect to fatal flaws in the site, if we judged that we could not transport the raw material to the site, then the site could not serve our purposes. An adequate electrical supply is absolutely necessary. And, usually, we like to have two separate sources of electricity, such as backup from on-site generators.

If we had found a fatal flaw in the site, we would have gone back to the government and explained this to them. Then we would have petitioned for permission to go to another area. The permitting process took about two years just to get the required okays on the site we are discussing. To go after another site might have delayed plant start-up by another two years. The timing was also a factor because there were three other companies that had already gotten licenses to produce the same product. We did not want to lose any more time.

**The Raw Materials:** But the main issue for the site-selection team had to do with our concern that the isocyanate would be a problem to the Indian government and the people of India after the chemical plant disaster in Bhopal. The isocyanate that would be used at this plant is not at all like the isocyanate involved in the Bhopal tragedy. Du Pont's isocyanate has a very high melting point; it is a solid. To make sure that it stayed solid during shipment, the chemical would be transported in 40-ft. refrigerated containers all the way from the manufacturer to the plant site.

Du Pont's principal supplier of NDI is Dow in the U.S. Alternatively, we could also get it from Bayer in Germany, which is, incidentally, already supplying a polymeric NDI, which is used by foam-product producers in India. When confronted with the Bhopal problem, the Indian government immediately banned all movement of NDI within the country, regardless of whether the chemical was the same one involved with Bhopal or not. And it took a month for the foam producers to convince the Indian government that the NDI that they used was entirely different from that which caused the Bhopal tragedy. Then they were able to resume their imports of it.

The other raw material used at this plant, PTMEG, is a glycol that presents no real environmental problem. It would be put into tanks at Du Pont's Niagara Falls plant and moved to the Indian site.

Part of the logistics problem of determining whether or not Du Pont could make this enterprise work in India has to do with who the NDI carriers would be, what Indian affiliates they have and what connection they would have with this prospective site, which is, as we indicated, 1,700 kilometers (900 miles) from port. The site-selection team found that there were several transportation candidates with good Indian contacts or subsidiaries. Failing shipping from the U.S., Du Pont had two alternates from Europe that also carry the polymeric NDI needed by the plant.

**Transportation:** One of the factors in considering this site is the long lead time required to get the raw materials to the site from the production point. But this factor would be the same for any site chosen in India or many other parts of the world. Shipment would require a certain number of days in the country of origin, plus time for an in-route port clearance. But in the case of India, the shipment process would also have a problem with monsoons. And when the site-

selection team was at the port in Bombay, there was a strike. So these are things we had to consider about working in a country like India.

En route to the site — along the 1,700 kilometers (900 miles) from port to the plant — the site-selection team assumed that the raw-material supply trucks would only run during daylight. And that meant the trucks would be traveling only eight hours a day, making the journey to the site from the port a six-day trip.

On the way to India, in Frankfurt, West Germany, the site-selection team stopped off to make sure that Du Pont could get refrigerated transportation containers. Even though the NDI has a high melting point, it will polymerize and become useless for Du Pont's purposes unless it is kept cold.

Now we will discuss the specifics of the prospective site with respect to the local transportation and how we would move the NDI through the area. The trucks carrying the NDI would come up through Bombay. In this region, the width of the road rapidly narrows from a maximum of 20 feet (six meters) down to 10 feet (three meters), and the course contains numerous sharp curves. That means that the trucks with 40-foot containers in tow would probably have trouble getting around some of those curves. And this was one of the main things that the site-selection team was worried about with respect to this particular site. Not only is it a long distance from port, but the last few kilometers are winding mountain roads.

Although there has not been a specific commitment to Du Pont to improve the roads, we noticed that the Indian government is widening some of the roads up to the site. Overall in India, the government is improving the road system, and we saw some of the crews, mostly women, carrying bricks and putting them down.

That basically sums up the logistics part of the site-selection study. Our conclusion was that with the right logistical controls, such as only driving during the day and having people on board the trucks who were capable of making any repairs, the site could work.

When there is a spill, the site-selection team was told that the Indian people along the road would think that the NDI is something that they could use for fuel. They will go out and scoop up the spillage in any kind of container that they can find. So, we would have to have somebody there to keep the local people away from the wreck.

**Other Site-Selection Considerations:** We considered the possibility of building a residential colony at the site. But it is remote and isolated and currently has no local amenities. Du Pont would have had to put in everything that the plant's staff would have there. An hour's drive from the plant over an adequate but heavily traveled road there is good family housing. This is the place where the British came to seek out cool weather in the hot season during the colonial days.

Two hours travel from the site within the city of Pontseib there is good family housing. However, the city people have to have guards in their houses. There is apparently a lot of thievery, and so all westerners living there hire guards. Grocery shopping in the city can be difficult for westerners. There are specialty stores, you might call them, but they are in a crowded part of town, and they are extremely unsanitary to our way of looking at them.

There is an excellent boys' school in the city, which goes to the secondary level. The city is the site of India's version of West Point or Sandhurst for training of army personnel. On the down side, the big problem with this area is that it contains no major medical facility.

Next, we will discuss the quality of the work force. The plant site is located in Seikh country. One of the important Seikh temples is located very close to the site. And there are many Seikhs living in the local area. Seikhs are, of course, among the best of the work force in India. So the site-selection team concluded that the labor pool was adequate and certainly trainable. There are people expert in mechanics from a large cement plant nearby. And there is a lot of light industry in the region.

Plant safety is a real problem because Seikhs will not give up their turbans, particularly in this area which is characterized by a high level of religious enthusiasm. A safety hat will not fit over a turban. And the site-selection team observed employees in local plants who needed hearing protection and hard-toe shoes according to our standards, but these safety precautions were not the custom. We would have to impose these safety programs on plant staff. Finally, under safety, the Indian custom of construction workers bringing their whole families on the site, with the women and children underfoot, caused some concern.

Another concern was the willingness of experienced staff to relocate to the area from the U.S. or Europe. There is a real reluctance on the part of many people to put their families into this kind of situation in which the schools and the healthcare are not always good.

To solve this problem, we decided to suggest that Du Pont repatriate an Indian person who had been with Du Pont, done well and had risen into a management position. The problem that we encountered on this score was that such people are sometimes not well-accepted by the indigenous Indian people. Du Pont-trained Indian managers would be returning to India at a relatively high salary, and it is difficult for them to re-enter the Indian social structure. So not only is it likely that such Indian repatriates will not want to work in India, but even if they did want to, they might not be accepted as managers.

Regarding environmental factors, the plant would need to dispose of some liquid waste. A river flows right by this site. But the plant would generate a liquid waste that could not be discharged into that river, which is the local source for drinking water. Solid waste disposal did not appear to be a problem.

But from a manufacturer's point of view, the dust generated by a nearby cement plant poses a problem. However the engineers said that the dust was not an issue in light of the normal wind directions. We would need to drill wells on the site, and there was a question of groundwater allocation rights. But the site-selection team concluded that the well would be okay if we got some local support.

The final issue for the site-selection team was the monsoon. In July and August, between 25 and 35 inches of rain fall in a single month. The site-selection team visited the site in the non-monsoon season. The team visited the site again during the monsoon season.

### The Site-Acquisition Process

The site had already been designated for industrial use by the state government, so the site-selection team did not have that hurdle to cross. Industrial sites in India can be acquired in two ways. First, under section 4616 of the law, the government can acquire it. And this would be akin to our laws of condemnation. This is, however, a very long process that must go through the courts. And the site-selection team learned that frequently this results in bad feelings by the

people since they may feel unfairly compensated and treated.

The second way of acquiring an industrial site involves direct negotiation with the property owners. But no one on the site-selection team spoke the local language. So what the team agreed to do there at the suggestion of our joint-venture partner was to hire an ex-army officer who spoke the local language and who, by virtue of his prior position, would have the respect of the people.

The 570-hectare (230-acre) property consisted of a hundred individual parcels owned by members of 27 different families. We estimated that it would cost a million dollars, or $4,300 per acre, to purchase the land and another $100,000 to relocate the people living there. Their homes were grass huts. We were required to give the displaced families a small piece of land for their sacred cow on a section of the site away from the plant. We also agreed that the plant's clinic would provide medical service to the community and that the plant would hire members of the displaced families. Du Pont did not have to hire all of the people who had lived on the site. Generally, one person from each family would be hired. These people would be placed in jobs such as landscaping, grounds maintenance and cleaning the plant — work appropriate for people who are not literate.

Du Pont's joint-venture partner felt that the land-purchase negotiations would take anywhere from one to six months but could take longer. Only seven of the 200 villagers were reported to be literate; negotiations would generally be held with the head of the village and his counselors, who would make the decision for others. If negotiations proved unsuccessful, then Du Pont would have to resort to the condemnation route for acquiring the land.

In addition to minimizing ill feelings among the many landowners, another advantage of privately acquiring the land was that Du Pont would then be free to dispose of it to another approved industry at a negotiated price. If the land was acquired by condemnation from the government, under the law, it could only be sold back to the government.

When the site-selection team got back to the U.S. and we put our heads together and talked to management, we had many concerns. But we thought that we could manage all of those concerns. The general conclusion was that the site-selection team found no fatal flaws in the site, and we recommended that Du Pont acquire it.

---

### SUGGESTED READING

1 Canary, Patrick H. "International Transportation Factors in Site Selection," *Industrial Development,* September/October 1988, vol. 157, no. 5, pp. 7-9.

2 Rees, Terry L. "Site Selection in Europe — A Case Study," *Industrial Development,* September/October 1988, vol. 157, no. 5, pp. 13-15.

# 6

# PERFORMANCE MEASUREMENT AND PORTFOLIO MANAGEMENT

Business performance is constantly measured to prove to the business owners that their investments are being wisely and profitability managed. Quarterly and annual reports, with special financial reports on special occasions, are prepared for stockholder review. Multinational corporations are no exception to this performance review and reporting pattern.

Part of the performance management of the multinational company will be a report on the profitability of individual product lines and important worldwide subsidiaries. Usually the multinational company does not report the return on its overall real estate portfolio or the return from individual properties. In recent years, though, it has been proven among U.S.-based multinationals that companies may profit more from their real estate portfolios than from their offerings of products and services.

## THE PROFITABILITY AND LEVERAGE OF A SAMPLE OF U.S.-BASED MULTINATIONAL COMPANIES

Multinational companies with large portfolios of worldwide real estate may be highly profitable. The operating revenues of a sample of U.S.-based multinational companies do not fall below U.S. $2.3 billion per company (Exhibit 6.1). The internationally oriented company, Morton Thiokol, had 16 percent of its total operating revenues represented by revenues from international company operations. Warner Lambert, in contrast, derived 48 percent of its operating revenues from international operations and almost U.S. $4 billion in revenues from total company business. Many multinational companies derive a quarter to a third—if not more—of their revenues from overseas operations.

The multinational company can be very profitable overall. The sample of Exhibit 6.2 shows returns on equity over 30 percent for several of the companies while three companies have negative or very low returns on equity. Relatively low or moderate financial leverage is represented by the

**Exhibit 6.1**

**Total Operating Revenues and Percentage Represented by International Operating Revenues of 14 Selected U.S.-Based Multinational Corporations, 1988**

| U.S.-Based Multinational Corporation | Total Operating Revenues (Millions of Dollars) | Percent Represented by International Operating Revenues |
|---|---|---|
| Philip Morris including Kraft General Foods Group | $31,742 | 25% |
| Motorola | 8,250 | 36 |
| Abbott Laboratories | 4,937 | 24 |
| McDonald's | 16,064 | 29 |
| Morton Thiokol | 2,316 | 16 |
| Amoco | 23,919 | 22 |
| Campbell Soup | 4,869 | 21 |
| Warner-Lambert | 3,908 | 48 |
| United Parcel Services | 11,032 | N/A |
| duPont | 32,917 | 39 |
| Xerox | 11,688 | 25 |
| Union Carbide | 8,324 | 31 |
| FMC Corporation | 3,287 | 37 |
| AT&T | 35,210 | N/A |

N/A = Not available

Source: 1988 corporate annual reports.

most profitable multinational companies (Exhibit 6.2). The least profitable companies are associated with relatively high or moderate amounts of leverage.

High earnings per share were generated in 1988 by two of the largest companies of the U.S.-based multinational company sample—Philip Morris Kraft General Foods and DuPont (Exhibit 6.2). The largest company, AT&T, with U.S. $35 billion in total revenues, generated negative earnings per share, according to its publicly distributed annual report. DuPont and Philip Morris Kraft General Foods were the second and third largest companies in the sample.

Even though the operating revenues, returns on equity, and net earnings per share for the multinational companies show reasonably good profitability on the whole, the returns from their worldwide real estate are not shown in their annual reports. Of course, the companies operate in many different industries. A good test of multinational company profitability is the comparison of the company results with industry results. The comparison of profitability of company product lines with returns from product lines of the particular industries shows more about profitability of individual

**Exhibit 6.2**
**Return on Equity, Leverage, and Earnings per Share of Selected Multinational Corporations, 1988**

| Selected Company | Return on Equity (Net Earnings to Total Equity Yearend) | Leverage Total Debt to Equity | Net Earnings per Share |
|---|---|---|---|
| Philip Morris | | | |
|   Kraft Gen. Foods | 30% | 3.8 | $10.03 |
| Motorola | 13 | 0.99 | 3.43 |
| Abbott Labs | 31 | 0.96 | 3.33 |
| McDonald's | 19 | 1.39 | 3.43 |
| Morton Thiokol | 20 | 0.80 | 3.04 |
| Amoco | 15 | 0.50 | 4.00 |
| Campbell Soup | 14 | 0.90 | 2.12 |
| Warner Lambert | 34 | 1.71 | 5.00 |
| United Parcel Service | 24 | 0.54 | 4.69 |
| duPont | 14 | 0.95 | 9.11 |
| Xerox | 6 | 3.08 | 3.50 |
| Union Carbide | 36 | 1.50 | 4.66 |
| FMC | Negative | 108.1 | 3.60 |
| AT&T | Negative | 2.07 | (1.55) |

*Source*: 1988 corporate annual reports.

product lines. Many multinational companies such as DuPont and Union Carbide have product lines that cross several basic industries. If the company's profitability comes from highly diversified product lines, the company's overall profitability should be compared with that of similar, highly diversified companies.

## THE DIVERSIFIED PRODUCT LINES AND WORLDWIDE LOCATIONS OF SELECTED MULTINATIONAL COMPANIES

While FMC, DuPont, and Union Carbide have widely diversified product lines, some multinationals like McDonald's, Campbell Soup, and United Parcel Service have narrow product lines to offer worldwide. So product diversification varies immensely within the Fortune 500 multinational corporations. And the extent of the product diversification is not particularly related to diversification of company locations across the globe.

AT&T has a relatively limited product line of telecommunications services and systems and business and consumer products. The company is expanding very rapidly into global marketplaces, but their 1989 corporate reports showed company locations in only nine countries. Philip Morris Kraft General Foods was not highly diversified on a worldwide locational basis in 1989, but was highly diversified by product line. This multinational conglomerate offered tobacco, food, and beverage products as well as financial services including real estate services. Philip Morris et al. was located in only five countries of the world but it marketed a wide product line. In terms of size of operating revenues, these two companies were the larger ones of the sample—first and third in the ranking of the 14 multinational companies. Philip Morris Kraft General Foods, like AT&T, may expand rapidly geographically once the merger is "digested." This major merger recently occurred. Even the corporate real estate organization is being revised for more effective administration.

## CORPORATE REAL ESTATE PERFORMANCE MEASUREMENT

We first must look at the extent of investment property among multinational companies. Then we can view the extent of real estate management for outside the corporate bounds. As soon as we understand the essential real estate operations of the company, we can more readily understand the current status of corporate real estate performance measurement through records management and property and portfolio analysis.

### Investment Property Management

Only a few multinational industrial corporations invest in real estate to generate real estate operating profits and capital gains. Most multinational corporations lease and buy industrial and commercial properties for their own use and residential properties for their corporate personnel use. A few multinational industrial corporations manage real estate funds for their investment and those of other investors outside the corporate funds. Amoco is considering the development of a real estate fund for outside investors. Philip Morris et al. has a real estate development subsidiary to generate investment properties for its real estate portfolio. Xerox is moving the opposite direction. Xerox is divesting itself of its joint-venture relationship with VMS Realty for the development of Xerox and investment properties. United Parcel Service has been considering management and development of properties for outside investors as an extra source of real estate profitability.

### Records and Asset Management

Recently most of the multinational companies have computerized their real estate records for better operation and administration. Some of the major multinational companies are still engaged in the switch from manual or bookkeeping methods to main frame and personal computer systems.

Real estate records management has a number of facets that corporate management did not consider in earlier years. First, corporations did not recognize the value of their corporate real estate portfolios. Integrated records management with relatively current values for the various worldwide properties helps top and middle management to see the value of their real assets. If a prospective acquiring corporation views these valuable management records, it can analyze the current worth of the target company assets and consider financing means for a corporate takeover, hostile or friendly. Therefore, corporations recognize the need for security for these valuable asset records. Some companies have computerized their real asset records so that no one person has access to all the real estate records. For example, a person may have access only to the real estate records for properties for which the manager is responsible.

In order to measure individual property profitability or global portfolio profitability, the real estate records must be complete and up to date for corporate reports. Today, most multinational companies have records on individual properties used for overall company operations and possibly on their few investment properties. Some companies keep complete records on their U.S.-located properties but have not recorded comprehensive information about their international properties. These corporate real estate managers need to computerize the information about the international properties.

### The Use of Records on International Corporate Properties

Once information about the inventory of international corporate properties is entered permanently into the computer systems used by the corporate real estate department, a number of uses can be made of the data:

1. Individual property performance can be measured.
2. International and domestic properties can be analyzed for
   a) Expansion
   b) Renovation and rehabilitation
2. International and domestic properties can be analyzed for
   a) Demolition and reconstruction
   b) Divestiture through property sale
3. Global portfolio analysis
   a) Global portfolio yield measurement
   b) Global portfolio yield variability analysis
      (1) U.S. dollar terms
      (2) Local currency terms

### Current Global Real Estate Performance Management

Most corporations have established management systems for their domestic properties. These systems involve management for property maintenance, construction, redevelopment, and sale versus lease analysis. Advance planning for property development, construction, or divestiture is rarely done for the corporation as a whole. The operating unit and divisional managers usually initiate a request for space or indicate the nature of unused or unusable space. The request for new space may involve the indication of space that is no longer useable due to building obsolescence, location, or other factors.

The acceptability of the company's real estate is determined by the profitability of company operations from use of that space. Profits from the offerings of corporate goods and services from the use of the particular space determine whether the property is performing well. The company-used properties are not assumed to provide property revenues. Only the operating expenses of the company-used properties are generally noted along with the profitability of the goods and services produced from the properties.

Corporate real estate department personnel may be compensated on client service, not property performance. The client service may be associated only with intercompany services. The individual's compensation may be linked to the corporate real estate department's performance of the corporate team assigned to each separate real estate problem, and the evaluation of the individual's client service by his or her clients and surrounding associates and management. Even the managers of the real estate functions may be evaluated for ultimate compensation purposes by the same method.

Increasingly the corporate real estate department is treated as a profit center that charges intercompany units for the services it provides. This profit unit may also derive income from real estate services provided clients outside the company. The outside client may care about the individual property performance and about the yield from the real estate portfolio that the corporate real estate department manages for the client.

In order to make management decisions involving a number of disparate corporate people, a case study on the subject property may be generated by the real estate department. The known factors associated with a defined real estate problem are interjected into the case study writeup. The problem may be introduced to the department by a company unit operating manager. From the case study analysis, the alternatives for the problem solution might be defined, each alternative analyzed, and the best solution for all parties involved might be selected. AT&T uses this real estate management technique to solve problems that involve significant funds and personnel.

The management of property divestitures is related to company business expansion or contraction, mergers and acquisitions, needed corporate takeover protection, and corporate restructuring. The operating unit manager usually determines when a property is obsolete or at least inadequate for forecasted business expansion or contraction. Properties may be sold to partially pay off major mergers and acquisitions. Top management often makes such major financial decisions with the advice of consultants from leading investment banking houses. For corporate takeover protection, the company may sell key properties and lease them back. As properties become superfluous in corporate restructuring, they may be sold off. The restructuring may lead to different marketing and manufacturing systems at different locations in the world. For example, manufacturing facilities in Asia have often been chosen over manufacturing locations in North America or Europe.

## Analysis of Lease versus Buy Decisions

Generally property performance measurement is associated with lease-versus-buy decisions in corporate real estate. The financial analysis may be based upon competitive rents and property prices from the current marketplace. The cost of capital needed in the analysis may be the local cost of funds at the general corporate credit rating, or it may be the current cost of corporate debt or other cost of funds. The exchange rate for the analysis is usually the current foreign exchange rate between the home office and the country of the property location. Comparable property operating costs from the local marketplace may be used. Revenues from the corporate property's operations are difficult to estimate. The lease payments may be estimated from local real estate rent indices and the general history of rent review changes. The residual value may be determined from an estimate of property value at the end of ten years. Construction costs can be estimated from local market conditions and local construction cost indices.

## The Performance of Global Properties in General

As multinational corporations consider measuring global property productivity and managing their global properties as a portfolio, the corporate real estate managers may note the trends in international real estate investment yields. The *1989 International Property Bulletin* of Hillier Parker May & Rowden of London, written with the assistance of the European Commercial Property Association, Landauer Associates, First Pacific Davies Properties and Baring Brothers of Tokyo, shows that the highest overall rates of return have been realized in Spain and West Germany. But the highest yields in Spain have been associated with retail and industrial properties while the highest yields in West Germany have been associated with retail and office properties. Other reasonably good property yields in Europe have been coming from Portugal office and industrial space and Swedish office, retail, and industrial space. This annual report from Hillier Parker shows relatively low yields from the other 12 European countries, the United States, and Australia. On the basis of first-year property yields, the income properties of Lisbon, Portugal rank very high. Reports in the London *Financial Times* report 35 percent yields in the City of London over the past year. At the same time, Hillier Parker reported for the first half of 1989 average property yields for the United Kingdom of more than 6 percent for shops and offices and nearly 9 percent for industrial properties. In the United Kingdom since 1982, property yields overall have surpassed yields from equities but have been lower than yields on gilts, government securities with indefinite maturity dates.

The Swiss government is proposing a ceiling on real estate investment by institutional investors because real estate prices have been soaring. The prices of properties in Geneva and Zurich have reached levels among the highest in Europe, according to banking analysts and institutional consultants. Swiss observations about its real estate market tend to substantiate the Hillier Parker reporting of relatively low overall rates of return and relatively low first-year yields in Switzerland.

Property yields in Japan and Hong Kong tend to be relatively low because property prices are continuing to increase even though they are already at high levels. Space is scarce in both countries. Yields are also relatively low in the Republic of Korea for the same reasons. The South Korean government is taking steps to reduce land speculation which has driven property prices unusually high.

## GLOBAL PORTFOLIO MANAGEMENT

Institutional and individual portfolio managers are increasingly adding international securities to their portfolios to gain yield and reduction of risk from assets that are relatively uncorrelated in price trends and yields. At the same time, real estate portfolio managers are seeking investment participation in global property funds and are seeking foreign commercial properties with relatively high investment yields and relatively low risk to develop well-diversified real estate portfolios. As multinational corporations continue to spread out worldwide, the corporate real estate portfolio takes on more width and depth. In a sense, corporate real estate managers become global real estate portfolio managers.

Most corporate real estate officials do not view their worldwide leased and owned properties as a global property portfolio. The company may not even have comprehensive records for its international properties. But Exhibit 6.3 shows that all of the selected companies have global portfolios. The managers tend not to think in terms of global real estate portfolio management because the multinational company focuses on manufacturing and/or distribution rather than on real estate investment.

In portfolio management, the major premise is that higher yields over the investment holding period will be gained from assets with relatively

**Exhibit 6.3**
**Sample Multinational Corporate Product Lines and Extent of Geographical Diversification Worldwide**

---

Some Geographical Diversification                    Product Lines/General Locations

AT&T          Product Lines
                    Telecommunications services and systems
                    Business, data, and consumer products
              General Locations:  9 countries in mid-1989

Philip Morris    Product Lines
  Kraft General         Tobacco:  Domestic and international
  Foods                 Food and drinks including beer
                        Financial services and real estate
                        Other products and services
                 General Locations:  5 countries in mid-1989

Highly Diversified Geographically

Abbott Labora-    Product Lines
  tories                 Pharmaceutical and nutritional products
                         Hospital and laboratory
                  General Locations:  Worldwide
                         U.S., Latin America, Eruope, Middle East,
                         Africa, Pacific, Far East, Canada

Amoco Oil Co.     Product Lines
                         Petroleum operations:  Exploration and production
                                                Refining, marketing, and
                                                      transportation
                         Chemical operations
                         Other operations
                  General Locations:  More than 40 foreign countries
                         including U.S., Egypt, U.K., Canada, Trinidad,
                         Brunei, Qatar, Jordan, Oman, Gabon, Kenya,
                         Argentina, India, People's Republic of China,
                         Norway, Belgium, Taiwan, South Korea, Papua New
                         Guinea, and the Netherlands

Campbell Soup     Product Lines
                         Food products:  Soups, groceries, convenience
                                         meals, fresh products, others
                  General Locations:  Worldwide
                         Argentinea, Australia, Belgium, Canada, England,
                         France, West Germany, Holland, Hong Kong, Italy,
                         Japan, Mexico, Puerto Rico

duPont            Product Lines
                         Agricultural and industrial chemicals, biomedical
                         products, coal, fibers, industrial and consumer pro-
                         ducts, petroleum exploration and production, petro-
                         leum refining, marketing, and transportation, polymer
                         products
                  General Locations:  200 plants in about 40 countries on
                                      6 continents

FMC               Product Lines
                         Industrial chemicals, precious metals, defense systems,
                         performance chemicals, and machinery and equipment
                  General Locations:  Worldwide
                         U.S., Latin America, Canada, Western Europe, Asia,
                         Africa, Other

**Exhibit 6.3** (continued)

| Some Geographical Diversification | Product Lines/General Locations |
|---|---|

McDonald's

Product Lines
    Restaurant operations and service
General Locations: Worldwide

Morton Thiokol
(split as of
July 1, 1989)

Product Lines
    Morton: Salt and other consumer products
    Thiokol: Primarily aerospace products
General Locations: Worldwide
    U.S., Canada, Bahamas, Europe including Denmark, France,
    West Germany, Italy, Belgium, and Holland, Far East
    including Japan, South Korea, Hong Kong and Singapore

Motorola

Product Lines
    Electronic equipment and semiconductor products, com-
    munications products, general systems products, infor-
    mations systems products, government electronic pro-
    ducts, and other products
General Locations: Worldwide - 21 countries

Union Carbide

Product Lines
    Chemicals and plastics
    Industrial gases
    Carbon products
General Locations: Worldwide
    Markets petrochemicals to more than 100 countries

United Parcel
Service

Product Lines
    Parcel delivery service
General Locations: Worldwide
    Service more than 160 countries through licenses,
    joint venture partners, and their own operations

Warner Lambert

Product Lines
    Health care:
        Ethical pharmaceutical products
        Non-prescription health care products
        Other health care products
    Gums and mints
General Locations: Worldwide
    U.S., Europe, Middle East, Africa, Americas,
    Far East

Xerox

Product Lines
    Business products and systems
    Financial services
General Locations: Worldwide
    North and Latin America, China and the South
    Pacific, Japan, India - by Xerox
    Rank Xerox of U.K. - 80 eastern hemisphere
                        countries
    Serve around 145 countries including 58 principal
    countries

**Exhibit 6.4**
**How Investment Returns Are Related**

|  | U.S. Stocks | Non-U.S. Stocks | Dollar Bonds | Non-Dollar Bonds | Real Estate | Cash |
|---|---|---|---|---|---|---|
| U.S. Stocks | 10.0 | 6.0 | 4.5 | 2.5 | 3.5 | - 1.0 |
| Non-U.S. Stocks | 6.0 | 10.0 | 2.5 | 6.0 | 3.0 | - 1.5 |
| Dollar Bonds | 4.5 | 2.5 | 10.0 | 3.0 | 2.0 | - 0.5 |
| Non-Dollar Bonds | 2.5 | 6.0 | 3.0 | 10.0 | 1.5 | - 1.0 |
| Real Estate | 3.5 | 3.0 | 2.0 | 1.5 | 10.0 | 2.5 |
| Cash | - 1.0 | - 1.5 | - 0.5 | - 1.0 | 2.5 | 10.0 |

Note: Forecasts return relationships for various investments over the long term. Anything below 9 indicates good diversification potential. Negative numbers indicate returns should move inversely, while O indicates there's no particular pattern. For example, returns on U.S. stocks and those on non-U.S. stocks are more closely tied (with a rating of 6) than returns on U.S. stocks and cash investments (with a rating of − 1), which should move in opposite directions.

Source: Brinson Partners, Inc. Reprinted with permission.

uncorrelated market prices and yields. It is assumed that markets do not move together in a concerted fashion so that all market prices will not move up or down together. If the marketplaces are relatively independent from each other, market prices will move partially or totally independent of other markets. A recent study of the First Chicago Investment Advisors indicates that returns from domestic and international stocks and bonds and cash are relatively uncorrelated with real estate returns (Exhibit 6.4). The lowest correlation related to real estate was found among nondollar bonds. In other words, the yields from bonds not denominated in U.S. dollars, U.S. stocks, and non-U.S. stocks. Therefore, global portfolio managers can increase yields and reduce return variability by diversifying into real estate.

The Hillier Parker, Jones Lang Wootton, and Richard Ellis reports tend to verify that property prices and yields do not move in a highly correlated manner among the countries of the world. It is true that most global portfolio managers wish to stay with securities and real assets from highly industrial countries where the debtors have relatively high credit ratings and with prime general-purpose properties with high long-term occupancy rates. For example, prime properties in Spain and Portugal are associated with relatively high yields while the prime properties of the United States and the United Kingdom are associated with relatively low yields.

## GENERAL REAL ESTATE GLOBAL PORTFOLIO MANAGEMENT

When corporate real estate executives are examining methods of measuring the productivity of their real estate holdings, whether leased or owned, they are considering real estate global portfolio management. But their focus normally is on the following policies:

Leasing property when the corporation is unsure of the profitability of the location for manufacturing, processing, or distribution

Buying the property if the corporate operating manager feels sure of the profit potential of the selected location

Even though real estate global diversification may have its strong points for institutional real estate investors, the multinational industrial corporation attains the same results through selection of properties in locations advantageous to overall company operations

If the multinational company had a real estate investment portfolio, portfolio diversification on a global basis might be a proper focus, but most multinational industrial corporations do not hold investment properties

## SUMMARY

While few of the sample multinational industrial companies have excessive leverage, their returns on equity range from negative to 34 percent. The companies selected for their international market exposure generally drew one quarter to one third of their revenues from abroad. Most of these firms marketed their products worldwide, though two of them—AT&T and Philip Morris Kraft General Foods—were represented in only a few overseas countries. Most of these firms have broad product lines, but there are exceptions. McDonald's has only fast-food restaurants, and United Parcel Service has only parcel and document delivery service to offer worldwide. Some of the companies own the majority of their global properties; others tend to lease the majority of their properties. Other global companies fall in between these two extreme positions.

Generally corporate real estate is evaluated on the basis of the profitability of the products associated with the particular real estate. Most corporate real estate officers measure and analyze profitability only in lease-versus-buy situations. Since they are increasing their use of computers for property management, they are considering productivity measurement for their global properties. Their global properties are not considered real estate portfolios of global corporations. But the companies benefit from the global diversification of property locations and the diversity among property types. Many multinational companies have office, warehouse, and industrial properties in many urban and suburban locations in single countries and in multiple countries across the world. Few multinational industrial corporations deliberately invest in real estate for its return, develop properties for other investors, administer real estate funds with managed global properties for various outside investors, or engage in other real estate activities for entities outside the corporation. And they rely on approved local and international sources of real estate information when conducting business associated with global properties.

## BIBLIOGRAPHY

*International Property Bulletin 1989*. London: Hillier Parker May & Rowden, 1989. Pp. 7–8.
*Property Market Returns (U.K.)*. London: Hillier Parker May & Rowden, 1989.

# SELECT BIBLIOGRAPHY

*Average Yields*. London: Hillier Parker May & Rowden, 1989.

Bingham, Bruce B. "Managing Corporate Real Estate in a Takeover." *Site Selection*, February 1989, pp. 6–9.

Burr, Barry B. "Riots Aside, Hong Kong Is Near Top." *Pensions & Investment Age*, August 21, 1989, p. 47.

Carrington, Tim. "Hungary Savoring Goulash Capitalism." *Wall Street Journal*, November 17, 1989, p. A10.

Cash, James I., Jr., E. Warren McFarlan, and James L. McKenney. *Corporate Information Systems Management: The Issues Facing Senior Executives*. 2nd ed. Homewood, Ill.: Dow Jones-Irwin, 1989.

Cheesright, Paul. "The Monday Interview: A Pirate Mourns Past Fun." *Financial Times*, August 21, 1989, p. 30.

Daniels, John D., and Lee H. Radebaugh. *International Business, Environments and Operations*. 5th ed. Reading, Mass.: Addison-Wesley Publishing Co., 1989.

Donahue, John J. "A Site-Selection Case in Sydney, Australia." *Site Selection Handbook*, June 1989, pp. 20–22.

Eiteman, David K., and Arthur I. Stonehill. *Multinational Business Finance*, 5th ed. Reading, Mass.: Addison-Wesley Publishing Co., 1989.

*Environmental Regulatory Compliance Guidebook*. Minneapolis, Minn.: Fidelity Products Company.

*Europe 1992: A Business Guide to U.S. Government Resources*. Washington, D.C.: Bureau of Public Affairs, U.S. Department of State, 1989.

Firstenberg, Paul B., and Charles H. Wurtzebach. "Managing Portfolio Risk and Reward." *Real Estate Review*, Summer 1989, pp. 61–65.

Ford, Maggie. "Breakneck Progress Turns S. Korea Green." *Financial Times*, August 24, 1989, p. 4.

———. "South Korea Plans Radical Reforms to Update Tax System." *Financial Times*, September 5, 1989, p. 4.

Gibson, Richard. "General Mills Would Like to Be Champion of Breakfasts in Europe." *Wall Street Journal*, December 1, 1989, p. B6.

————. "Personal 'Chemistry' Abruptly Ended Rise of Kellogg President." *Wall Street Journal*, November 28, 1989, pp. 1, A6.

"Global Survey Reveals Widespread Relaxation of Restrictions." *Site Selection*, October 1988, pp. 1344, 1346–1347.

Graham, George. "France Cuts Top Rate of VAT to 25%." *Financial Times*, September 7, 1989, p. 3.

Granwell, Alan W. *International Tax Planning for the U.S. Multinational Corporation*. New York: Practising Law Institute, 1988.

Hemmerick, Steve. "Foreign Realty Draws Attention." *Pensions & Investment Age*, October 2, 1989, pp. 2, 69.

Hilder, David B., and Linda Sandler. "Mega-Merger Game Will Survive, Some Say, But Tone Will Change." *Wall Street Journal*, October 16, 1989, p. C2.

Hines, Mary Alice. *Guide to International Real Estate Investment*. Westport, Conn.: Quorum Books, 1988.

————. *Income Property Development, Financing and Investment*. Lexington, Mass.: Lexington Books, 1984.

————. "Investing in the Booming Japanese Real Estate Market." *Corporate Real Estate Executive*, November/December 1988, pp. 38–40.

————. *Investing in Japanese Real Estate*. Westport, Conn.: Quorum Books, 1987.

————. *Marketing Real Estate Internationally*. Westport, Conn.: Quorum Books, 1988.

————. *An Overview of Global Real Estate Finance*. Scottsdale, Ariz.: International Real Estate Institute, 1989.

————. "Winning a Share of the New Common Market." *Corporate Real Estate Executive*, February 1989, pp. 54–56.

"Institutional Investor's 1989 Country Credit Ratings." *Institutional Investor*, September 1989, p. 302.

*International Property Bulletin 1989*. London: Hillier Parker May & Rowden, 1989.

"International Transportation Factor in Site Selection." *Site Selection*, October 1988, pp. 7+.

Jarman, David L. "Becoming a Corporate Asset While You Manage the Company's Assets." *Corporate Real Estate Executive*, February 1989, pp. 14–17.

"Joint Venture in Budapest." *Wall Street Journal*, December 14, 1989, p. A14.

"Joint Ventures See Profits, China Says." *Indianapolis Star*, November 25, 1989, p. B6.

Kaplan, Lawrence E. "A Compendium of Hazardous Substance Laws and Issues Involving Real Estate." *Site Selection Handbook*, January/February 1988, pp. 13–21.

Love, John F. *McDonald's: Behind the Arches*. New York: Bantam Books, 1986.

Lyne, Jack. "Ed Lewis: An Inside Look at the Man Behind Motorola's Real Estate Management." *Site Selection Handbook*, February 1988, pp. 34–36, 38.

Manning, Christopher A. "Is Ownership of Corporate Real Property Better than Leasing?" *Site Selection Handbook*, January/February 1988, pp. 8–12.

Mapes, Glynn, and Philip Revzin. "British Spat With EC over Pollution Shows What 1992 May Bring." *Wall Street Journal*, December 14, 1989, pp. 1, A14.

Marsh, Peter. "No Time or Place for Waste." *Financial Times*, September 23, 1989, p. 7.

Marzutto, Tito. "Innovative Japanese Design/Build Techniques." *Site Selection*, April 1989, pp. 8+.

"Merrill Lynch International Bond Indexes, September, 1989." *Wall Street Journal*, October 13, 1989, p. C1.

Mitchell, Constance. "Investors Brave Currency Risks for Higher Bond Yields." *Wall Street Journal*, October 10, 1989, pp. C1, C19.

Monroe, Linda K., "The Big Chill: How the CFC Ban Will Affect HVAC Operations." *Buildings*, November 1989, pp. 40–41.

————. "Industry Innovator: Tishman Realty & Construction Co., Inc. Takes the Term Full Service Beyond the Norm." *Buildings*, July 1989, pp. 50–54.

Moore, Philip. "Spend, Spend, Spend, Main Street Europe is Booming." *Global Investor*, December 1988/January 1989, pp. 31–40.

Naj, Amal Kumar, and Barry Newman. "GE to Buy 50% of Hungarian Lighting Firm." *Wall Street Journal*, November 16, 1989, p. A2.

Nomani, Asra Q. "Pritzkers Acquire Hungarian Firm under New Law." *Wall Street Journal*, August 21, 1989, p. B1.

Nourse, Hugh O. *Managerial Real Estate: Corporate Real Estate Asset Management.* Englewood Cliffs, N.J.: Prentice-Hall, 1990.

Ogan, Mark F. "Developing Cooperation Between the Corporate Real Estate and Legal Departments." *Site Selection*, December 1988, p. 1.

Pae, Peter. "Eastman Kodak Plans to Eliminate Minilab Division." *Wall Street Journal*, December 5, 1989, p. A15.

Parker, Joel R. "Characteristics of New Corporate Facility Investments." *Site Selection*, June 1989, pp. 25+.

————. "The Corporate Real Estate Profession: Tasks and Resources." *Site Selection*, February 1989, pp. 24+.

————. "Surplus Corporate Real Estate—Who Handles It and How It Has Changed." *Site Selection*, April 1989.

Parker, Marcia. "Extending the Reach." *Pensions & Investment Age*, October 2, 1989, pp. 2, 66.

Patner, Andrew. "VMS Announces Management Shake-Up, New Credit in Drive to Improve Finances." *Wall Street Journal*, November 16, 1989, p. A3.

*The Property Index.* London: Jones Lang Wootton, Healey & Baker, Hillier Parker, and Richard Ellis, 1989.

Rees, Terry L. "Site Selection in Europe—A Case Study." *Site Selection Handbook*, October 1988, pp. 13–15.

Reinbach, Andrew. "Riots Shake Asian Realty Projects." *Pensions & Investment Age*, June 12, 1989, pp. 3, 54.

Richard, Bill. "Abbott Labs Chief Schoellhorn to Retire in Surprise Move; Burnham is Successor." *Wall Street Journal*, December 11, 1989, p. A4.

Riddell, Peter. "Tax Will Still Be Among World's Highest." *Financial Times*, October 2, 1989, p. 3.

"Science Parks around the Globe." *Site Selection*, June 1989, pp. 660+.

Silverman, Robert A., ed. *Corporate Real Estate Handbook.* New York: McGraw-Hill, 1987.

"Sites for Science Enter New Era of Global Competition for High-Tech Locations." *Site Selection*, June 1989, pp. 652+.

Smith, David A. "Investor Protection Against Environmental Risks." *Real Estate Review*, Summer 1989, pp. 14–19.

Solnik, Bruno. *International Investments*. Reading, Mass.: Addison-Wesley, 1988.

Swasy, Alecia. "P&G in Surprise, Appoints Artxzt Chairman and Chief." *Wall Street Journal*, October 12, 1989, pp. B1, B5.

*Taxes on Immovable Property*. Paris: Organization for Economic Cooperation and Development, 1983.

"Tax Rules 'Drive Holding Groups to Foreign Havens.' " *Financial Times*, August 14, 1989, p. 6.

Tomsett, Eric. *The Management of Corporate Taxes*. London: Euromoney Publications, 1989.

Turner, Richard. "MCA to Propose Site Near London for Theme Park." *Wall Street Journal*, November 30, 1989, p. B6.

Vosti, Curtis. "U.S. Firms See Cash in Eastern Europe." *Pension & Investment Age*, October 2, 1989, pp. 29–30.

"Which Facility Management Software Systems Fit Your Operations?" *Buildings*, September 1988, pp. 62–69.

Williams, Terry. "Salomon Unveils Global Benchmark." *Pensions & Investment Age*, November 13, 1989, pp. 15–16.

Winkler, Matthew. "Ford Revamps Firm to Realize Big Tax Savings." *Wall Street Journal*, October 12, 1989, pp. A3, A20.

Wood, Allen R. "Site Selection Trends—1989–2000." *Site Selection*, June 1989, pp. 12–13.

# INDEX

## About the Author

M. A. HINES holds the Clarence W. King Endowed Chair of Finance and Real Estate at Washburn University of Topeka. Her 26 previous books include *Guide to International Real Estate Investment* (Quorum, 1988), *Marketing Real Estate Internationally* (Quorum, 1988), and *Investing in Japanese Real Estate* (Quorum, 1987).